GREAT LIVES

LEONARDO DA VINCI

First edition for the United States, Canada, and the Philippines
published in 2019 by B.E.S. Publishing

All inquiries should be addressed to:
B.E.S. Publishing
250 Wireless Boulevard
Hauppauge, NY 11788
www.bes-publishing.com

ISBN: 978-1-4380-1203-2

Library of Congress Control No.: 2018963804

Conceived, designed, and produced by The Bright Press,
an imprint of The Quarto Group.
The Old Brewery, 6 Blundell Street,
London, N7 9BH, United Kingdom
T (0) 20 7700 6700 F (0) 20 7700 8066
www.QuartoKnows.com

Publisher: Mark Searle
Creative Director: James Evans
Managing Editor: Jacqui Sayers
Editor: Judith Chamberlain
Project Editors: Anna Southgate, Lucy York
Art Director: Katherine Radcliffe
Design: Lyndsey Harwood and Geoff Borin

Date of Manufacture: March 2019
Manufactured by: Hung Hing Printing, Shenzhen, China

Printed in China

9 8 7 6 5 4 3 2 1

GREAT LIVES
LEONARDO DA VINCI

By Tammy L. Enz
with illustrations by Dave Shephard

PUBLISHING

CONTENTS

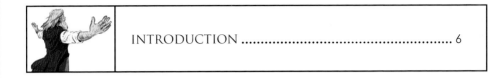

INTRODUCTION

The term "Renaissance Man" was coined to describe a person with a broad range of abilities in many different areas. A true Renaissance Man knew no boundaries in learning, expressing artistic or musical talent, or developing skills in architecture and engineering. Leonardo da Vinci was perhaps the person who best symbolizes the meaning of the term "Renaissance Man."

Renaissance is a French word meaning "rebirth," and Leonardo was born at a time in which society was undergoing great change. A new culture was emerging that saw exciting advancements in the arts and the sciences. Leonardo was in the right place at the right time. From humble beginnings in a small village called Vinci, Italy, this great man known only as Leonardo of Vinci (da Vinci) burst onto the scene bringing revolutionary ideas in art, science, engineering, music, and thought.

It would be impossible for a single book to capture the many facets of this amazing man's life. Leonardo was ahead of his time, and his life and works forever shaped the world as we know it. Thanks to his ceaseless curiosity and his skill at capturing his thoughts in writing and sketches, we can reconstruct a bit of his life, and we can hope to understand some of his incredible thought processes. Leonardo left more than 7,000 pages of writings and sketches upon his death. While many have been lost over the years, those that remain tell a great story.

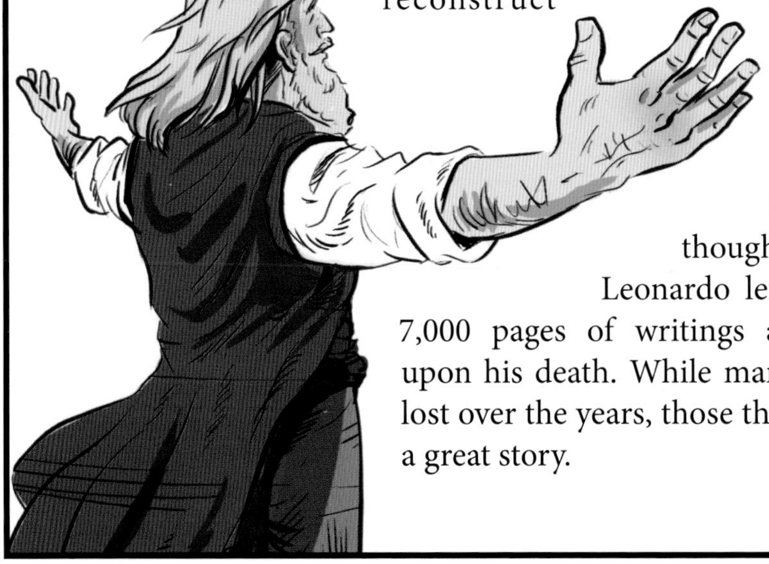

While few of Leonardo's feelings or details of his personal life were recorded in his notebooks, we can make assumptions about the man based on his subjects and methods of study. We can also glean valuable insights from the writings of people who knew Leonardo or interviewed his friends and acquaintances. While some of his writings hint at a dark and troubled side—Leonardo suffered many setbacks—there is little doubt that he was a kind and generous man who surrounded himself with friends. Giorgio Vasari first published a biography of Leonardo just a few decades after his death. In it he describes Leonardo:

"He was striking and handsome, and his great presence brought comfort to the most troubled soul. His disposition was so loveable that he commanded everyone's affection. He was so pleasing in conversation that he attracted himself to the hearts of men."

Leonardo was never afraid to pick the minds of the great thinkers of his day, and he let nothing hold him back in the pursuit of knowledge. This book shares glimpses of the people he encountered and the amazing challenges he undertook. Above all, it shares the breadth of his interests and the feats he realized as a result of the one thing we can all foster in ourselves—relentless curiosity.

CHAPTER 1

THE NOTEBOOKS

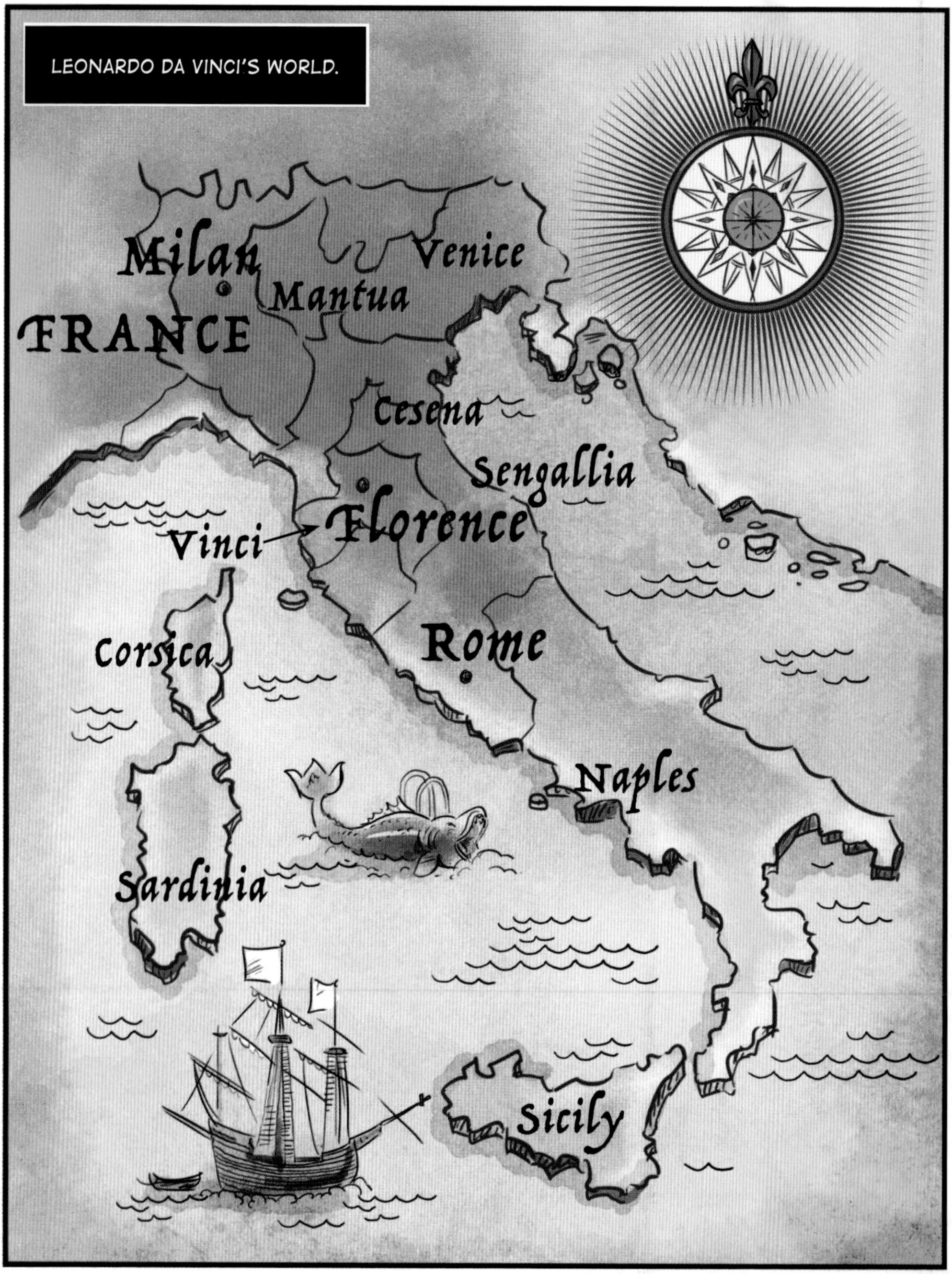
LEONARDO DA VINCI'S WORLD.
Milan
Venice
Mantua
FRANCE
Cesena
Sengallia
Vinci
Florence
Corsica
Rome
Naples
Sardinia
Sicily

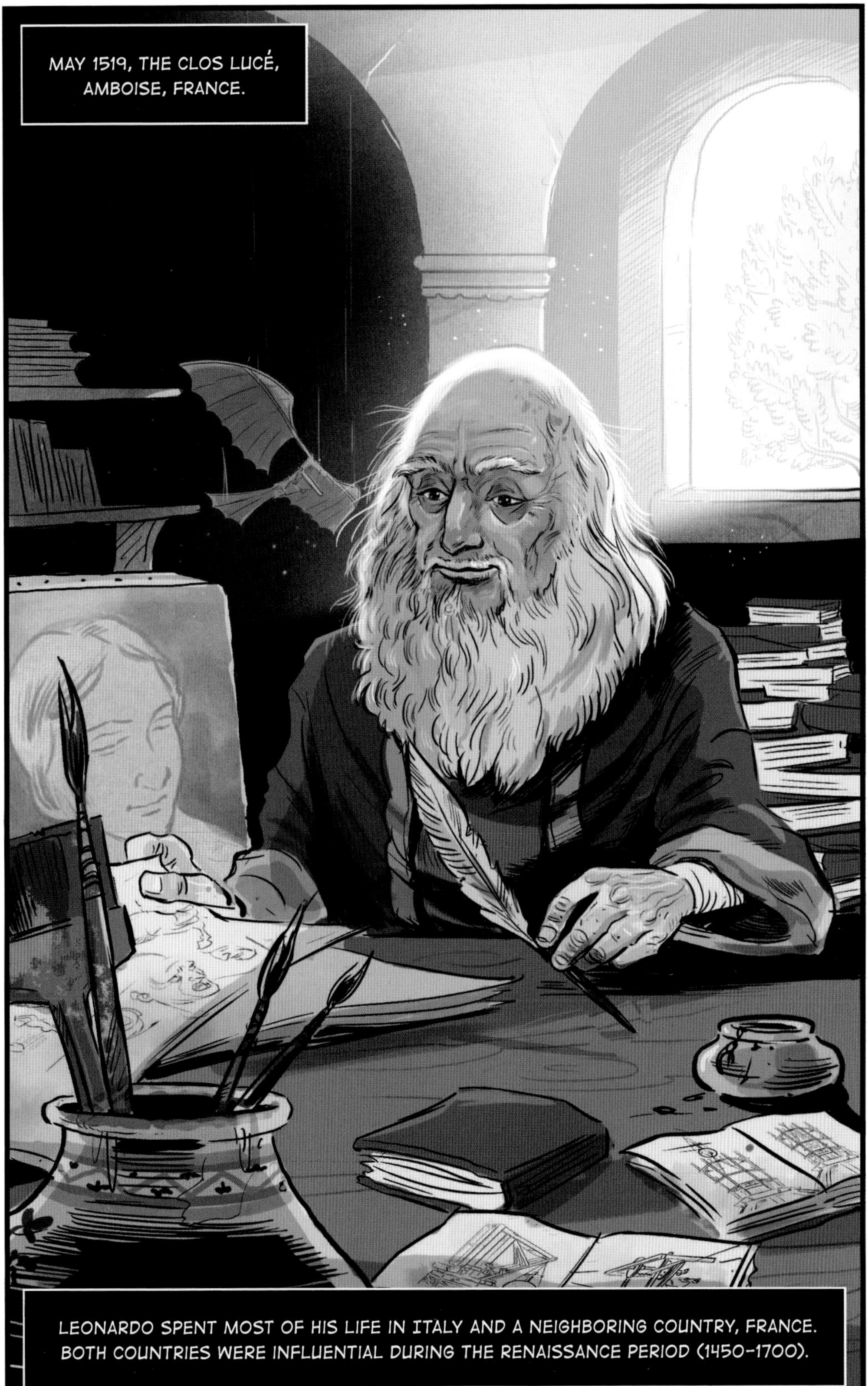
MAY 1519, THE CLOS LUCÉ, AMBOISE, FRANCE.
LEONARDO SPENT MOST OF HIS LIFE IN ITALY AND A NEIGHBORING COUNTRY, FRANCE. BOTH COUNTRIES WERE INFLUENTIAL DURING THE RENAISSANCE PERIOD (1450–1700).

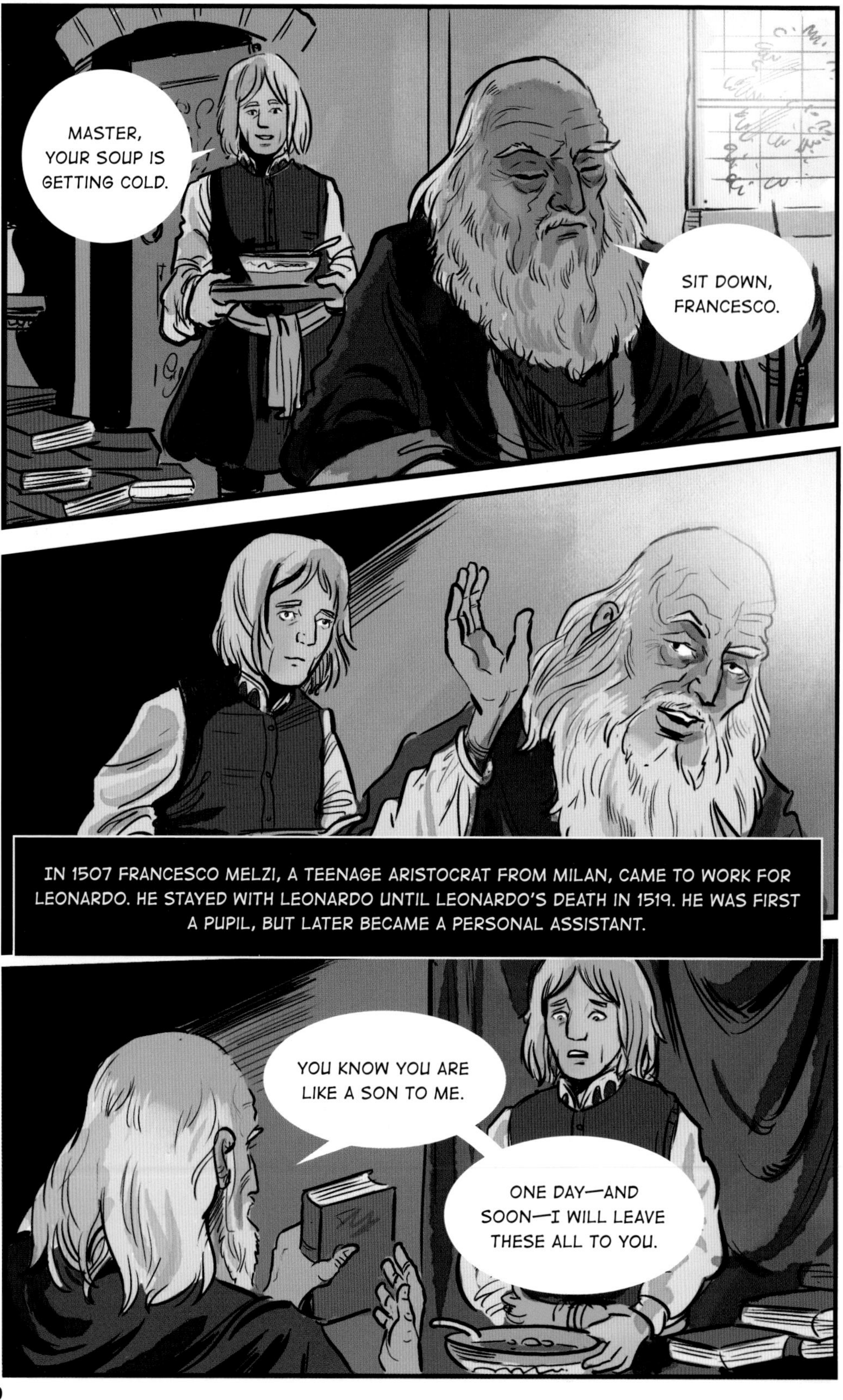
MASTER, YOUR SOUP IS GETTING COLD.
SIT DOWN, FRANCESCO.
IN 1507 FRANCESCO MELZI, A TEENAGE ARISTOCRAT FROM MILAN, CAME TO WORK FOR LEONARDO. HE STAYED WITH LEONARDO UNTIL LEONARDO'S DEATH IN 1519. HE WAS FIRST A PUPIL, BUT LATER BECAME A PERSONAL ASSISTANT.
YOU KNOW YOU ARE LIKE A SON TO ME.
ONE DAY—AND SOON—I WILL LEAVE THESE ALL TO YOU.

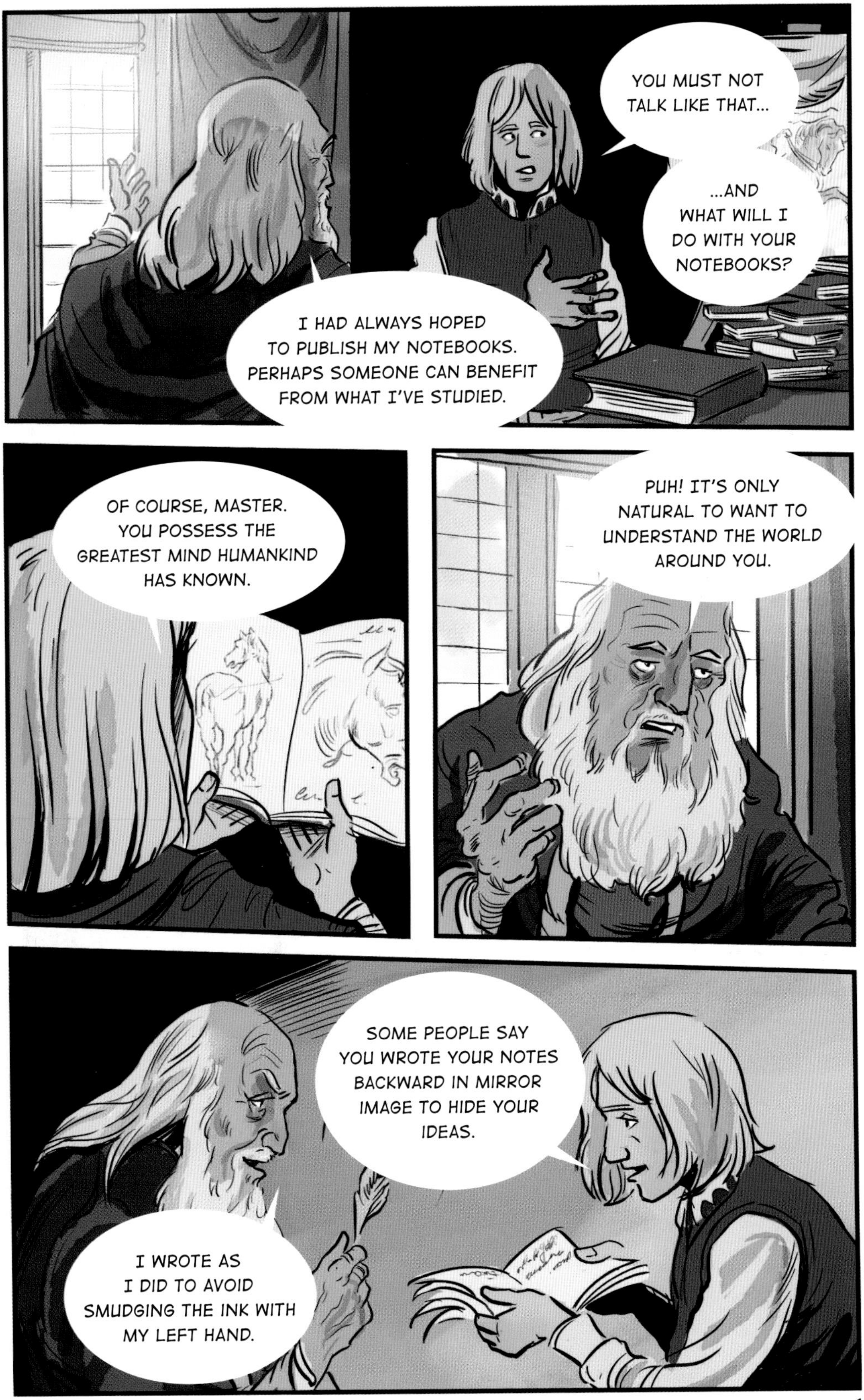
YOU MUST NOT TALK LIKE THAT...
...AND WHAT WILL I DO WITH YOUR NOTEBOOKS?
I HAD ALWAYS HOPED TO PUBLISH MY NOTEBOOKS. PERHAPS SOMEONE CAN BENEFIT FROM WHAT I'VE STUDIED.
OF COURSE, MASTER. YOU POSSESS THE GREATEST MIND HUMANKIND HAS KNOWN.
PUH! IT'S ONLY NATURAL TO WANT TO UNDERSTAND THE WORLD AROUND YOU.
SOME PEOPLE SAY YOU WROTE YOUR NOTES BACKWARD IN MIRROR IMAGE TO HIDE YOUR IDEAS.
I WROTE AS I DID TO AVOID SMUDGING THE INK WITH MY LEFT HAND.

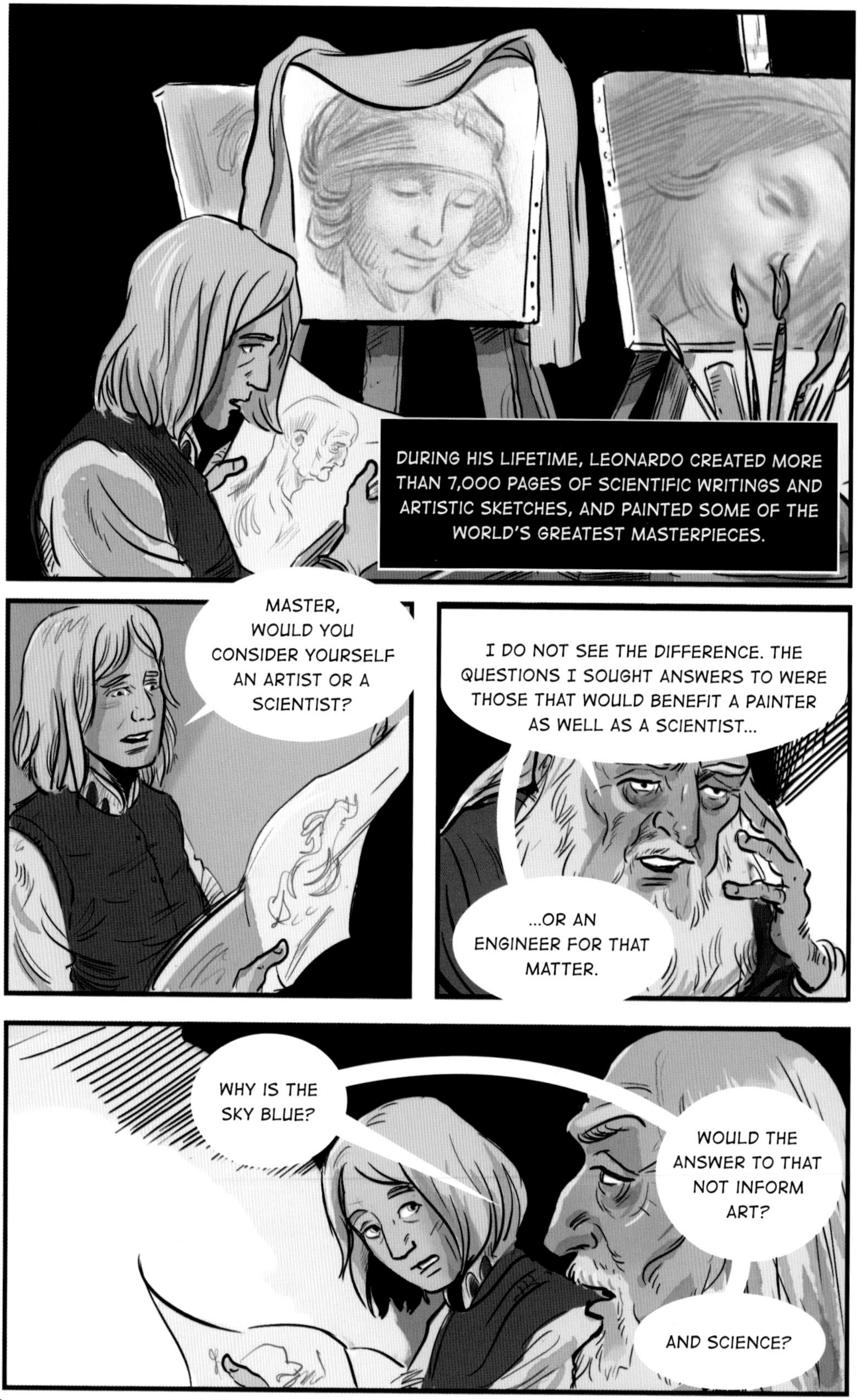
DURING HIS LIFETIME, LEONARDO CREATED MORE THAN 7,000 PAGES OF SCIENTIFIC WRITINGS AND ARTISTIC SKETCHES, AND PAINTED SOME OF THE WORLD'S GREATEST MASTERPIECES.
MASTER, WOULD YOU CONSIDER YOURSELF AN ARTIST OR A SCIENTIST?
I DO NOT SEE THE DIFFERENCE. THE QUESTIONS I SOUGHT ANSWERS TO WERE THOSE THAT WOULD BENEFIT A PAINTER AS WELL AS A SCIENTIST...
...OR AN ENGINEER FOR THAT MATTER.
WHY IS THE SKY BLUE?
WOULD THE ANSWER TO THAT NOT INFORM ART?
AND SCIENCE?

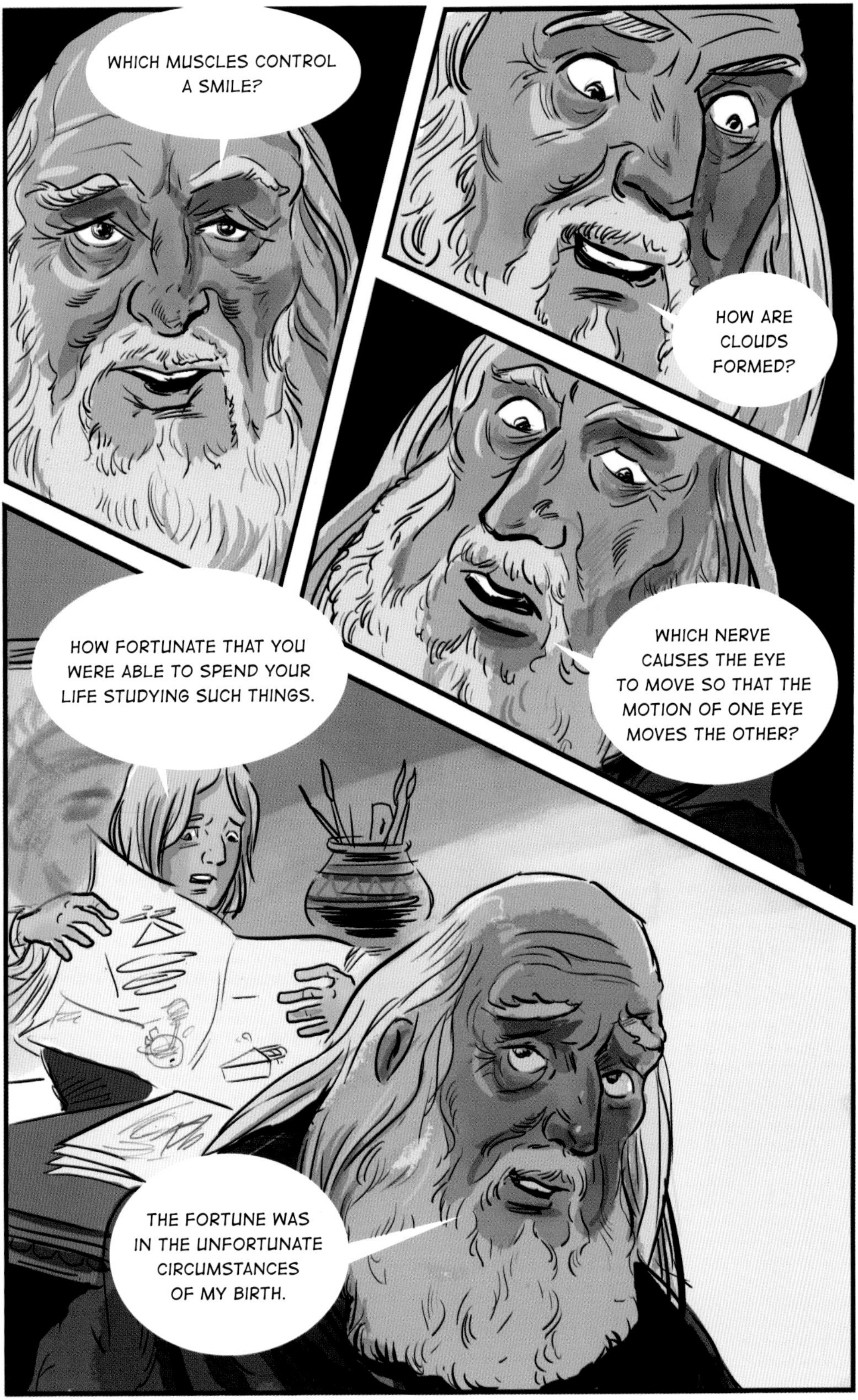
WHICH MUSCLES CONTROL A SMILE?
HOW ARE CLOUDS FORMED?
WHICH NERVE CAUSES THE EYE TO MOVE SO THAT THE MOTION OF ONE EYE MOVES THE OTHER?
HOW FORTUNATE THAT YOU WERE ABLE TO SPEND YOUR LIFE STUDYING SUCH THINGS.
THE FORTUNE WAS IN THE UNFORTUNATE CIRCUMSTANCES OF MY BIRTH.

CHAPTER 2

LEONARDO'S CHILDHOOD

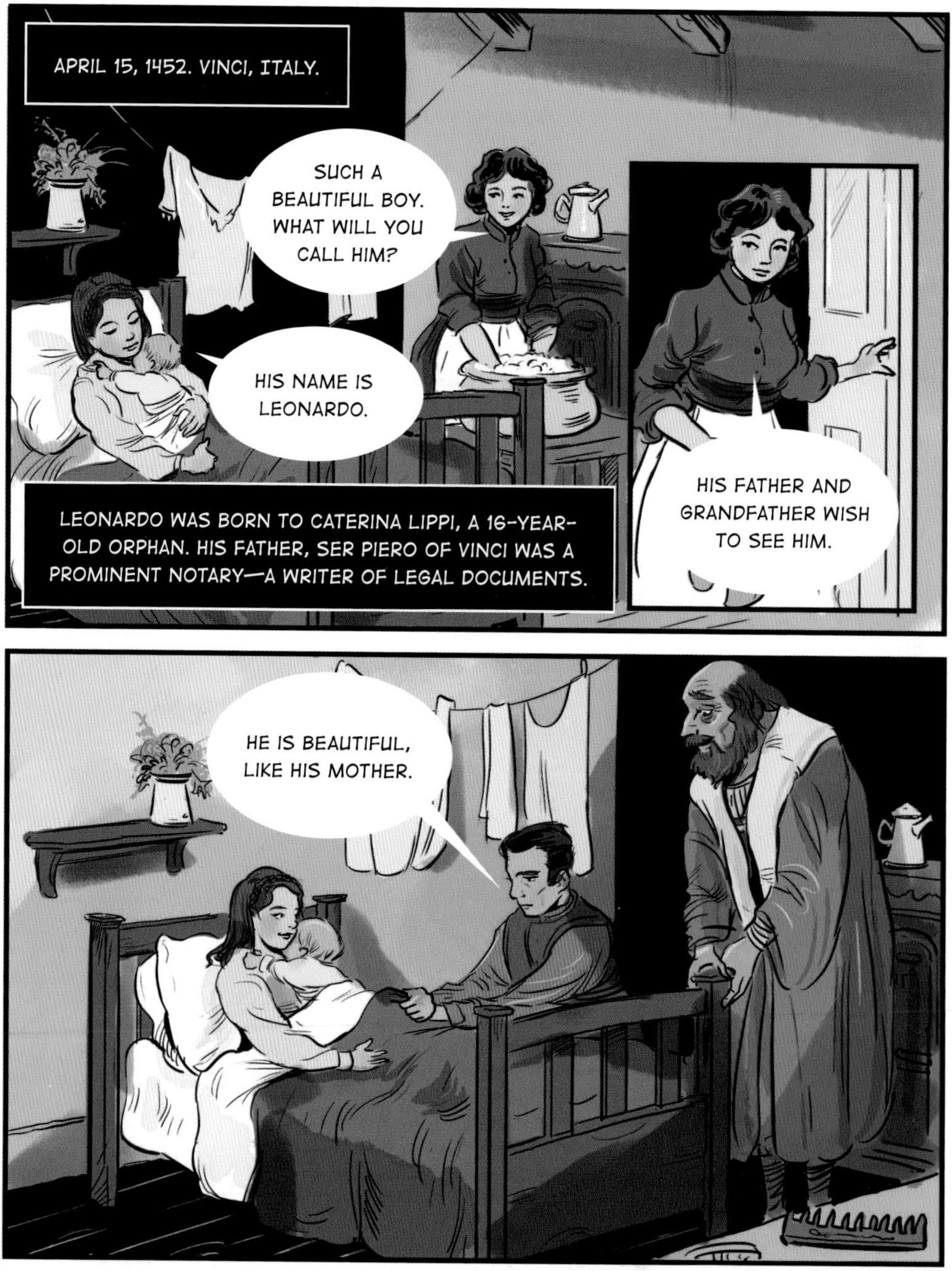

APRIL 15, 1452. VINCI, ITALY.
SUCH A BEAUTIFUL BOY. WHAT WILL YOU CALL HIM?
HIS NAME IS LEONARDO.
LEONARDO WAS BORN TO CATERINA LIPPI, A 16-YEAR-OLD ORPHAN. HIS FATHER, SER PIERO OF VINCI WAS A PROMINENT NOTARY—A WRITER OF LEGAL DOCUMENTS.
HIS FATHER AND GRANDFATHER WISH TO SEE HIM.
HE IS BEAUTIFUL, LIKE HIS MOTHER.

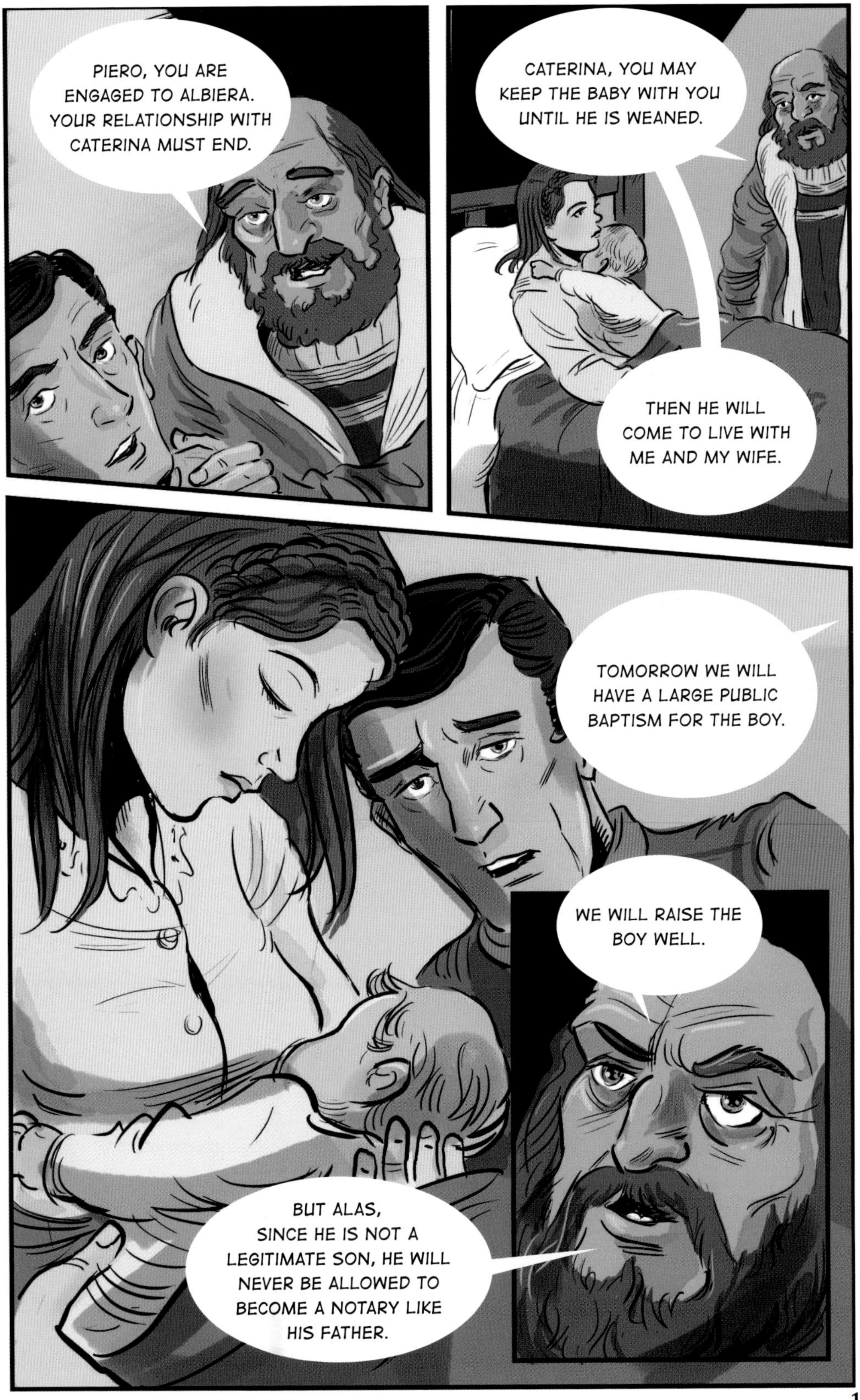
PIERO, YOU ARE ENGAGED TO ALBIERA. YOUR RELATIONSHIP WITH CATERINA MUST END.
CATERINA, YOU MAY KEEP THE BABY WITH YOU UNTIL HE IS WEANED.
THEN HE WILL COME TO LIVE WITH ME AND MY WIFE.
TOMORROW WE WILL HAVE A LARGE PUBLIC BAPTISM FOR THE BOY.
WE WILL RAISE THE BOY WELL.
BUT ALAS, SINCE HE IS NOT A LEGITIMATE SON, HE WILL NEVER BE ALLOWED TO BECOME A NOTARY LIKE HIS FATHER.

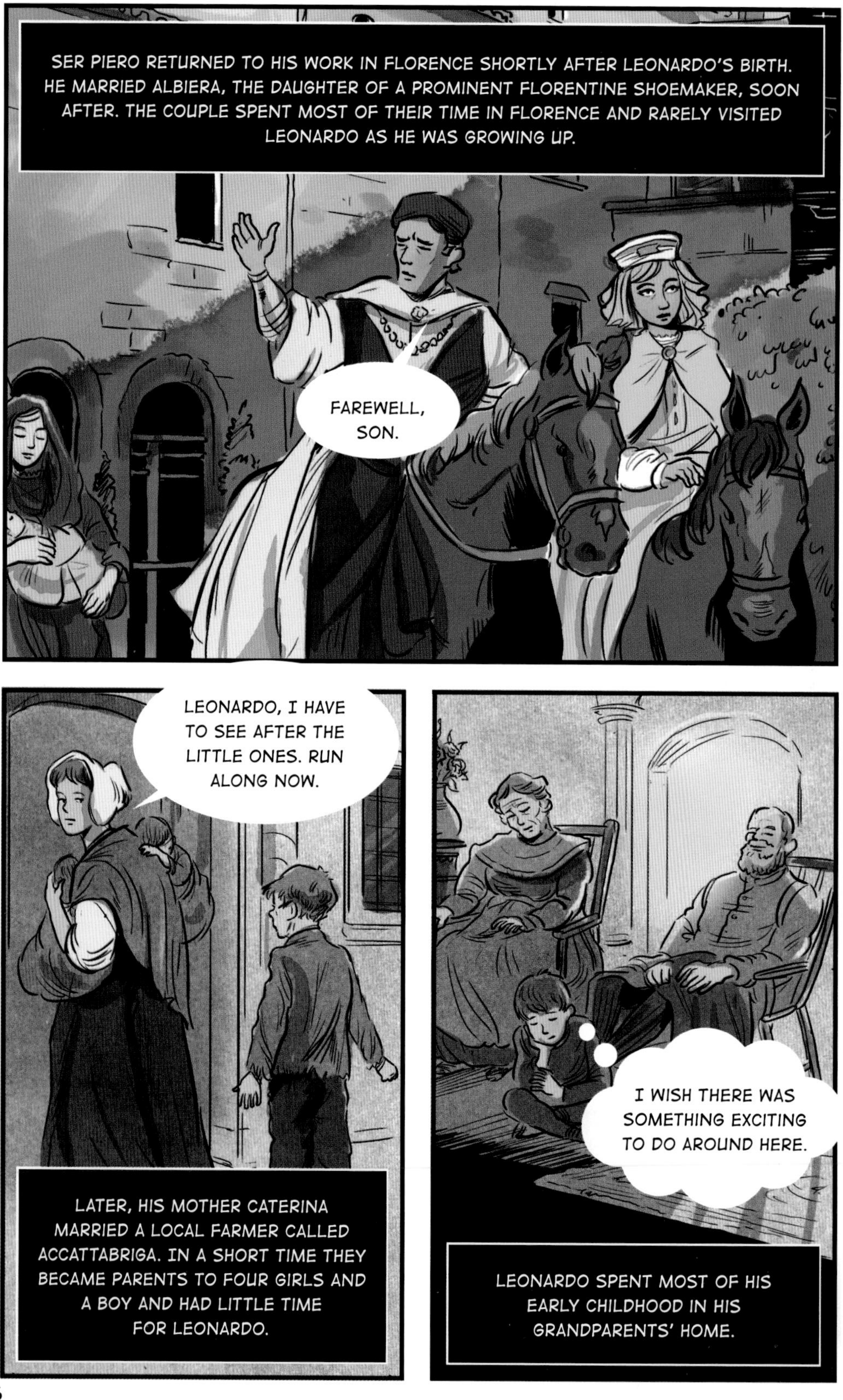
SER PIERO RETURNED TO HIS WORK IN FLORENCE SHORTLY AFTER LEONARDO'S BIRTH. HE MARRIED ALBIERA, THE DAUGHTER OF A PROMINENT FLORENTINE SHOEMAKER, SOON AFTER. THE COUPLE SPENT MOST OF THEIR TIME IN FLORENCE AND RARELY VISITED LEONARDO AS HE WAS GROWING UP.
FAREWELL, SON.
LEONARDO, I HAVE TO SEE AFTER THE LITTLE ONES. RUN ALONG NOW.
LATER, HIS MOTHER CATERINA MARRIED A LOCAL FARMER CALLED ACCATTABRIGA. IN A SHORT TIME THEY BECAME PARENTS TO FOUR GIRLS AND A BOY AND HAD LITTLE TIME FOR LEONARDO.
I WISH THERE WAS SOMETHING EXCITING TO DO AROUND HERE.
LEONARDO SPENT MOST OF HIS EARLY CHILDHOOD IN HIS GRANDPARENTS' HOME.

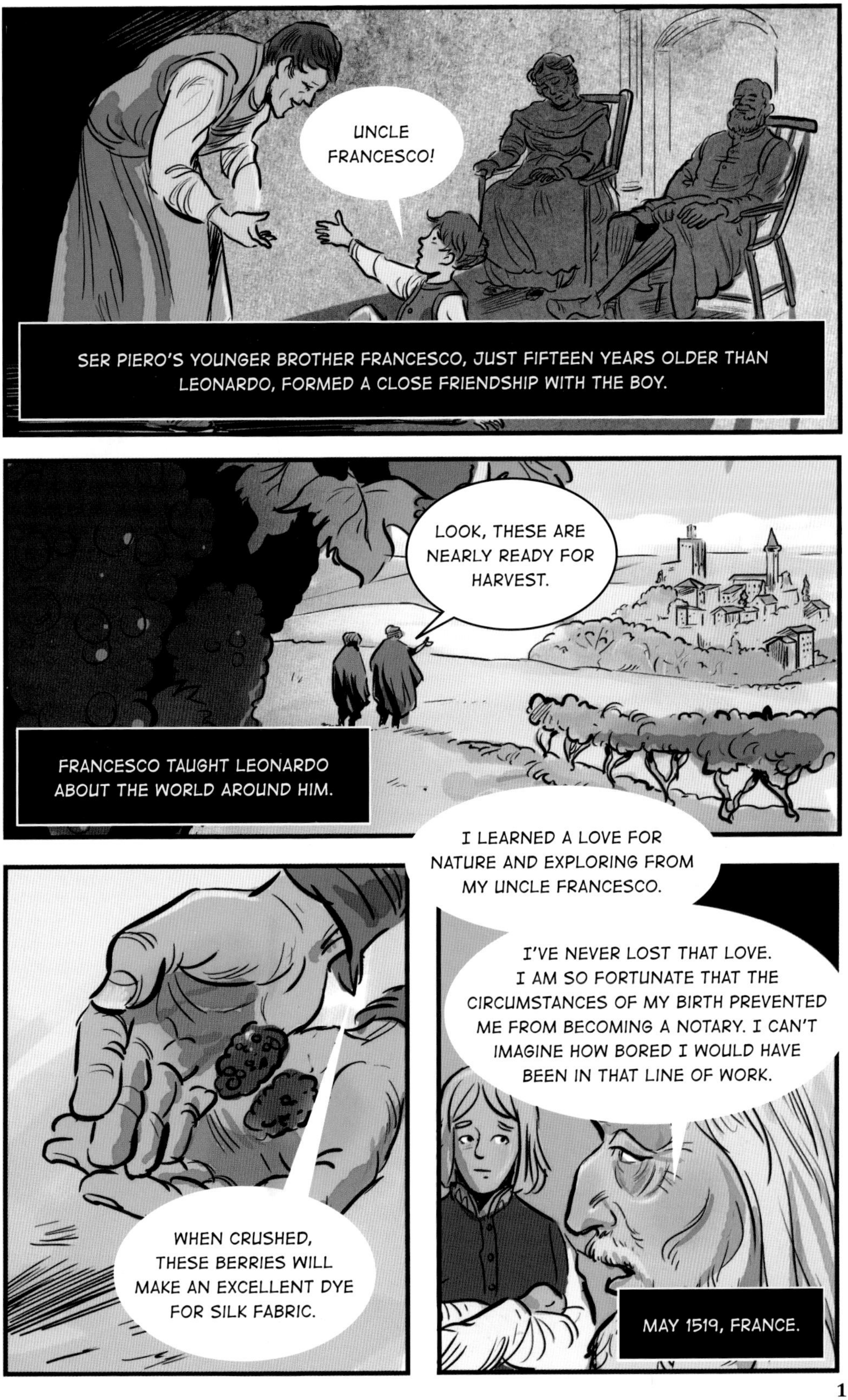
UNCLE FRANCESCO!
SER PIERO'S YOUNGER BROTHER FRANCESCO, JUST FIFTEEN YEARS OLDER THAN LEONARDO, FORMED A CLOSE FRIENDSHIP WITH THE BOY.
LOOK, THESE ARE NEARLY READY FOR HARVEST.
FRANCESCO TAUGHT LEONARDO ABOUT THE WORLD AROUND HIM.
WHEN CRUSHED, THESE BERRIES WILL MAKE AN EXCELLENT DYE FOR SILK FABRIC.
I LEARNED A LOVE FOR NATURE AND EXPLORING FROM MY UNCLE FRANCESCO.
I'VE NEVER LOST THAT LOVE. I AM SO FORTUNATE THAT THE CIRCUMSTANCES OF MY BIRTH PREVENTED ME FROM BECOMING A NOTARY. I CAN'T IMAGINE HOW BORED I WOULD HAVE BEEN IN THAT LINE OF WORK.
MAY 1519, FRANCE.

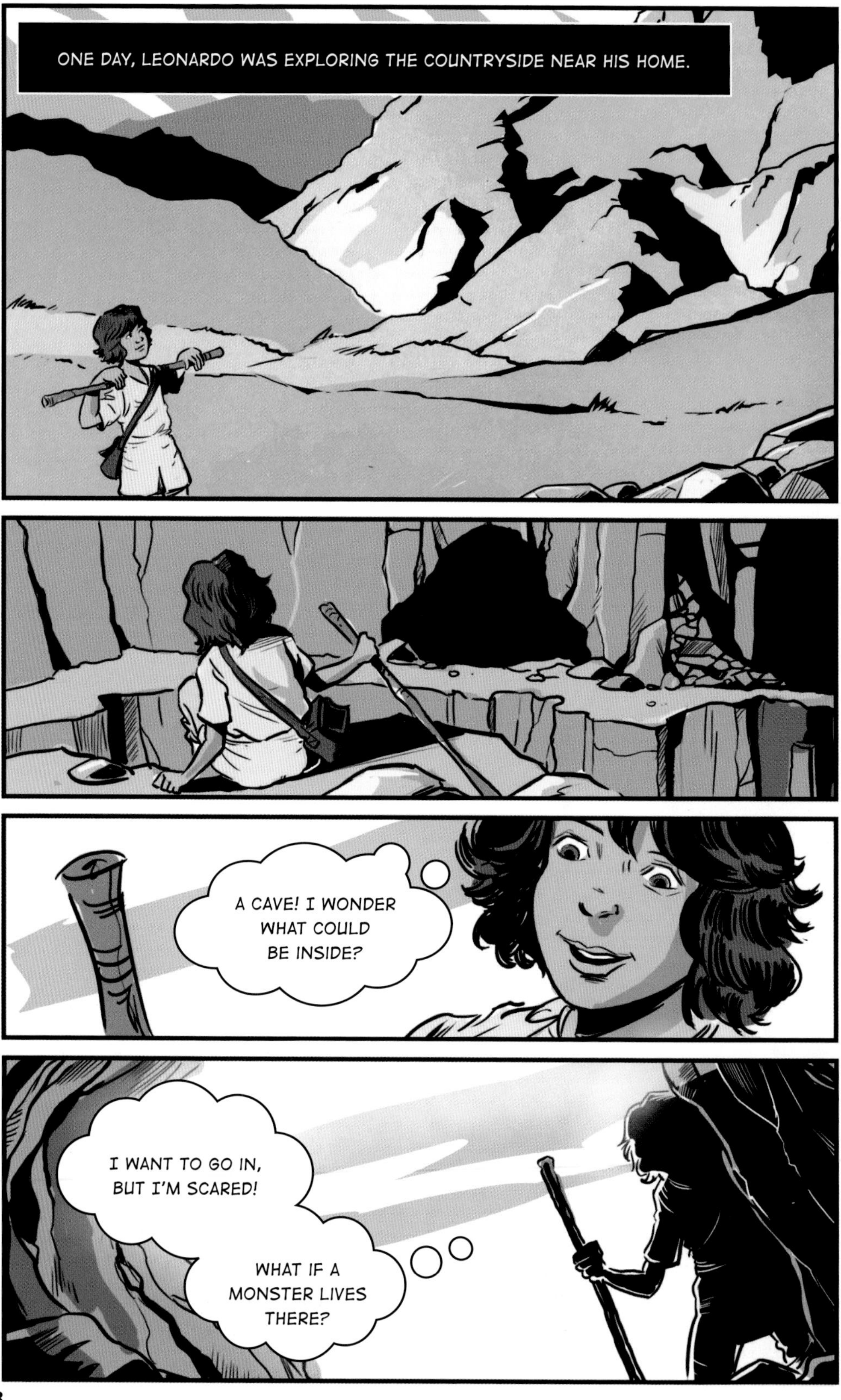
ONE DAY, LEONARDO WAS EXPLORING THE COUNTRYSIDE NEAR HIS HOME.
A CAVE! I WONDER WHAT COULD BE INSIDE?
I WANT TO GO IN, BUT I'M SCARED!
WHAT IF A MONSTER LIVES THERE?

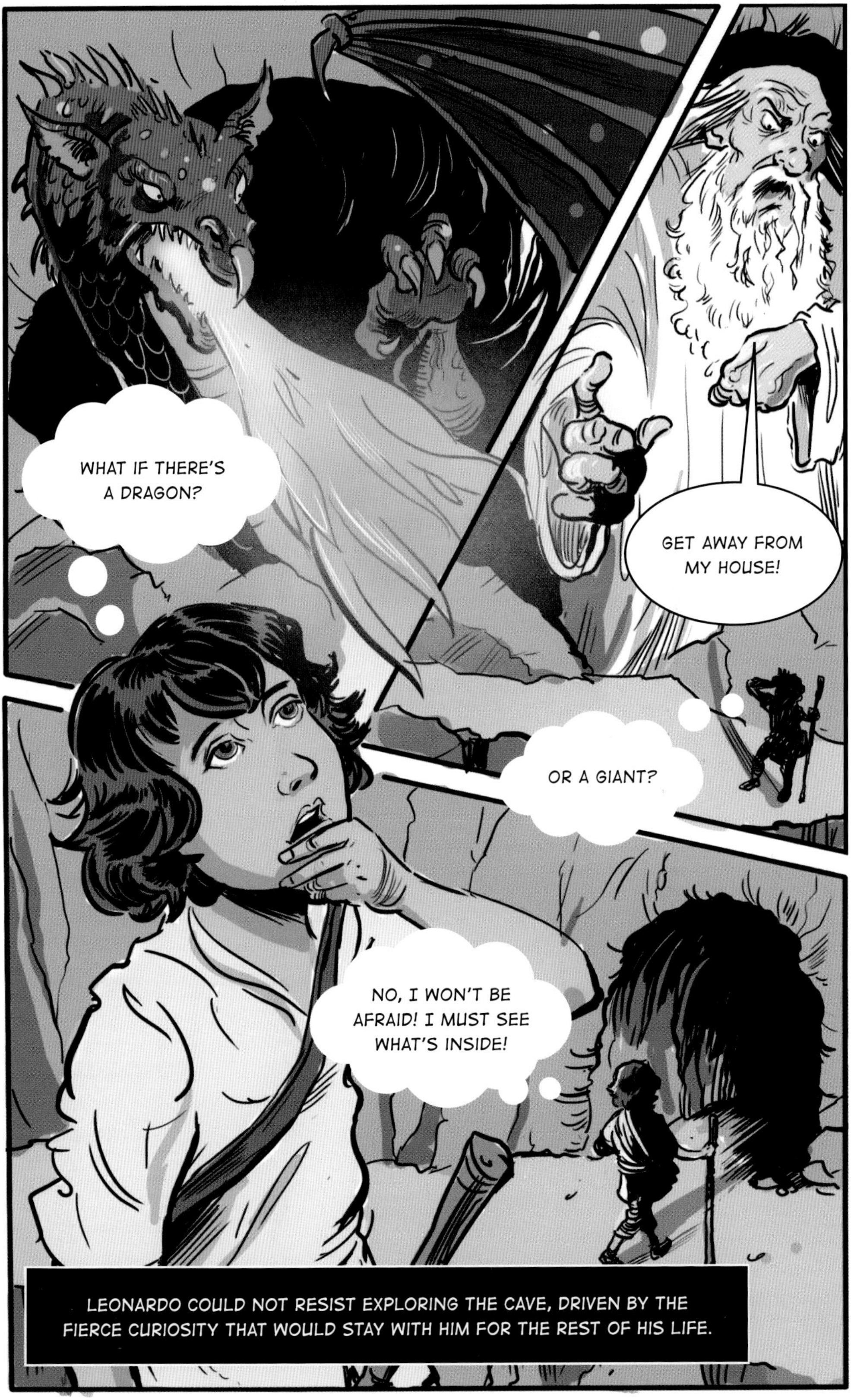
WHAT IF THERE'S A DRAGON?
GET AWAY FROM MY HOUSE!
OR A GIANT?
NO, I WON'T BE AFRAID! I MUST SEE WHAT'S INSIDE!
LEONARDO COULD NOT RESIST EXPLORING THE CAVE, DRIVEN BY THE FIERCE CURIOSITY THAT WOULD STAY WITH HIM FOR THE REST OF HIS LIFE.

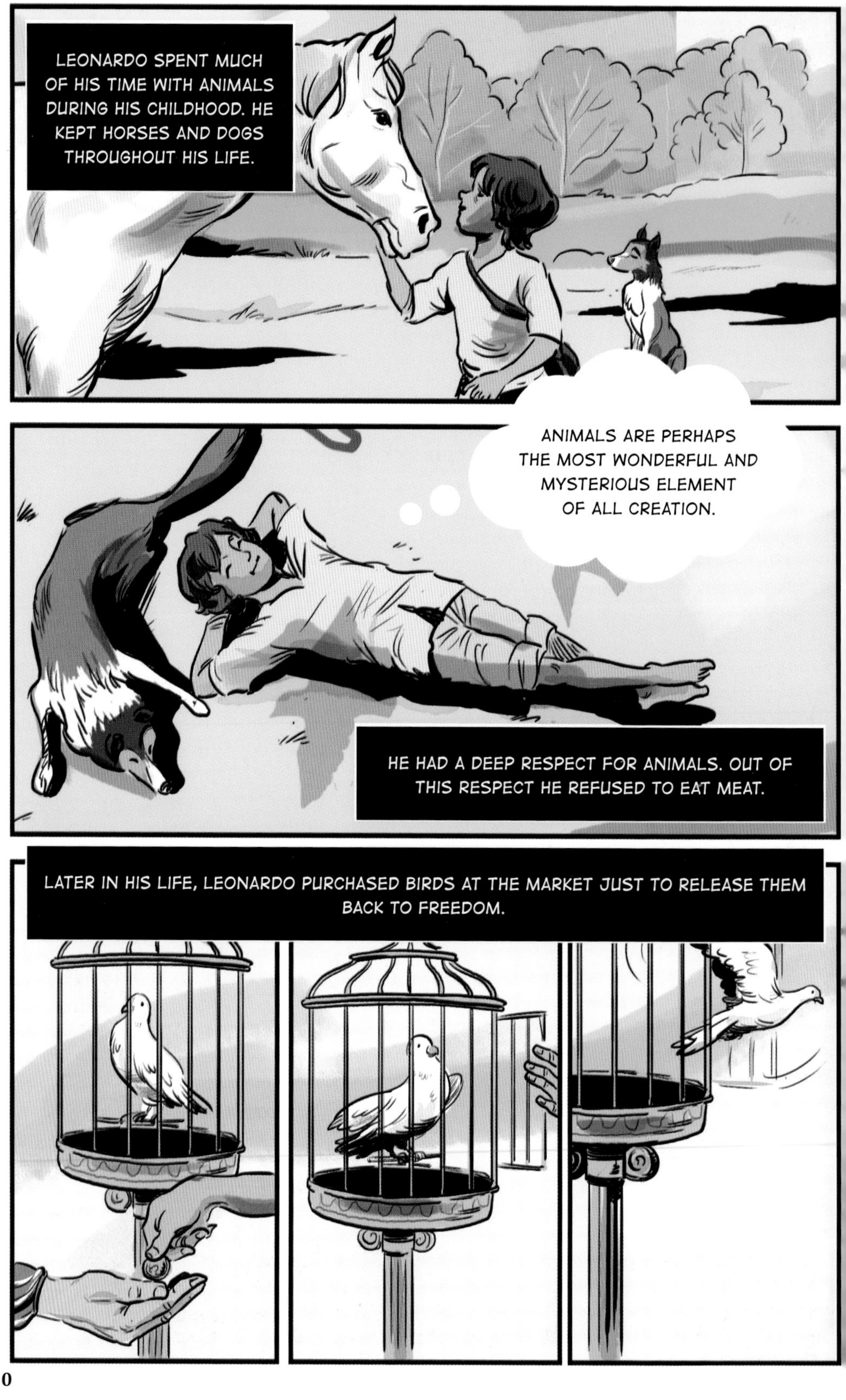
LEONARDO SPENT MUCH OF HIS TIME WITH ANIMALS DURING HIS CHILDHOOD. HE KEPT HORSES AND DOGS THROUGHOUT HIS LIFE.
ANIMALS ARE PERHAPS THE MOST WONDERFUL AND MYSTERIOUS ELEMENT OF ALL CREATION.
HE HAD A DEEP RESPECT FOR ANIMALS. OUT OF THIS RESPECT HE REFUSED TO EAT MEAT.
LATER IN HIS LIFE, LEONARDO PURCHASED BIRDS AT THE MARKET JUST TO RELEASE THEM BACK TO FREEDOM.

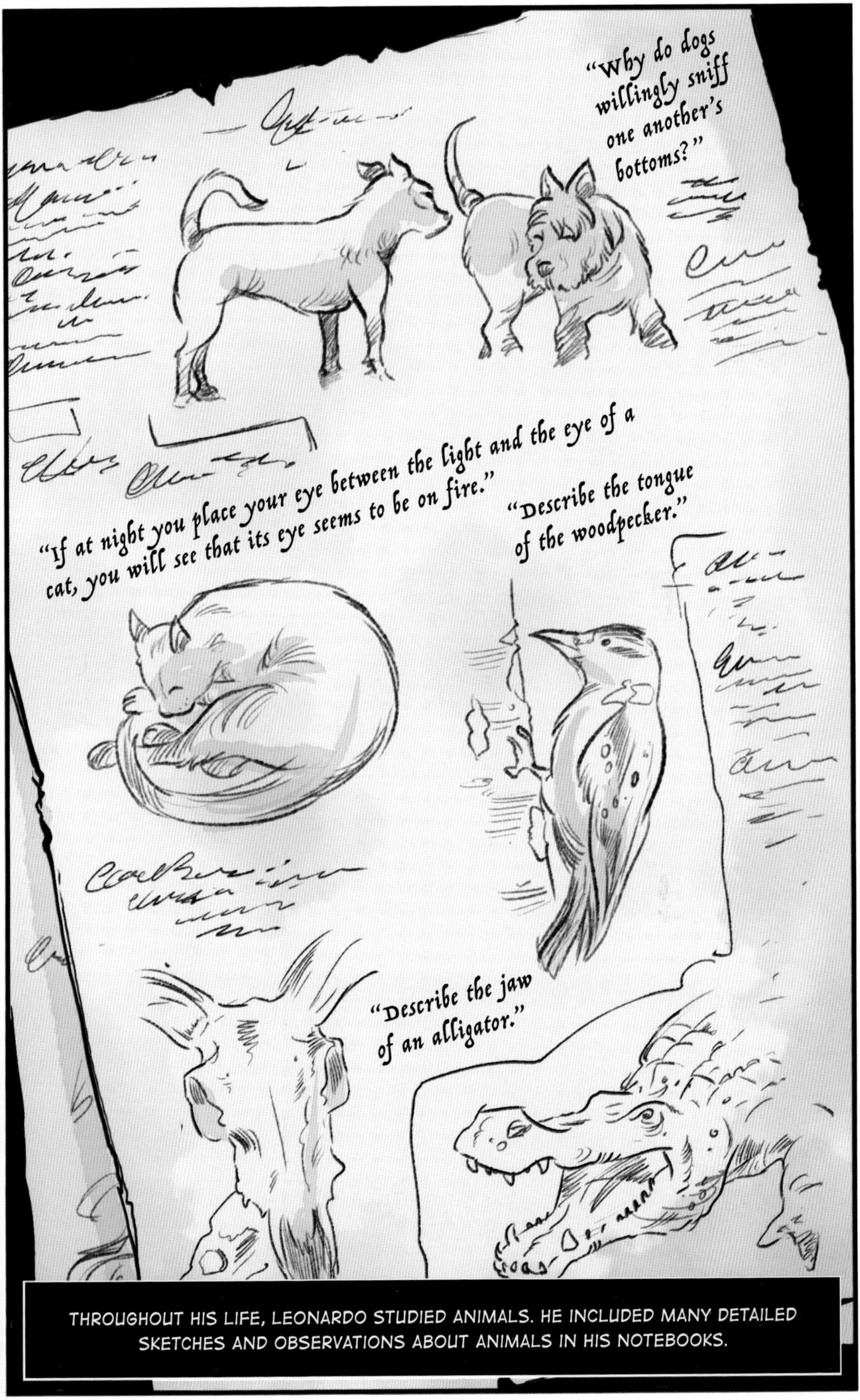
"Why do dogs willingly sniff one another's bottoms?"
"If at night you place your eye between the light and the eye of a cat, you will see that its eye seems to be on fire."
"Describe the tongue of the woodpecker."
"Describe the jaw of an alligator."

THROUGHOUT HIS LIFE, LEONARDO STUDIED ANIMALS. HE INCLUDED MANY DETAILED SKETCHES AND OBSERVATIONS ABOUT ANIMALS IN HIS NOTEBOOKS.

CHAPTER 3

LIFE IN FLORENCE

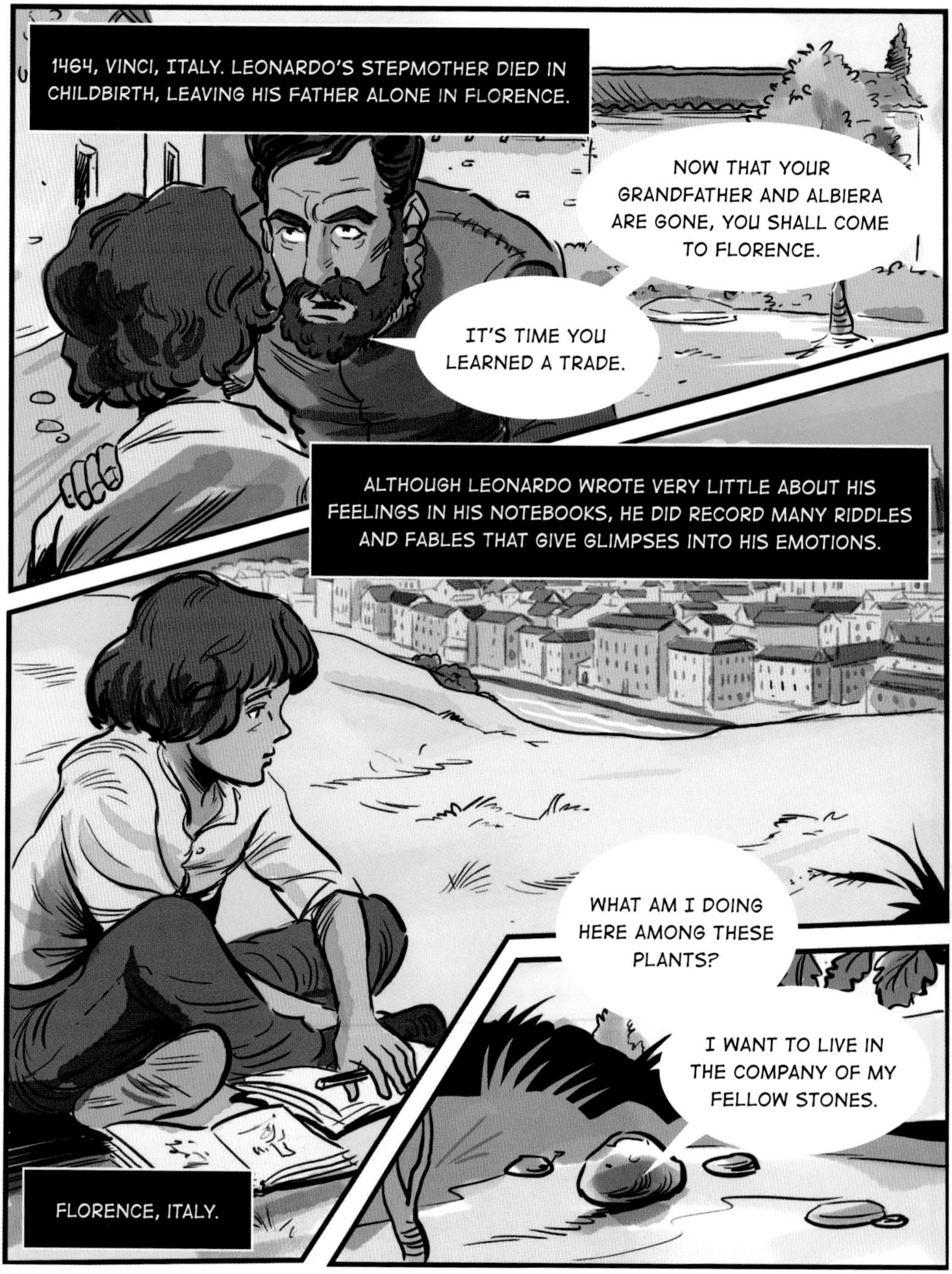
1464, VINCI, ITALY. LEONARDO'S STEPMOTHER DIED IN CHILDBIRTH, LEAVING HIS FATHER ALONE IN FLORENCE.
NOW THAT YOUR GRANDFATHER AND ALBIERA ARE GONE, YOU SHALL COME TO FLORENCE.
IT'S TIME YOU LEARNED A TRADE.
ALTHOUGH LEONARDO WROTE VERY LITTLE ABOUT HIS FEELINGS IN HIS NOTEBOOKS, HE DID RECORD MANY RIDDLES AND FABLES THAT GIVE GLIMPSES INTO HIS EMOTIONS.
FLORENCE, ITALY.
WHAT AM I DOING HERE AMONG THESE PLANTS?
I WANT TO LIVE IN THE COMPANY OF MY FELLOW STONES.

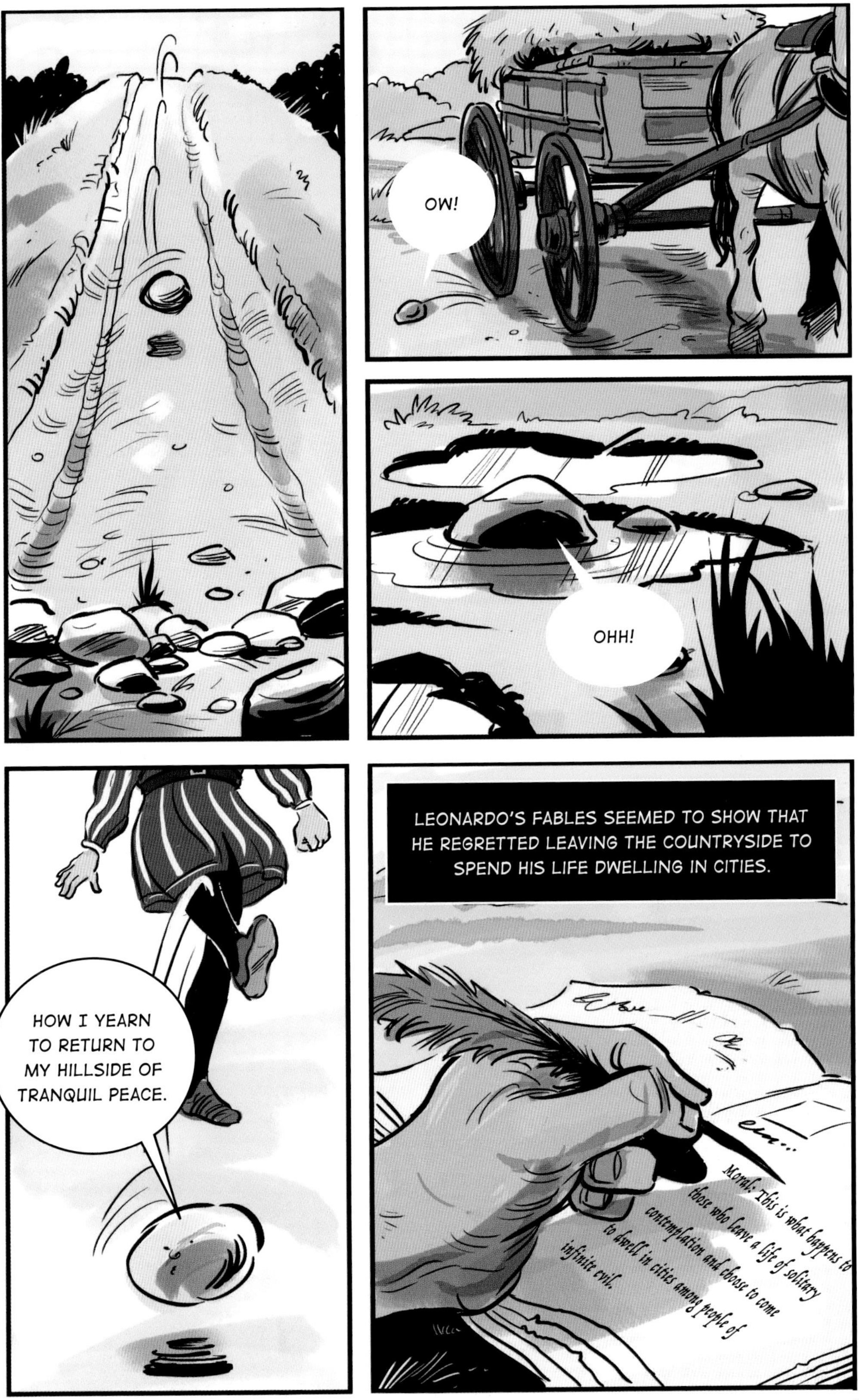
OW!
OHH!
HOW I YEARN TO RETURN TO MY HILLSIDE OF TRANQUIL PEACE.
LEONARDO'S FABLES SEEMED TO SHOW THAT HE REGRETTED LEAVING THE COUNTRYSIDE TO SPEND HIS LIFE DWELLING IN CITIES.
Moral: This is what happens to those who leave a life of solitary contemplation and choose to come to dwell in cities among people of infinite evil.

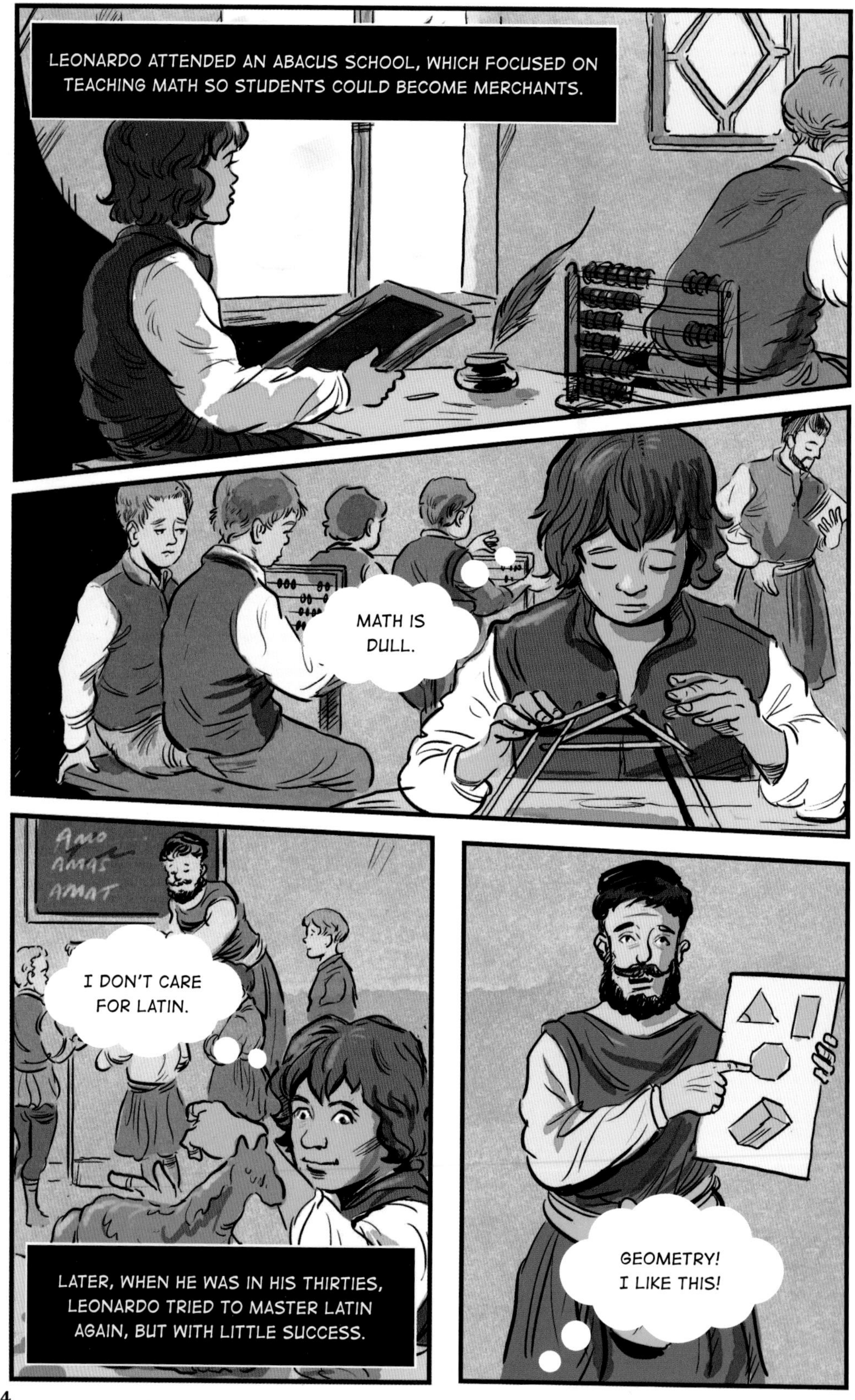
LEONARDO ATTENDED AN ABACUS SCHOOL, WHICH FOCUSED ON TEACHING MATH SO STUDENTS COULD BECOME MERCHANTS.
MATH IS DULL.
AMO
AMAS
AMAT
I DON'T CARE FOR LATIN.
LATER, WHEN HE WAS IN HIS THIRTIES, LEONARDO TRIED TO MASTER LATIN AGAIN, BUT WITH LITTLE SUCCESS.
GEOMETRY! I LIKE THIS!

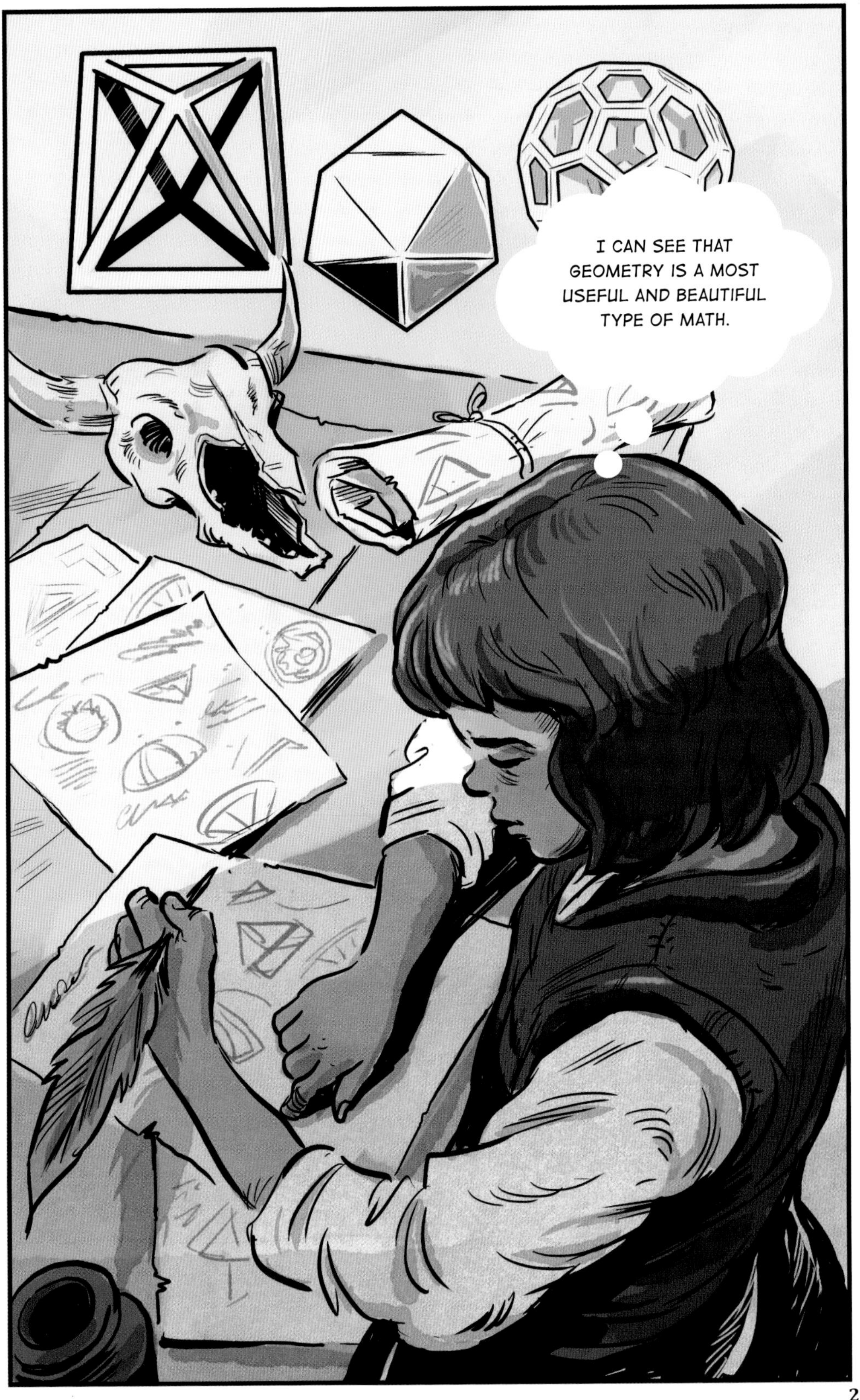
I CAN SEE THAT GEOMETRY IS A MOST USEFUL AND BEAUTIFUL TYPE OF MATH.

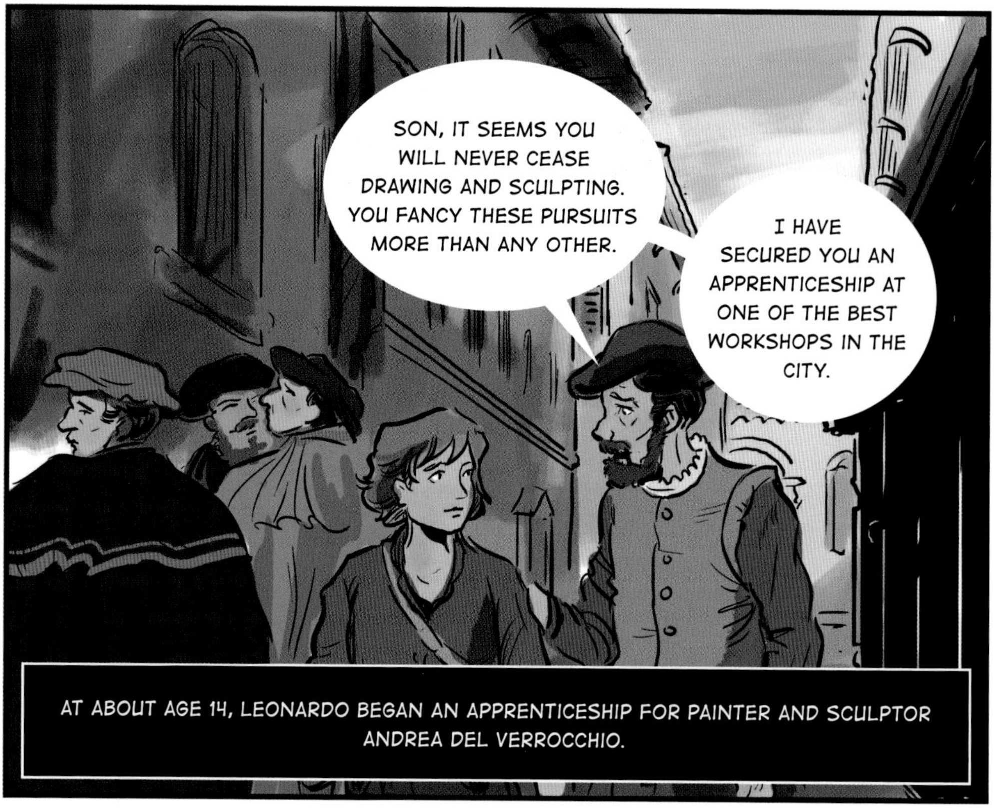
SON, IT SEEMS YOU WILL NEVER CEASE DRAWING AND SCULPTING. YOU FANCY THESE PURSUITS MORE THAN ANY OTHER.
I HAVE SECURED YOU AN APPRENTICESHIP AT ONE OF THE BEST WORKSHOPS IN THE CITY.
AT ABOUT AGE 14, LEONARDO BEGAN AN APPRENTICESHIP FOR PAINTER AND SCULPTOR ANDREA DEL VERROCCHIO.

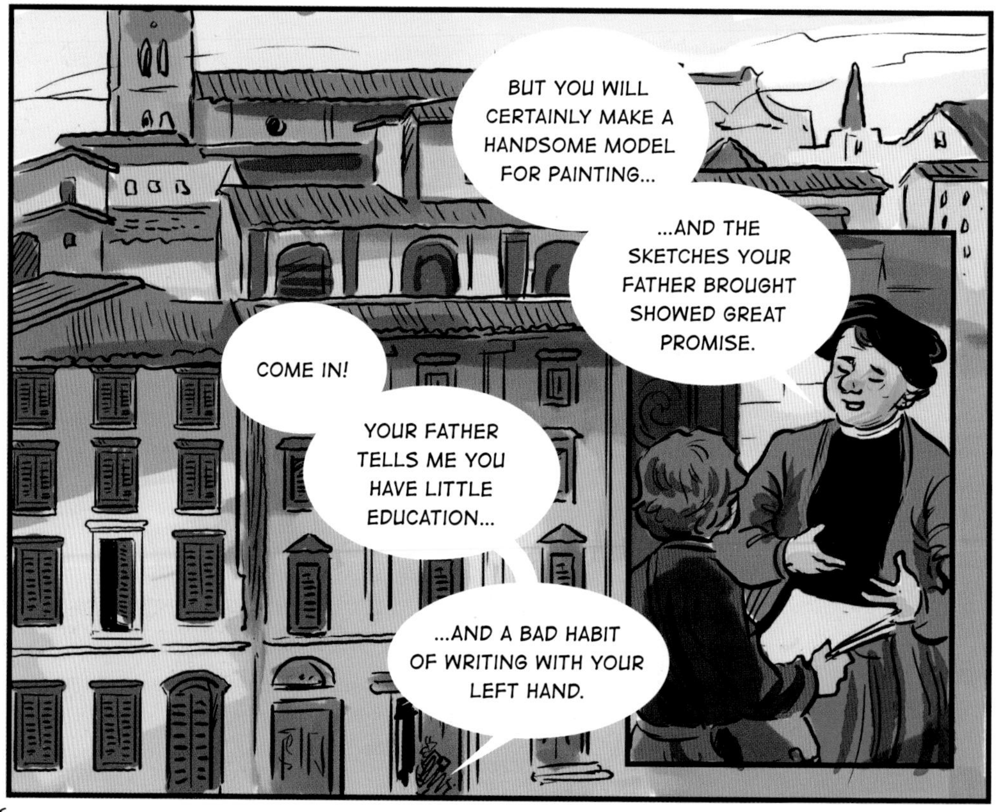
BUT YOU WILL CERTAINLY MAKE A HANDSOME MODEL FOR PAINTING...
...AND THE SKETCHES YOUR FATHER BROUGHT SHOWED GREAT PROMISE.
COME IN!
YOUR FATHER TELLS ME YOU HAVE LITTLE EDUCATION...
...AND A BAD HABIT OF WRITING WITH YOUR LEFT HAND.

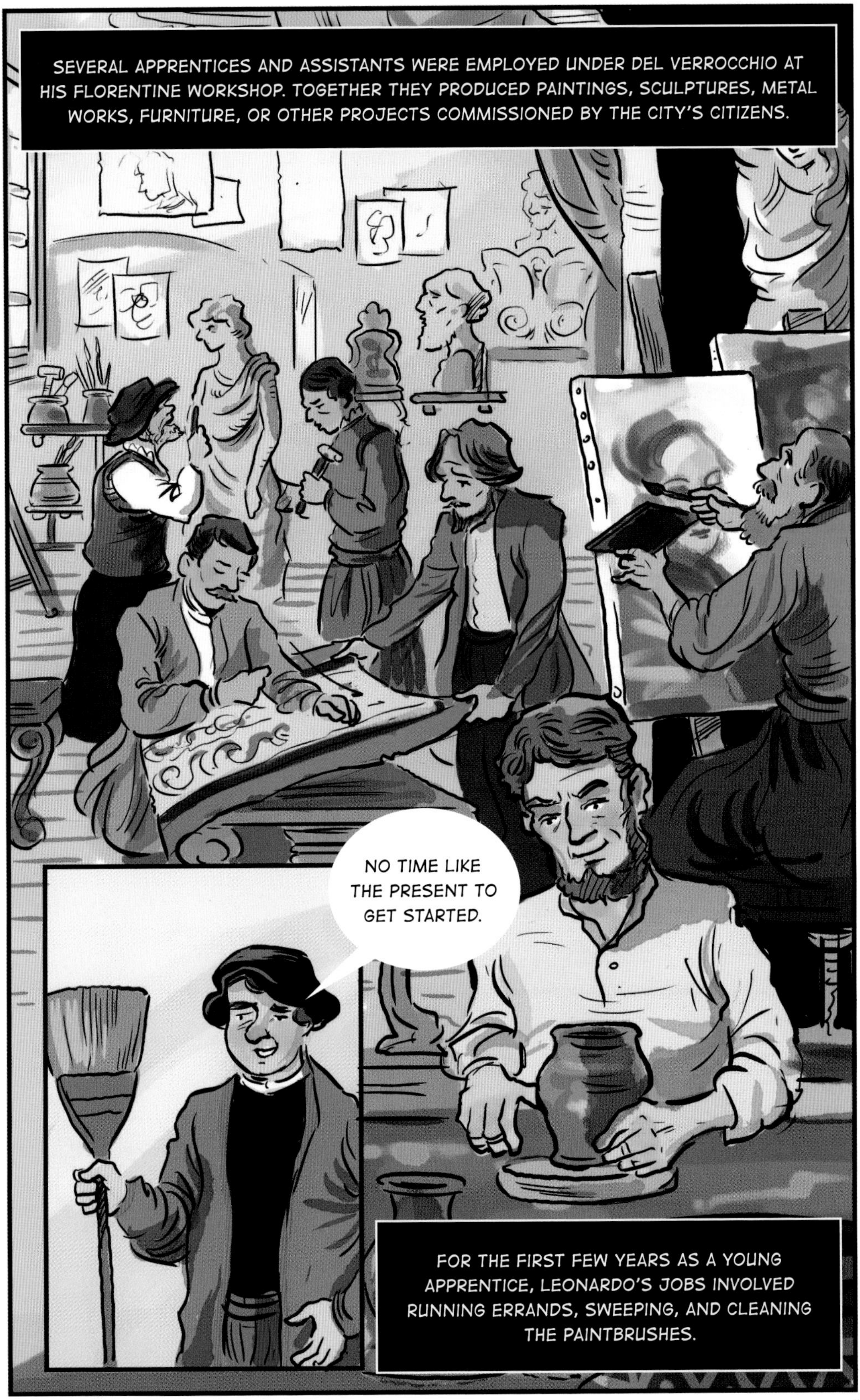
SEVERAL APPRENTICES AND ASSISTANTS WERE EMPLOYED UNDER DEL VERROCCHIO AT HIS FLORENTINE WORKSHOP. TOGETHER THEY PRODUCED PAINTINGS, SCULPTURES, METAL WORKS, FURNITURE, OR OTHER PROJECTS COMMISSIONED BY THE CITY'S CITIZENS.
NO TIME LIKE THE PRESENT TO GET STARTED.
FOR THE FIRST FEW YEARS AS A YOUNG APPRENTICE, LEONARDO'S JOBS INVOLVED RUNNING ERRANDS, SWEEPING, AND CLEANING THE PAINTBRUSHES.

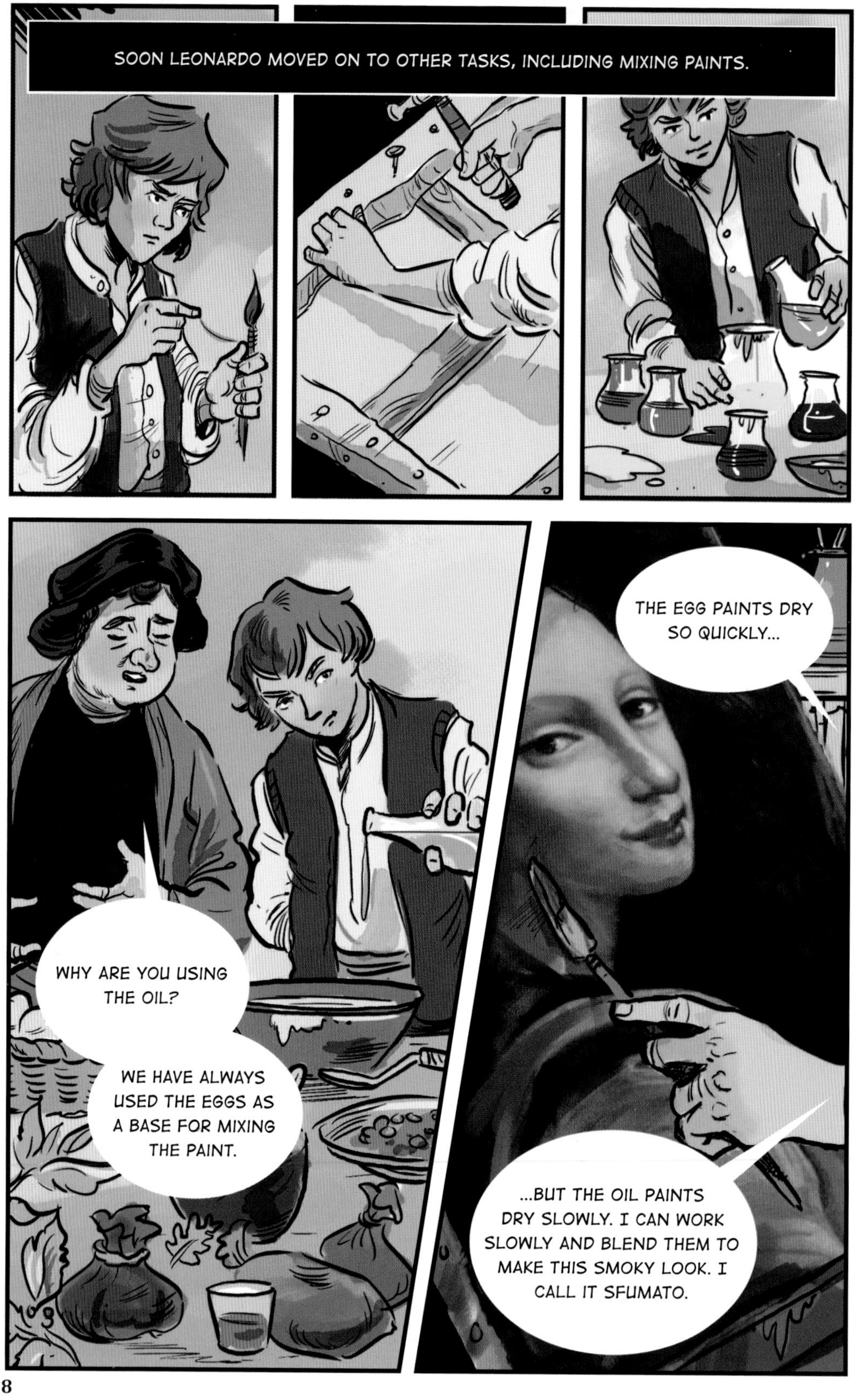
SOON LEONARDO MOVED ON TO OTHER TASKS, INCLUDING MIXING PAINTS.
WHY ARE YOU USING THE OIL?
WE HAVE ALWAYS USED THE EGGS AS A BASE FOR MIXING THE PAINT.
THE EGG PAINTS DRY SO QUICKLY...
...BUT THE OIL PAINTS DRY SLOWLY. I CAN WORK SLOWLY AND BLEND THEM TO MAKE THIS SMOKY LOOK. I CALL IT SFUMATO.

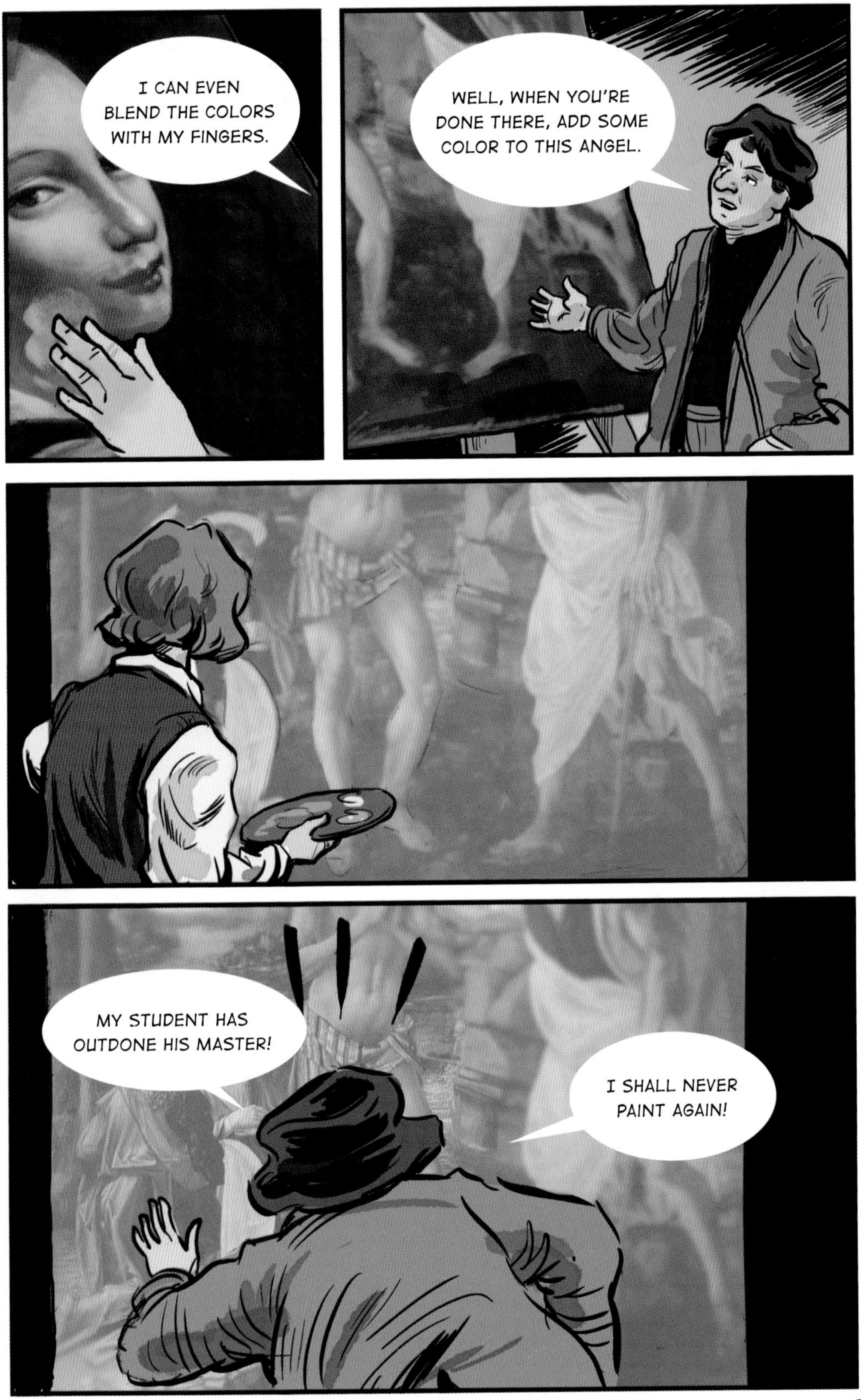
I CAN EVEN BLEND THE COLORS WITH MY FINGERS.
WELL, WHEN YOU'RE DONE THERE, ADD SOME COLOR TO THIS ANGEL.
MY STUDENT HAS OUTDONE HIS MASTER!
I SHALL NEVER PAINT AGAIN!

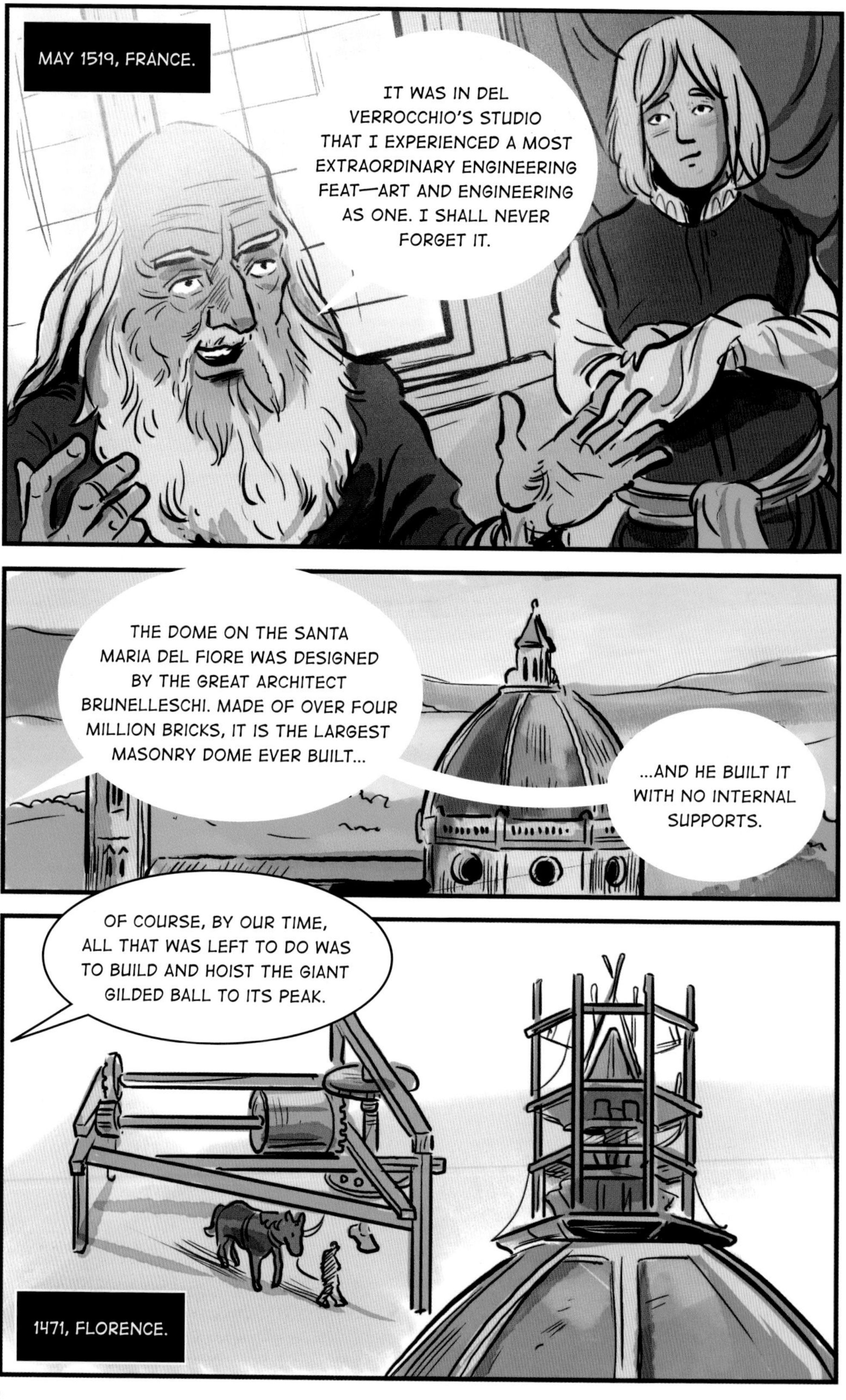
MAY 1519, FRANCE.
IT WAS IN DEL VERROCCHIO'S STUDIO THAT I EXPERIENCED A MOST EXTRAORDINARY ENGINEERING FEAT—ART AND ENGINEERING AS ONE. I SHALL NEVER FORGET IT.
THE DOME ON THE SANTA MARIA DEL FIORE WAS DESIGNED BY THE GREAT ARCHITECT BRUNELLESCHI. MADE OF OVER FOUR MILLION BRICKS, IT IS THE LARGEST MASONRY DOME EVER BUILT...
...AND HE BUILT IT WITH NO INTERNAL SUPPORTS.
OF COURSE, BY OUR TIME, ALL THAT WAS LEFT TO DO WAS TO BUILD AND HOIST THE GIANT GILDED BALL TO ITS PEAK.
1471, FLORENCE.

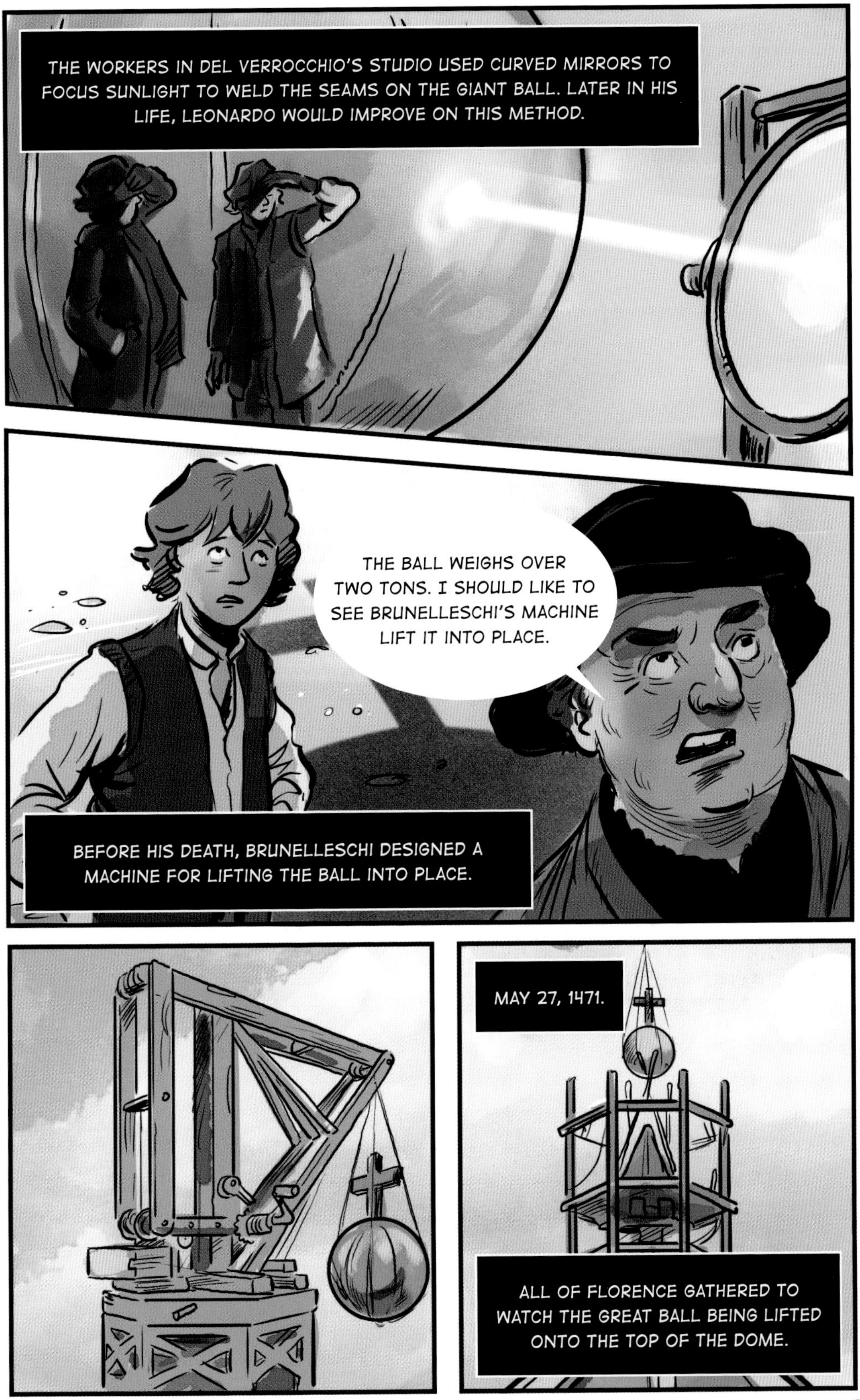
THE WORKERS IN DEL VERROCCHIO'S STUDIO USED CURVED MIRRORS TO FOCUS SUNLIGHT TO WELD THE SEAMS ON THE GIANT BALL. LATER IN HIS LIFE, LEONARDO WOULD IMPROVE ON THIS METHOD.
THE BALL WEIGHS OVER TWO TONS. I SHOULD LIKE TO SEE BRUNELLESCHI'S MACHINE LIFT IT INTO PLACE.
BEFORE HIS DEATH, BRUNELLESCHI DESIGNED A MACHINE FOR LIFTING THE BALL INTO PLACE.
MAY 27, 1471.
ALL OF FLORENCE GATHERED TO WATCH THE GREAT BALL BEING LIFTED ONTO THE TOP OF THE DOME.

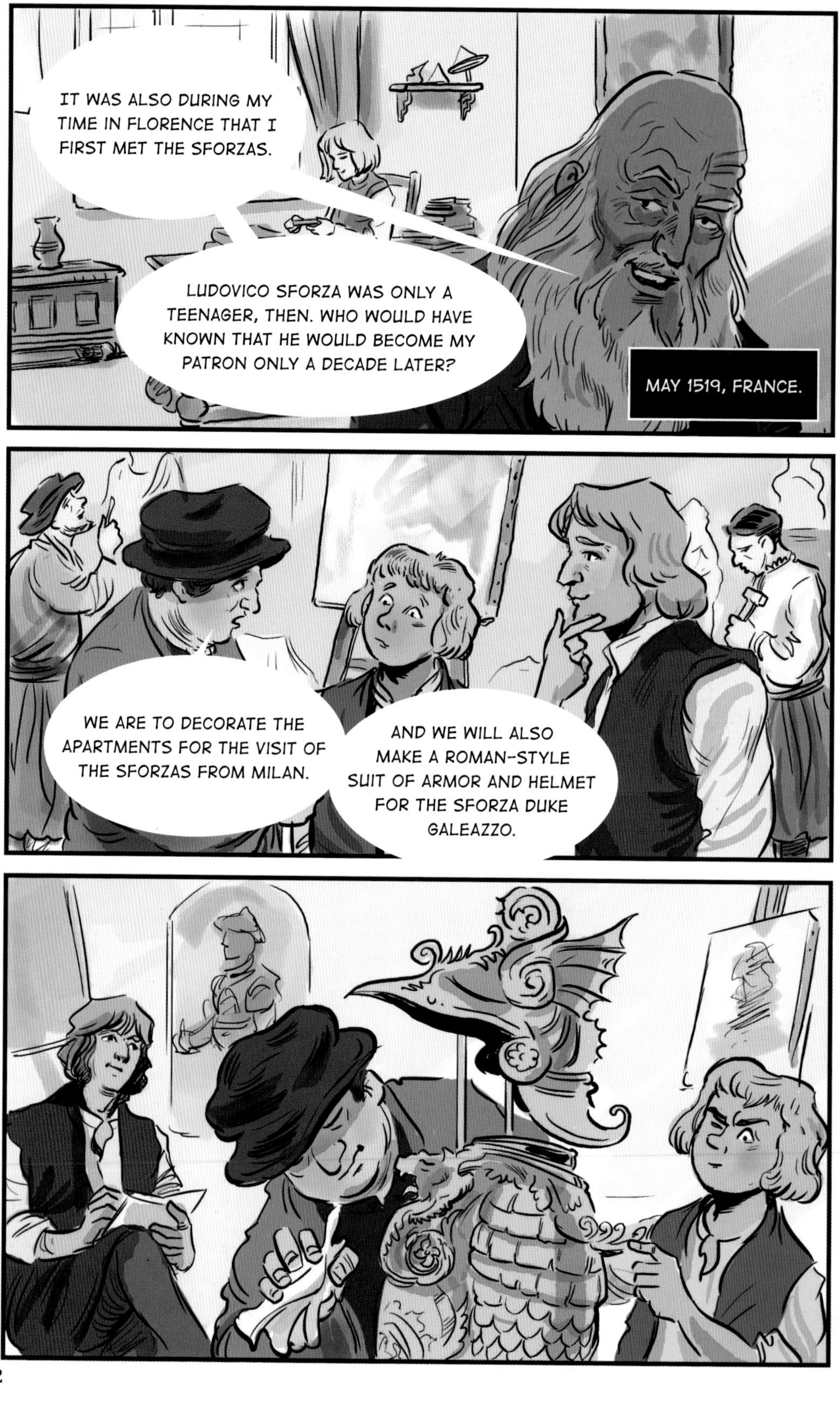
IT WAS ALSO DURING MY TIME IN FLORENCE THAT I FIRST MET THE SFORZAS.
LUDOVICO SFORZA WAS ONLY A TEENAGER, THEN. WHO WOULD HAVE KNOWN THAT HE WOULD BECOME MY PATRON ONLY A DECADE LATER?
MAY 1519, FRANCE.
WE ARE TO DECORATE THE APARTMENTS FOR THE VISIT OF THE SFORZAS FROM MILAN.
AND WE WILL ALSO MAKE A ROMAN-STYLE SUIT OF ARMOR AND HELMET FOR THE SFORZA DUKE GALEAZZO.

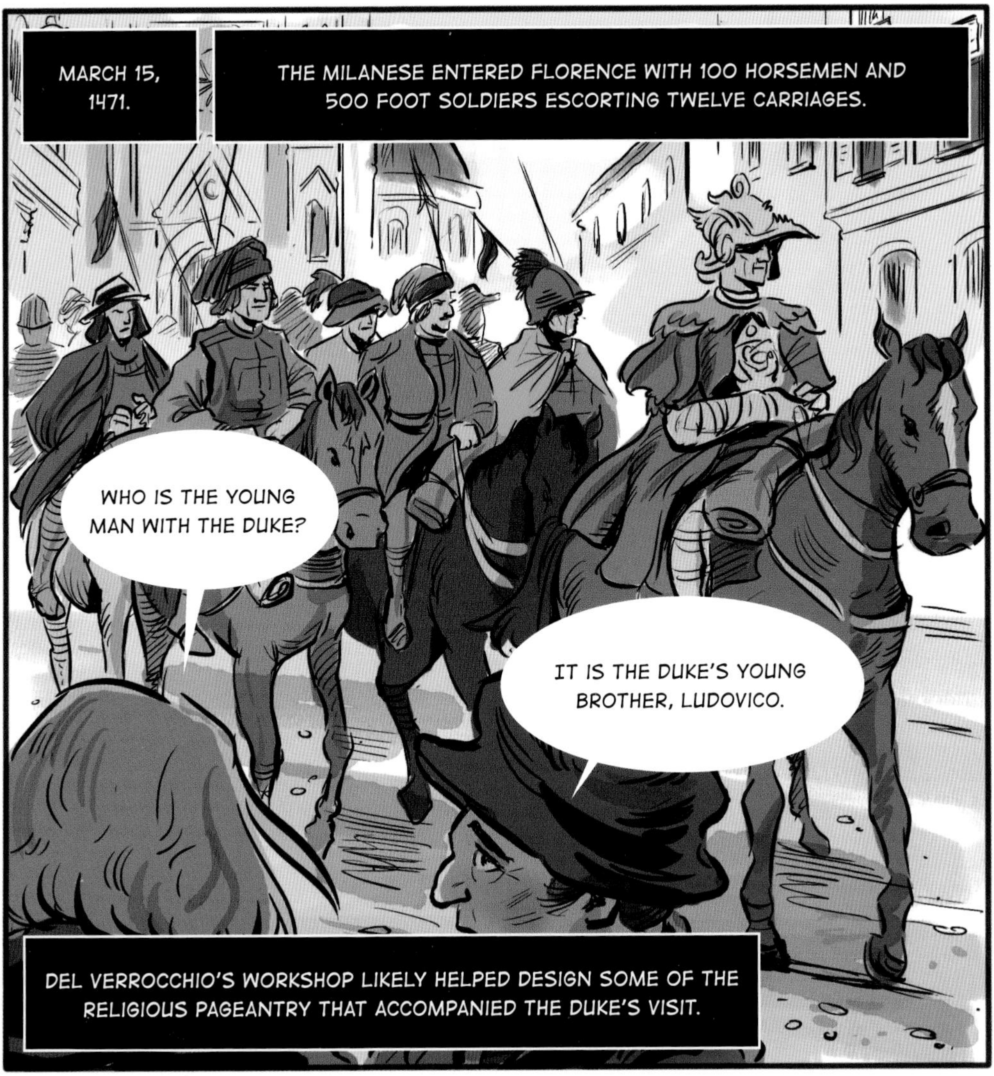
MARCH 15, 1471.
THE MILANESE ENTERED FLORENCE WITH 100 HORSEMEN AND 500 FOOT SOLDIERS ESCORTING TWELVE CARRIAGES.
WHO IS THE YOUNG MAN WITH THE DUKE?
IT IS THE DUKE'S YOUNG BROTHER, LUDOVICO.
DEL VERROCCHIO'S WORKSHOP LIKELY HELPED DESIGN SOME OF THE RELIGIOUS PAGEANTRY THAT ACCOMPANIED THE DUKE'S VISIT.

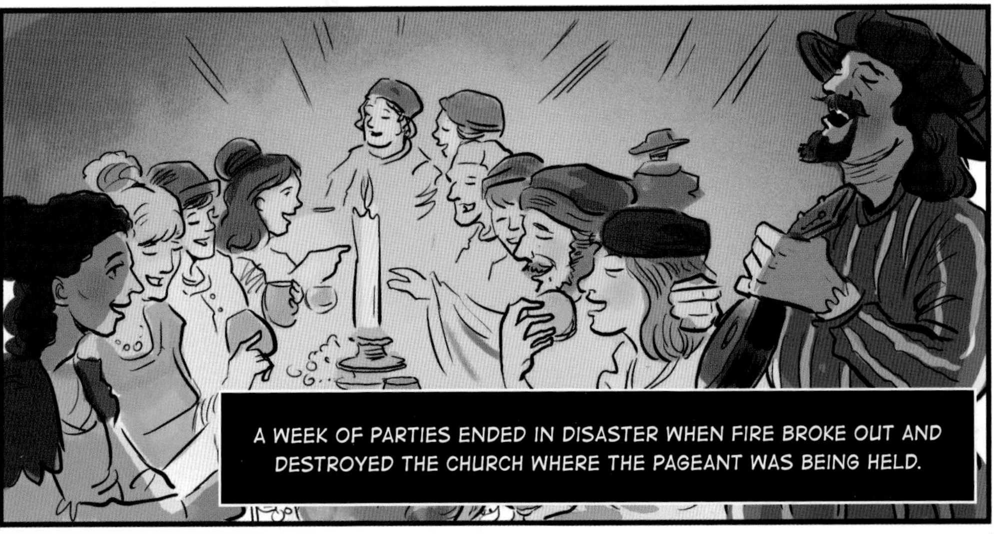
A WEEK OF PARTIES ENDED IN DISASTER WHEN FIRE BROKE OUT AND DESTROYED THE CHURCH WHERE THE PAGEANT WAS BEING HELD.

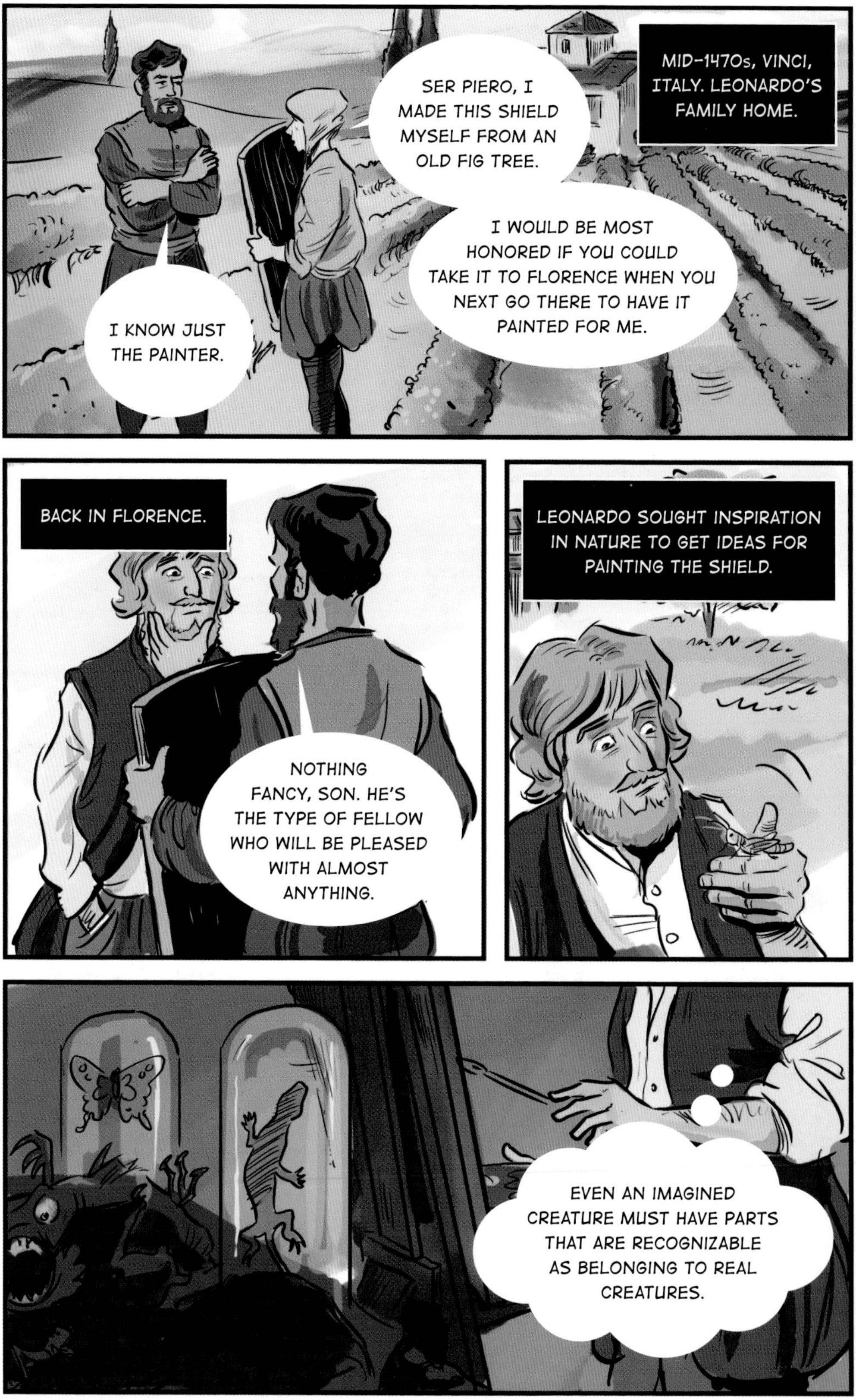
MID-1470s, VINCI, ITALY. LEONARDO'S FAMILY HOME.
SER PIERO, I MADE THIS SHIELD MYSELF FROM AN OLD FIG TREE.
I WOULD BE MOST HONORED IF YOU COULD TAKE IT TO FLORENCE WHEN YOU NEXT GO THERE TO HAVE IT PAINTED FOR ME.
I KNOW JUST THE PAINTER.
BACK IN FLORENCE.
NOTHING FANCY, SON. HE'S THE TYPE OF FELLOW WHO WILL BE PLEASED WITH ALMOST ANYTHING.
LEONARDO SOUGHT INSPIRATION IN NATURE TO GET IDEAS FOR PAINTING THE SHIELD.
EVEN AN IMAGINED CREATURE MUST HAVE PARTS THAT ARE RECOGNIZABLE AS BELONGING TO REAL CREATURES.

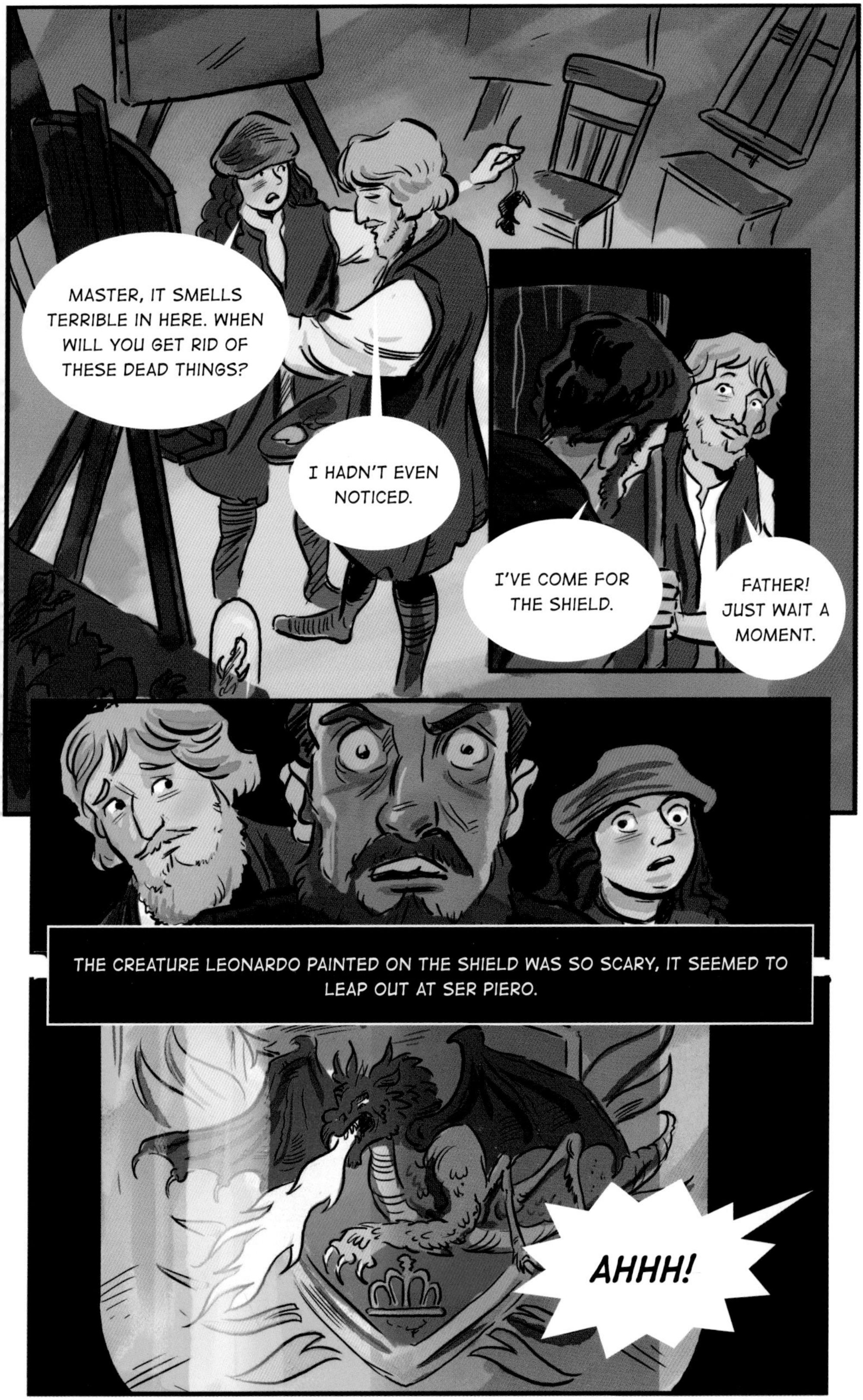
MASTER, IT SMELLS TERRIBLE IN HERE. WHEN WILL YOU GET RID OF THESE DEAD THINGS?
I HADN'T EVEN NOTICED.
I'VE COME FOR THE SHIELD.
FATHER! JUST WAIT A MOMENT.
THE CREATURE LEONARDO PAINTED ON THE SHIELD WAS SO SCARY, IT SEEMED TO LEAP OUT AT SER PIERO.
AHHH!

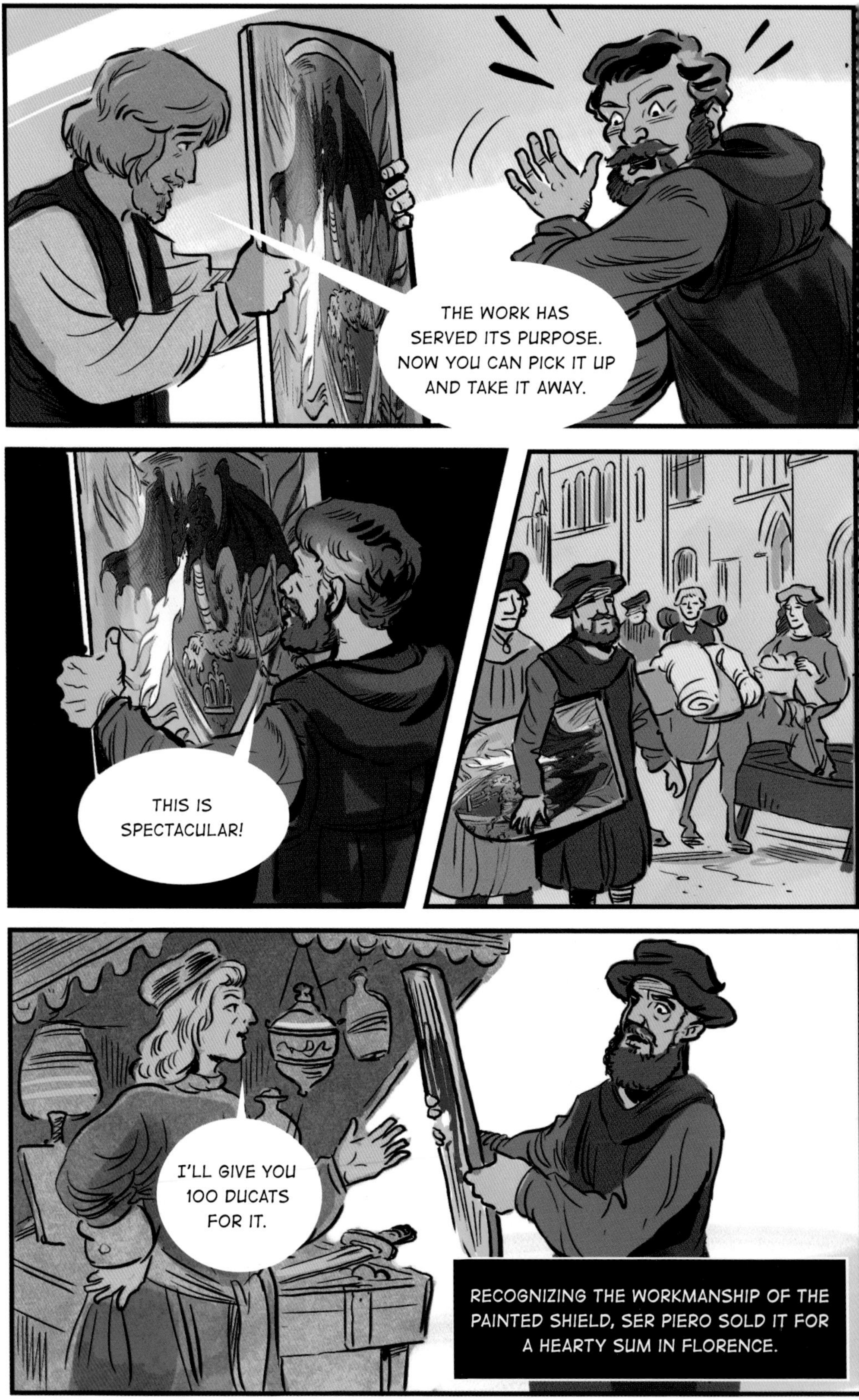
THE WORK HAS SERVED ITS PURPOSE. NOW YOU CAN PICK IT UP AND TAKE IT AWAY.
THIS IS SPECTACULAR!
I'LL GIVE YOU 100 DUCATS FOR IT.
RECOGNIZING THE WORKMANSHIP OF THE PAINTED SHIELD, SER PIERO SOLD IT FOR A HEARTY SUM IN FLORENCE.

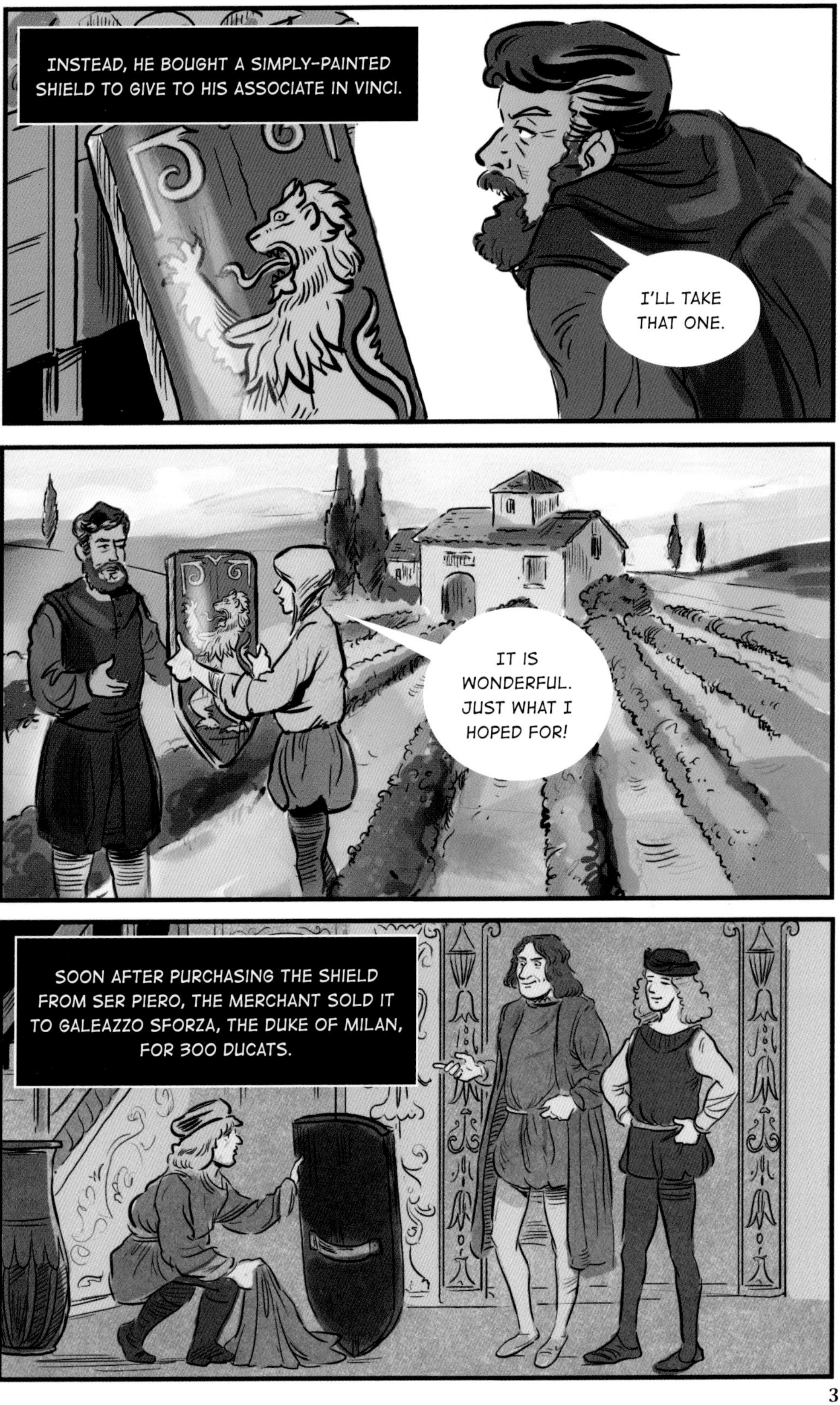
INSTEAD, HE BOUGHT A SIMPLY-PAINTED SHIELD TO GIVE TO HIS ASSOCIATE IN VINCI.
I'LL TAKE THAT ONE.
IT IS WONDERFUL. JUST WHAT I HOPED FOR!
SOON AFTER PURCHASING THE SHIELD FROM SER PIERO, THE MERCHANT SOLD IT TO GALEAZZO SFORZA, THE DUKE OF MILAN, FOR 300 DUCATS.

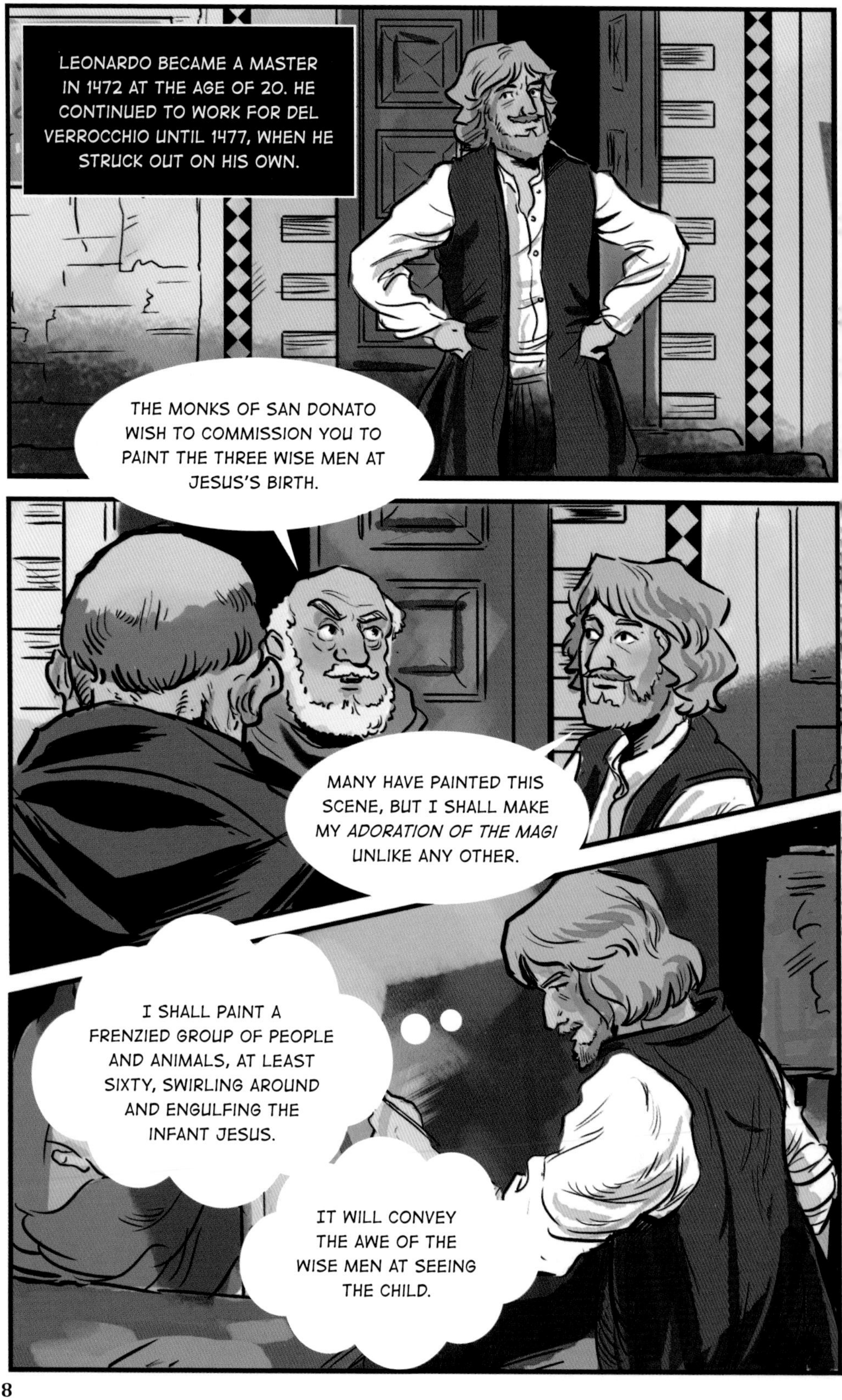
LEONARDO BECAME A MASTER IN 1472 AT THE AGE OF 20. HE CONTINUED TO WORK FOR DEL VERROCCHIO UNTIL 1477, WHEN HE STRUCK OUT ON HIS OWN.
THE MONKS OF SAN DONATO WISH TO COMMISSION YOU TO PAINT THE THREE WISE MEN AT JESUS'S BIRTH.
MANY HAVE PAINTED THIS SCENE, BUT I SHALL MAKE MY *ADORATION OF THE MAGI* UNLIKE ANY OTHER.
I SHALL PAINT A FRENZIED GROUP OF PEOPLE AND ANIMALS, AT LEAST SIXTY, SWIRLING AROUND AND ENGULFING THE INFANT JESUS.
IT WILL CONVEY THE AWE OF THE WISE MEN AT SEEING THE CHILD.

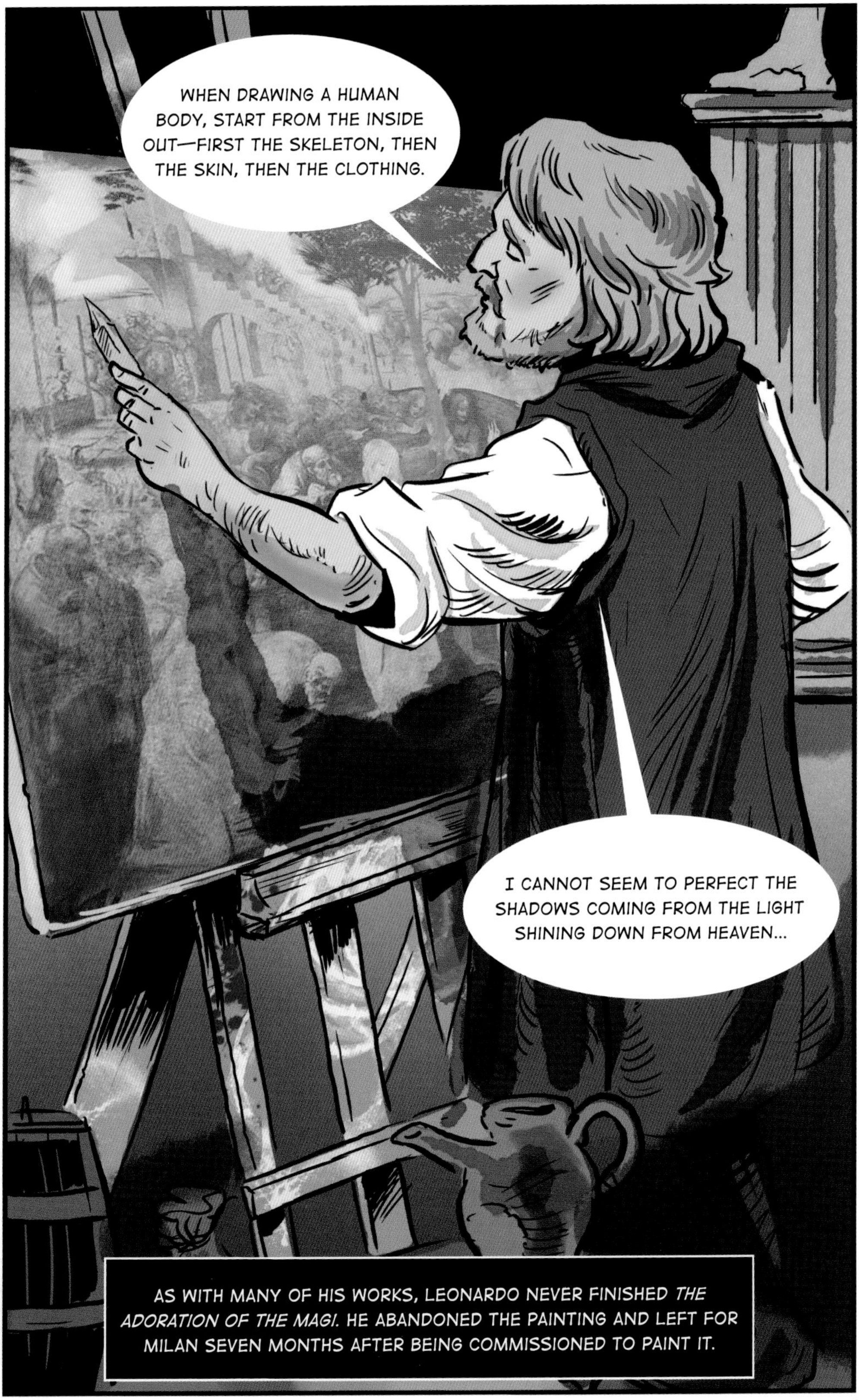
WHEN DRAWING A HUMAN BODY, START FROM THE INSIDE OUT—FIRST THE SKELETON, THEN THE SKIN, THEN THE CLOTHING.
I CANNOT SEEM TO PERFECT THE SHADOWS COMING FROM THE LIGHT SHINING DOWN FROM HEAVEN...
AS WITH MANY OF HIS WORKS, LEONARDO NEVER FINISHED *THE ADORATION OF THE MAGI.* HE ABANDONED THE PAINTING AND LEFT FOR MILAN SEVEN MONTHS AFTER BEING COMMISSIONED TO PAINT IT.

CHAPTER 4

AT COURT IN MILAN

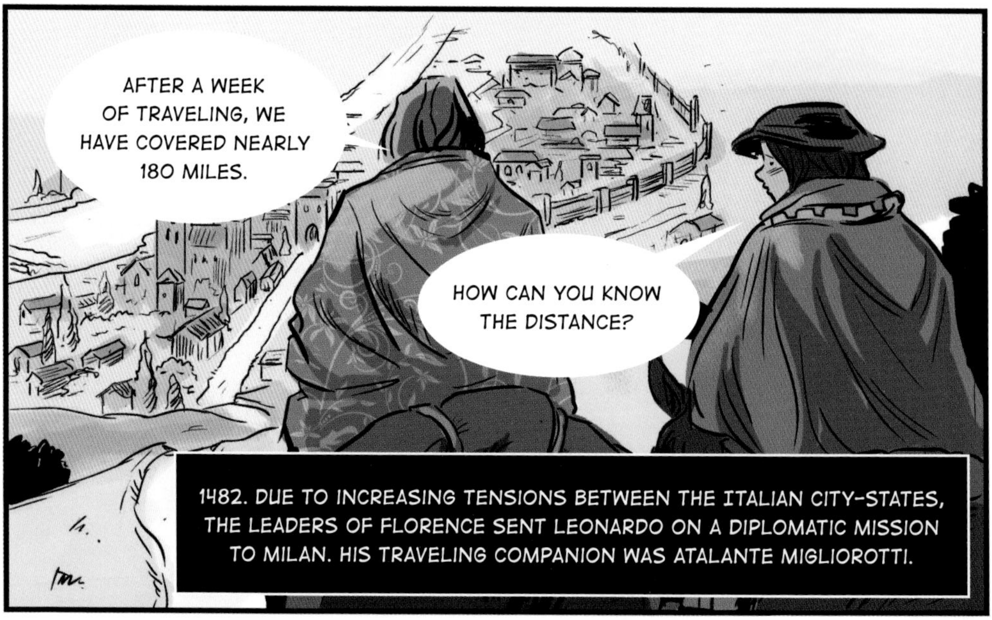
AFTER A WEEK OF TRAVELING, WE HAVE COVERED NEARLY 180 MILES.
HOW CAN YOU KNOW THE DISTANCE?
1482. DUE TO INCREASING TENSIONS BETWEEN THE ITALIAN CITY-STATES, THE LEADERS OF FLORENCE SENT LEONARDO ON A DIPLOMATIC MISSION TO MILAN. HIS TRAVELING COMPANION WAS ATALANTE MIGLIOROTTI.

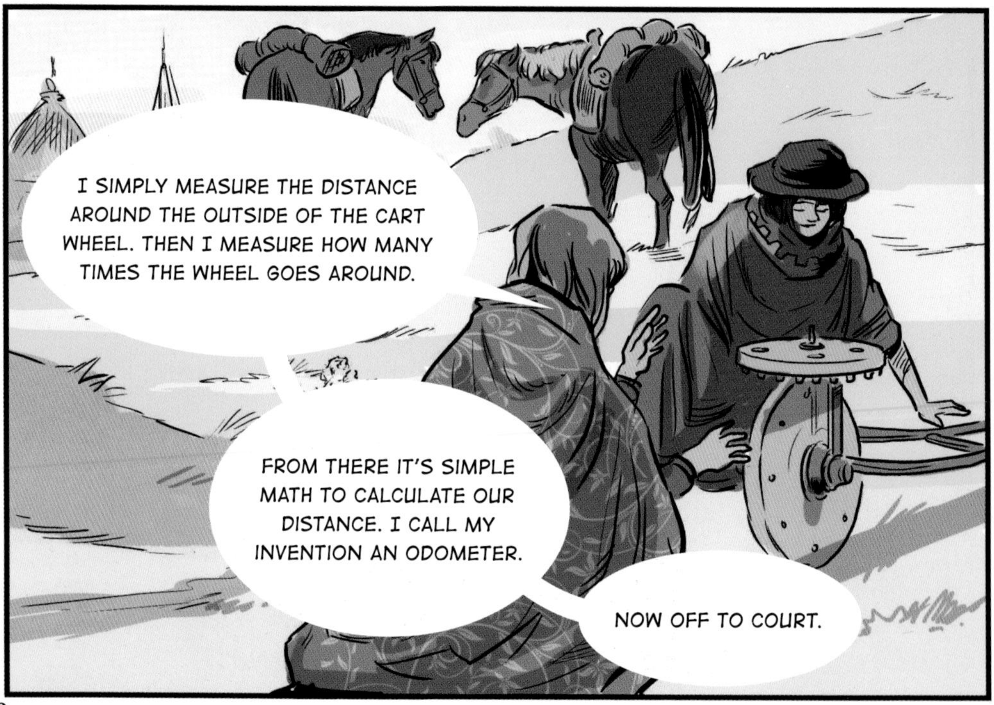
I SIMPLY MEASURE THE DISTANCE AROUND THE OUTSIDE OF THE CART WHEEL. THEN I MEASURE HOW MANY TIMES THE WHEEL GOES AROUND.
FROM THERE IT'S SIMPLE MATH TO CALCULATE OUR DISTANCE. I CALL MY INVENTION AN ODOMETER.
NOW OFF TO COURT.

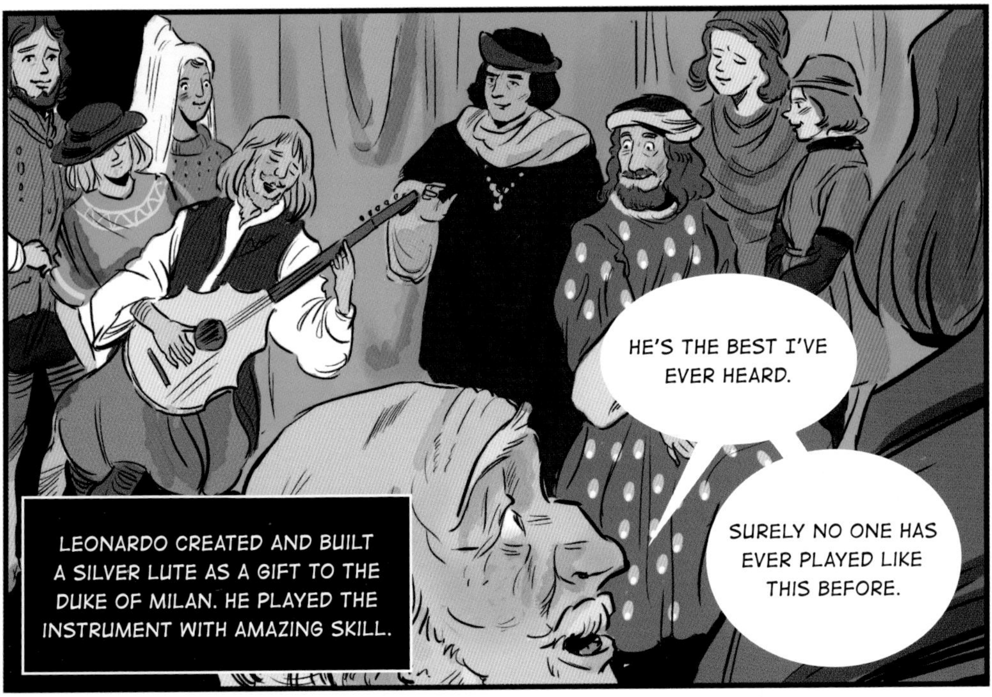
LEONARDO CREATED AND BUILT A SILVER LUTE AS A GIFT TO THE DUKE OF MILAN. HE PLAYED THE INSTRUMENT WITH AMAZING SKILL.
HE'S THE BEST I'VE EVER HEARD.
SURELY NO ONE HAS EVER PLAYED LIKE THIS BEFORE.

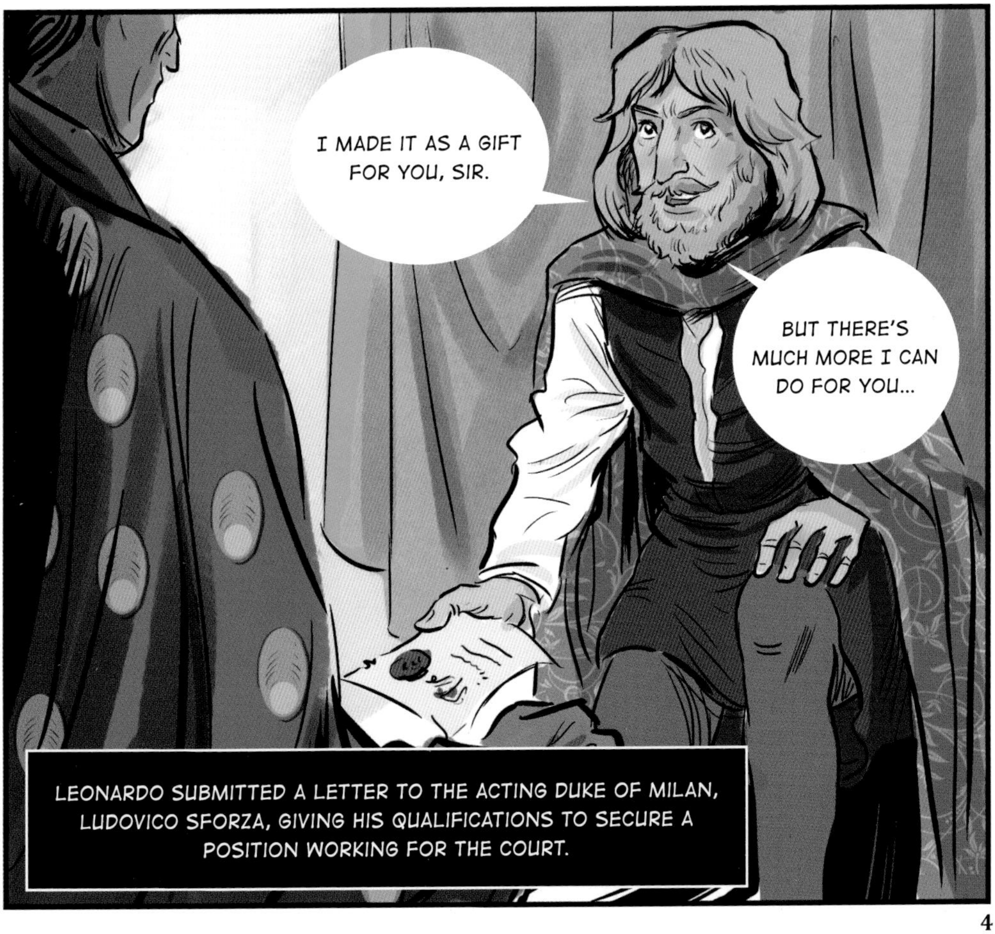
I MADE IT AS A GIFT FOR YOU, SIR.
BUT THERE'S MUCH MORE I CAN DO FOR YOU...
LEONARDO SUBMITTED A LETTER TO THE ACTING DUKE OF MILAN, LUDOVICO SFORZA, GIVING HIS QUALIFICATIONS TO SECURE A POSITION WORKING FOR THE COURT.

Most Illustrious Lord,

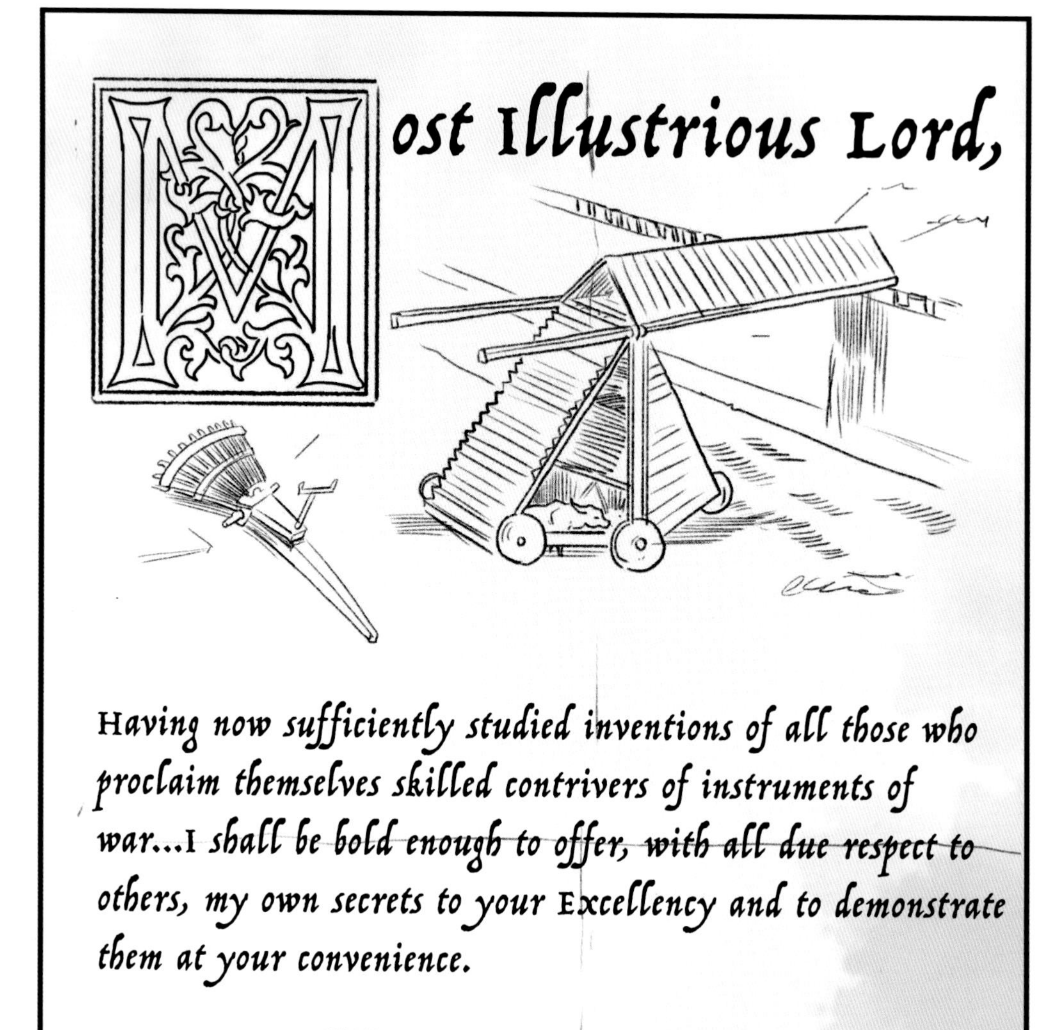

Having now sufficiently studied inventions of all those who proclaim themselves skilled contrivers of instruments of war...I shall be bold enough to offer, with all due respect to others, my own secrets to your Excellency and to demonstrate them at your convenience.

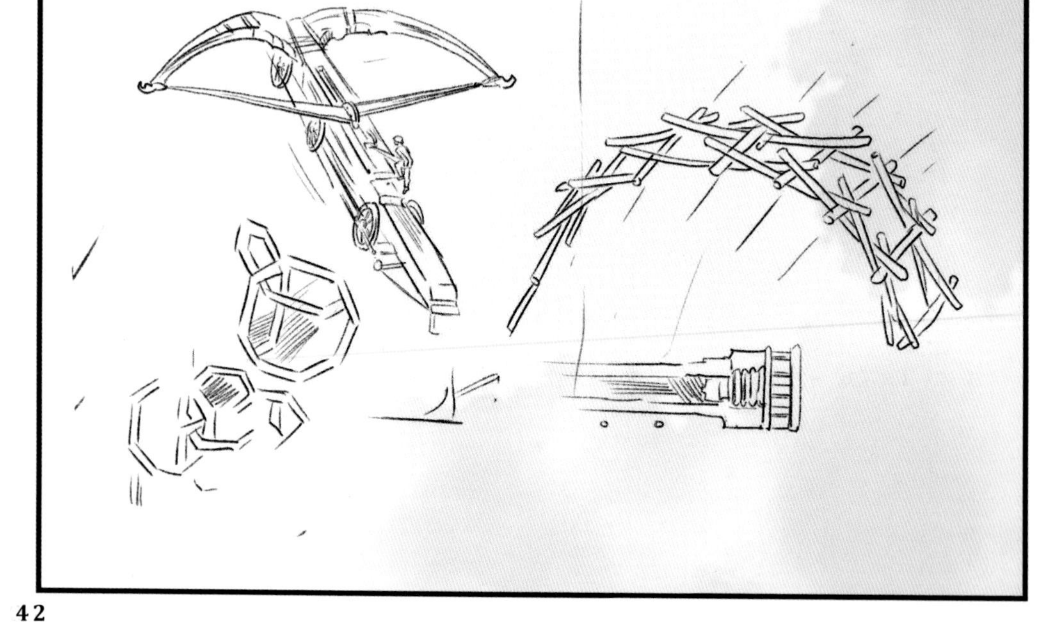

I have designed extremely light and strong bridges, easily carried, indestructible by fire and battle, easy to lift and place.

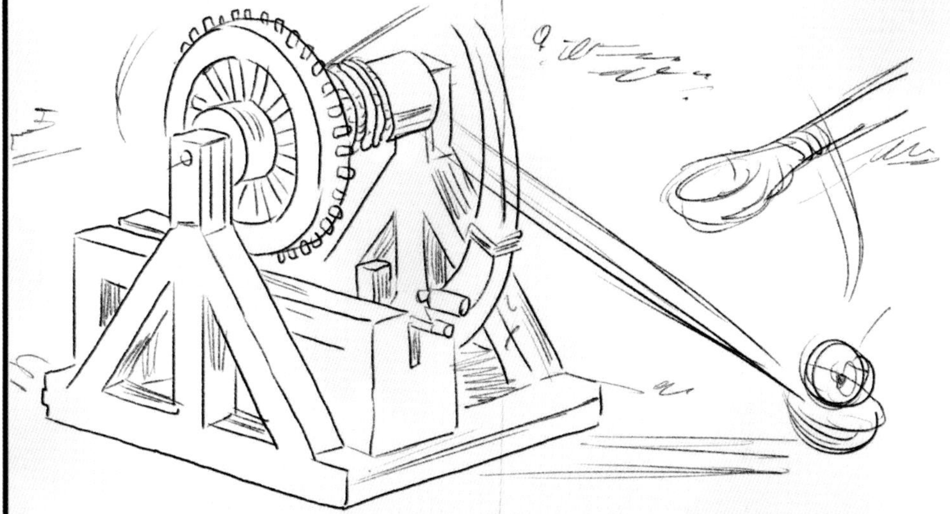

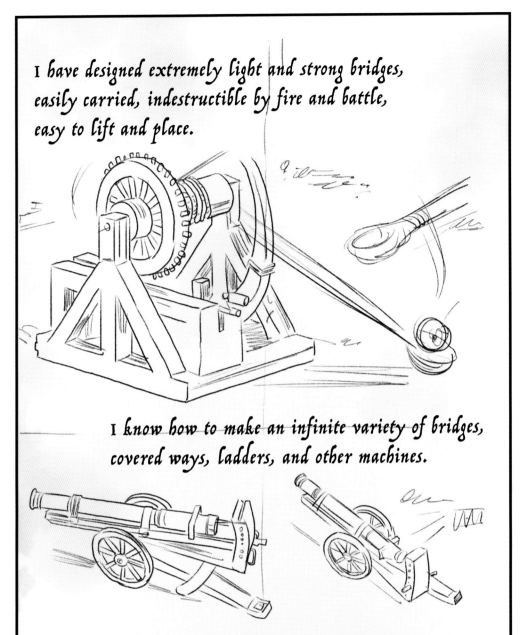

I know how to make an infinite variety of bridges, covered ways, ladders, and other machines.

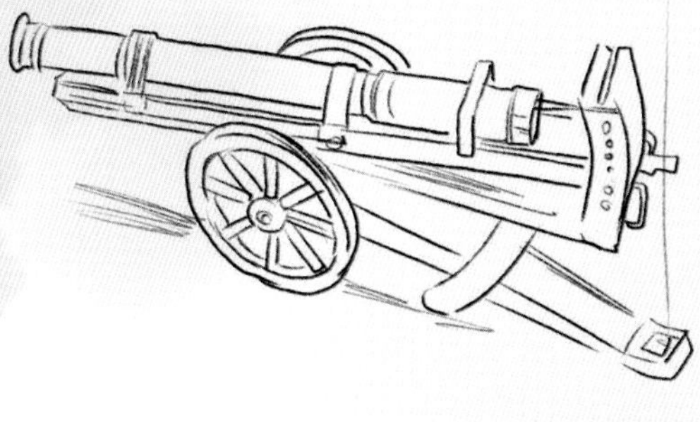

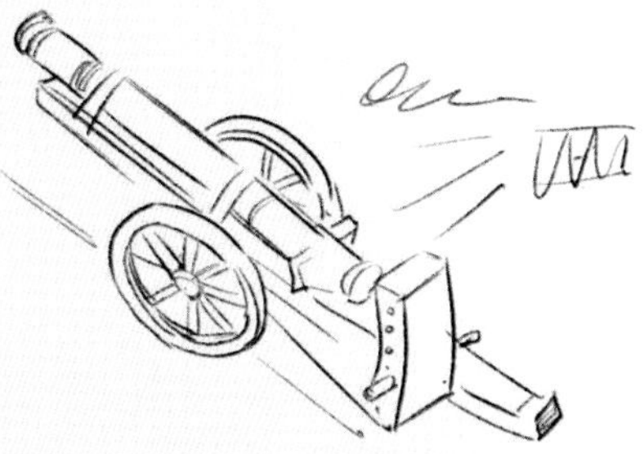

I have cannons, convenient and easy to carry, that can fling small stones almost resembling a hailstorm: the smoke will cause great terror to the enemy, to his great detriment and confusion...

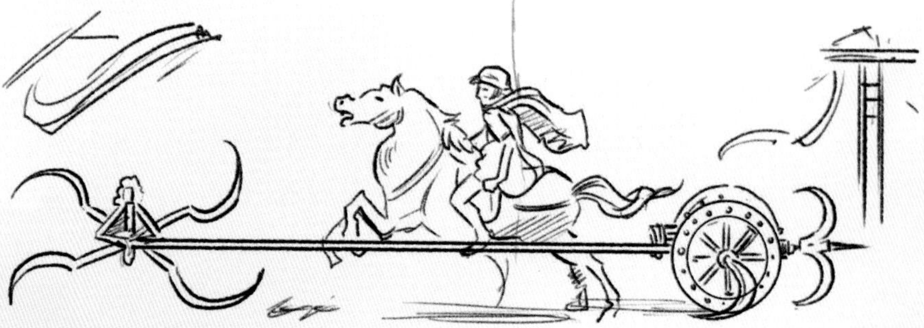

I will make unassailable armored chariots that can penetrate the ranks of the enemy with their artillery, and there is no body of soldiers so great that it could withstand them.

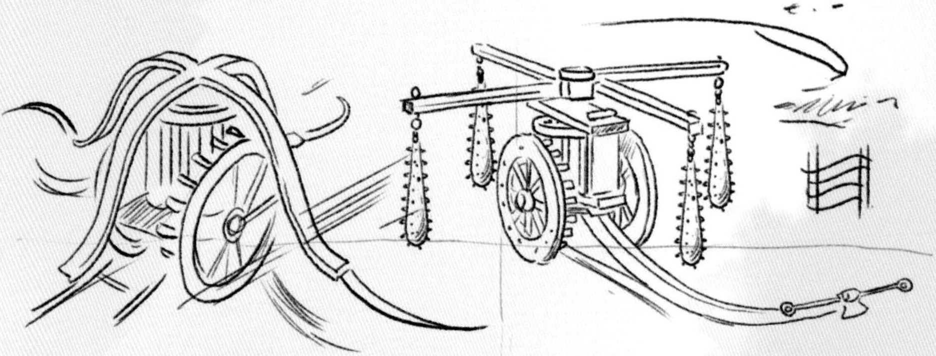

I will make cannons and artillery of beautiful and useful design.

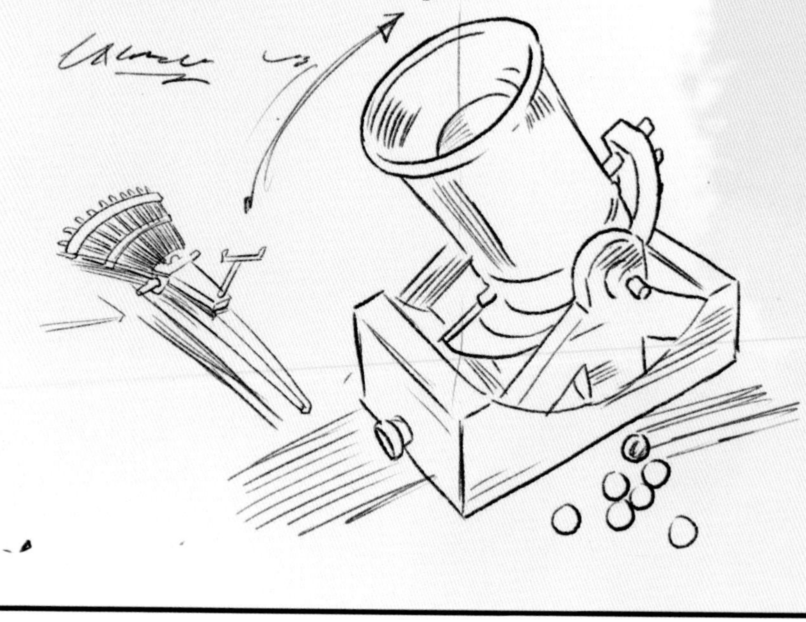

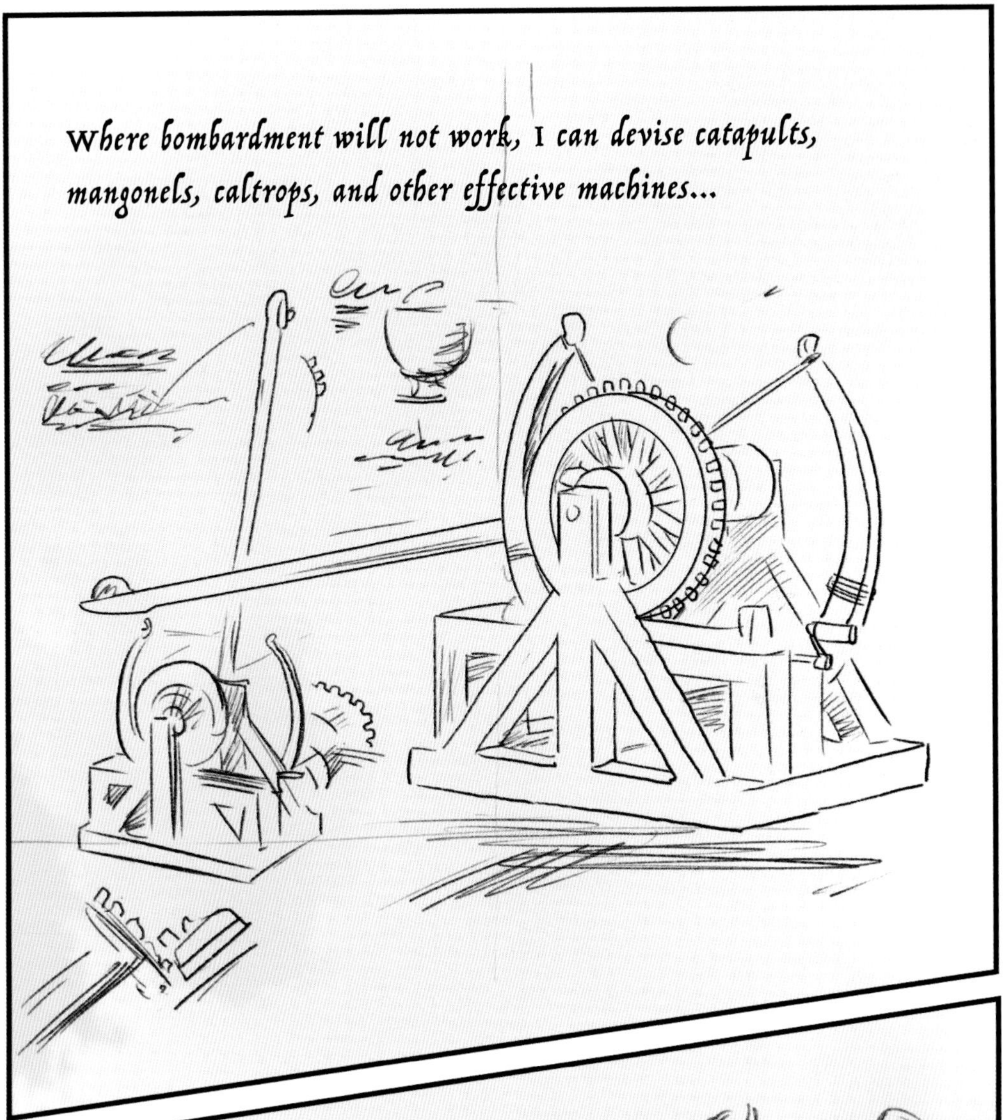
Where bombardment will not work, I can devise catapults, mangonels, caltrops, and other effective machines...

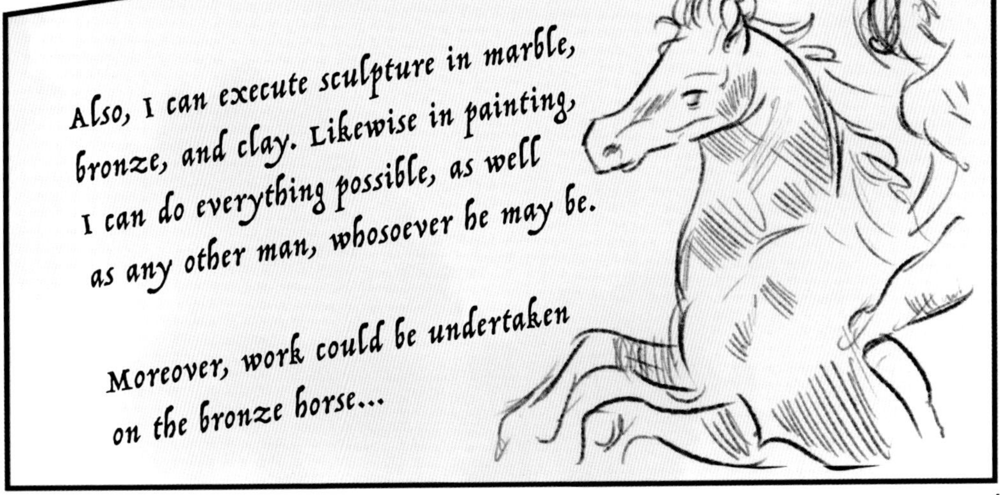
Also, I can execute sculpture in marble, bronze, and clay. Likewise in painting, I can do everything possible, as well as any other man, whosoever he may be.
Moreover, work could be undertaken on the bronze horse...

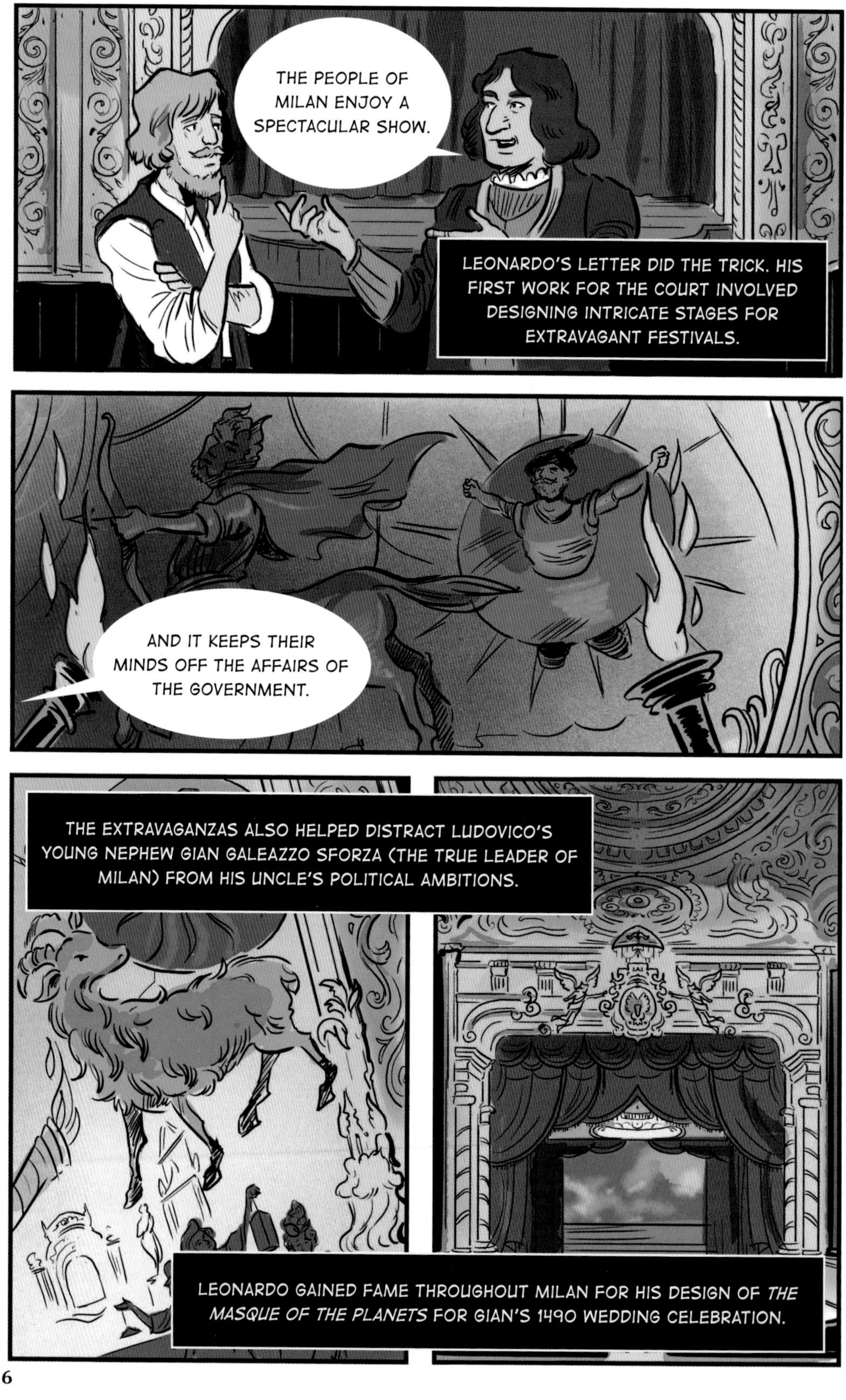
THE PEOPLE OF MILAN ENJOY A SPECTACULAR SHOW.
LEONARDO'S LETTER DID THE TRICK. HIS FIRST WORK FOR THE COURT INVOLVED DESIGNING INTRICATE STAGES FOR EXTRAVAGANT FESTIVALS.
AND IT KEEPS THEIR MINDS OFF THE AFFAIRS OF THE GOVERNMENT.
THE EXTRAVAGANZAS ALSO HELPED DISTRACT LUDOVICO'S YOUNG NEPHEW GIAN GALEAZZO SFORZA (THE TRUE LEADER OF MILAN) FROM HIS UNCLE'S POLITICAL AMBITIONS.
LEONARDO GAINED FAME THROUGHOUT MILAN FOR HIS DESIGN OF *THE MASQUE OF THE PLANETS* FOR GIAN'S 1490 WEDDING CELEBRATION.

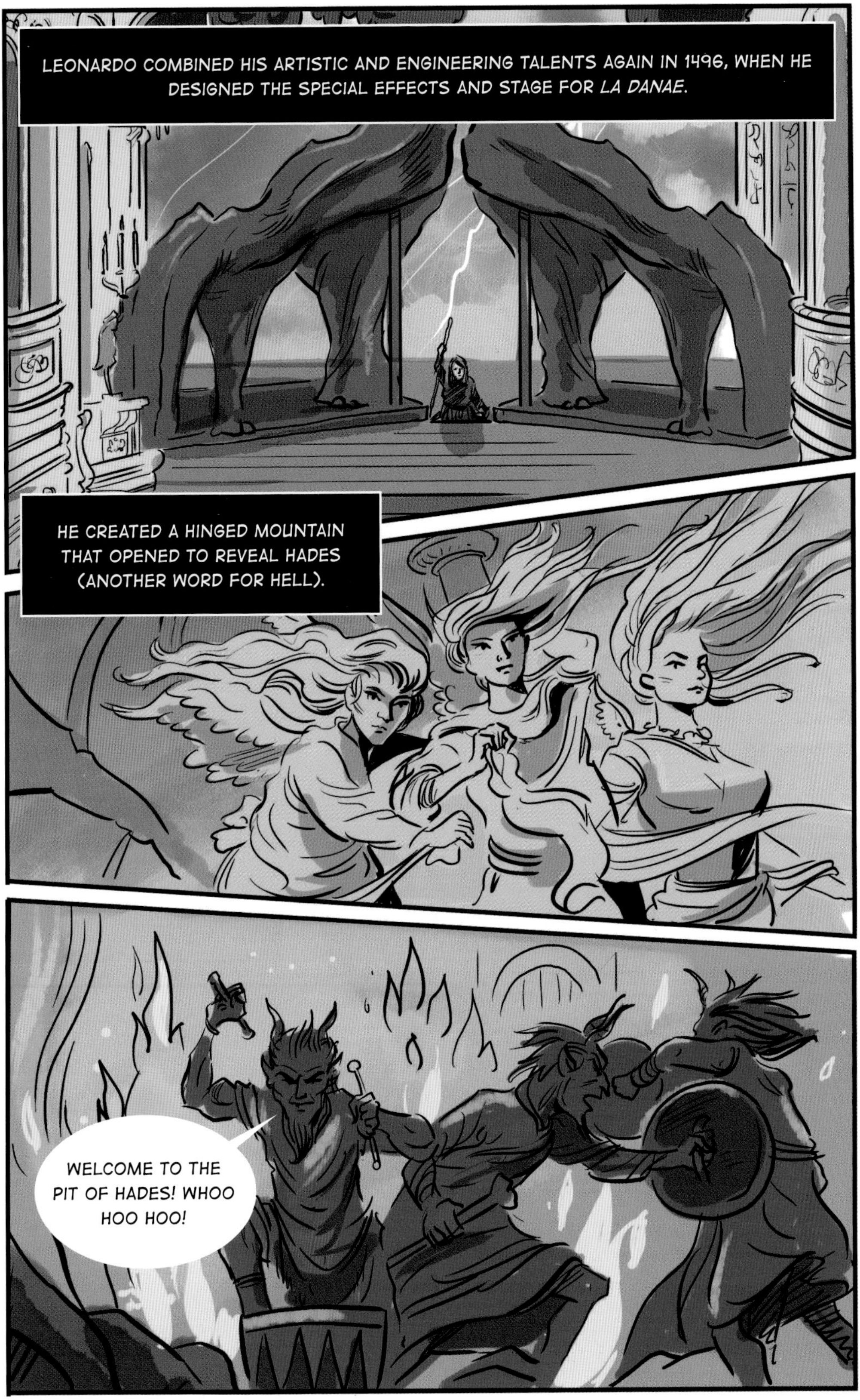
LEONARDO COMBINED HIS ARTISTIC AND ENGINEERING TALENTS AGAIN IN 1496, WHEN HE DESIGNED THE SPECIAL EFFECTS AND STAGE FOR *LA DANAE*.
HE CREATED A HINGED MOUNTAIN THAT OPENED TO REVEAL HADES (ANOTHER WORD FOR HELL).
WELCOME TO THE PIT OF HADES! WHOO HOO HOO!

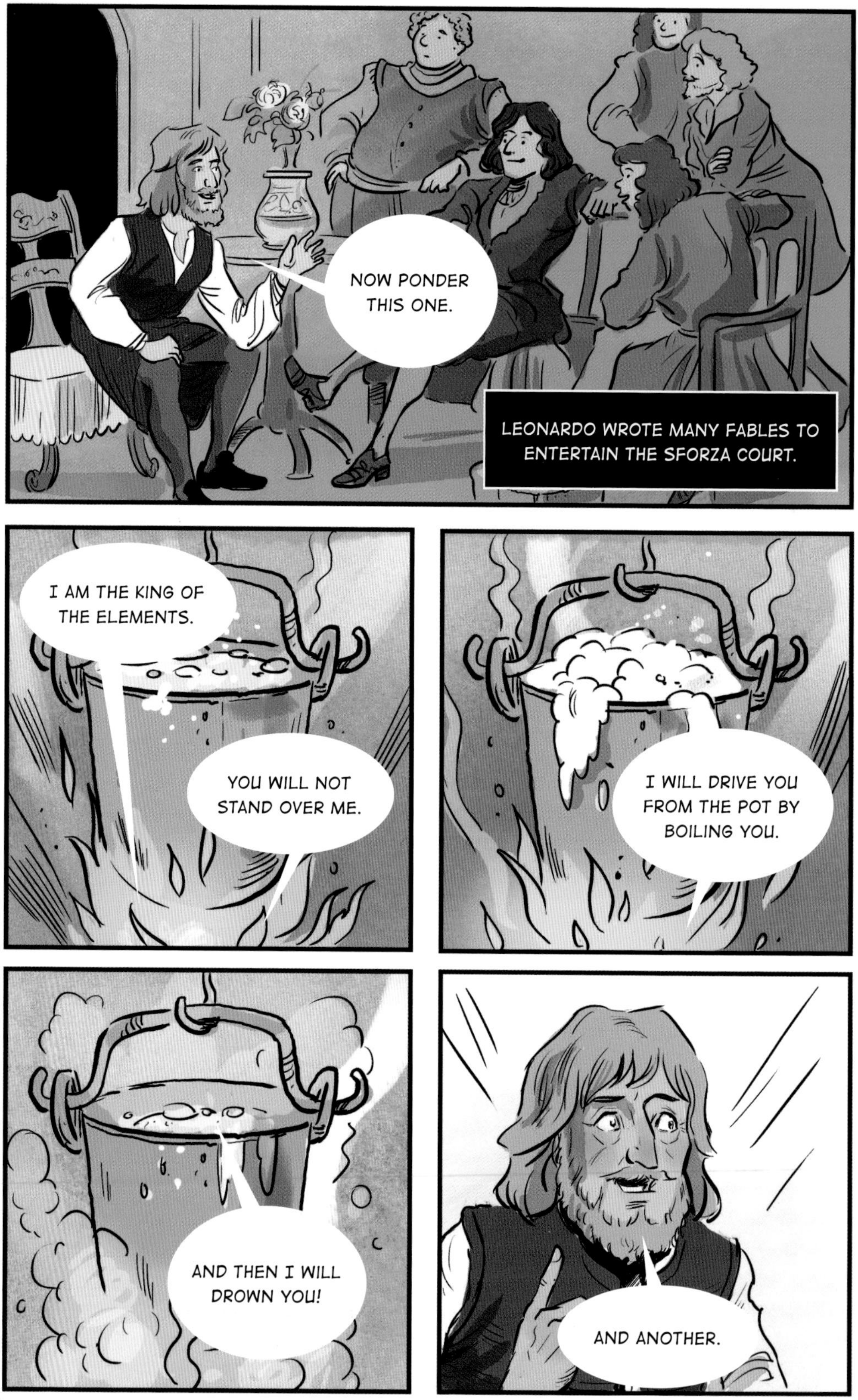
NOW PONDER THIS ONE.
LEONARDO WROTE MANY FABLES TO ENTERTAIN THE SFORZA COURT.
I AM THE KING OF THE ELEMENTS.
YOU WILL NOT STAND OVER ME.
I WILL DRIVE YOU FROM THE POT BY BOILING YOU.
AND THEN I WILL DROWN YOU!
AND ANOTHER.

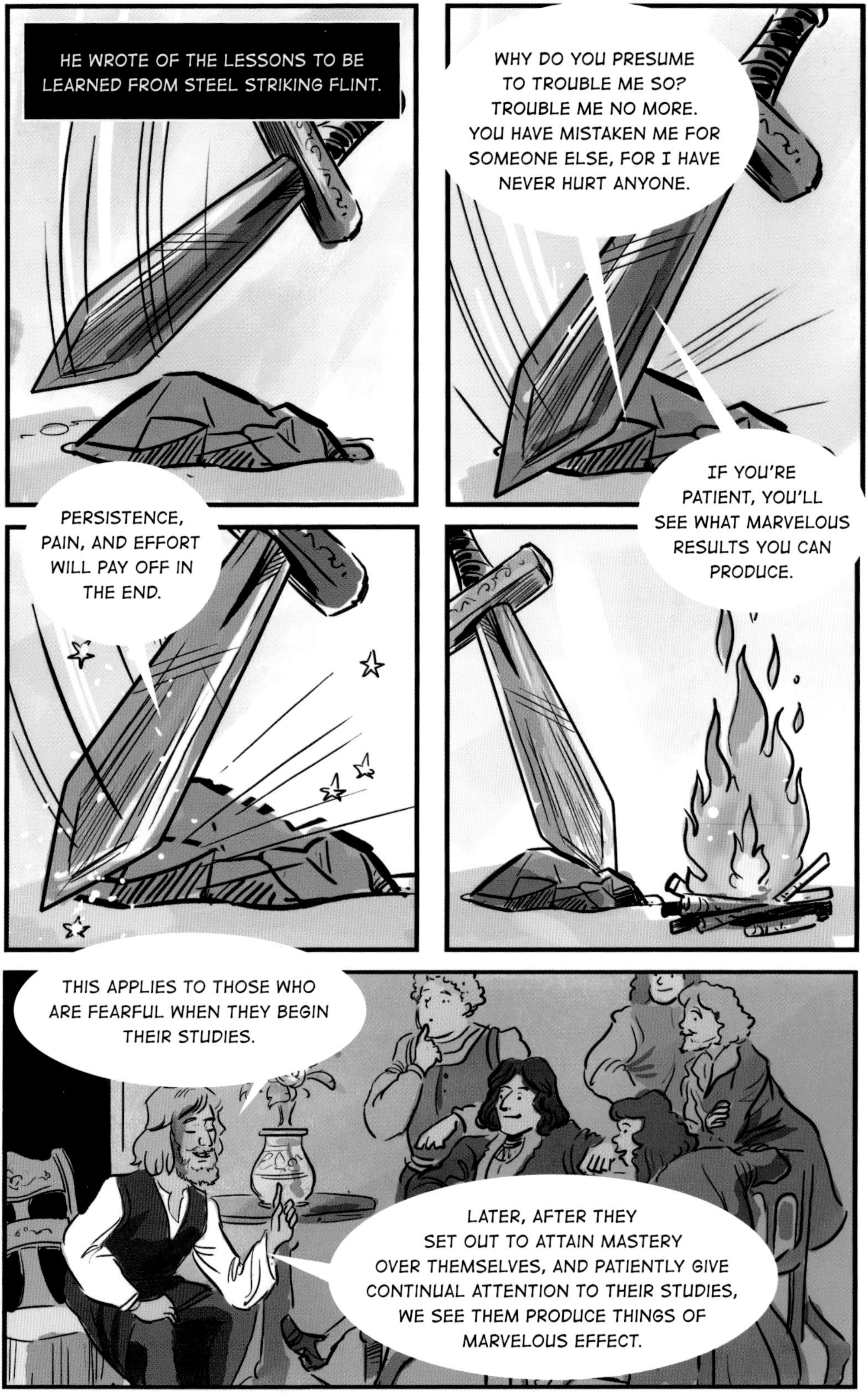
HE WROTE OF THE LESSONS TO BE LEARNED FROM STEEL STRIKING FLINT.
WHY DO YOU PRESUME TO TROUBLE ME SO? TROUBLE ME NO MORE. YOU HAVE MISTAKEN ME FOR SOMEONE ELSE, FOR I HAVE NEVER HURT ANYONE.
IF YOU'RE PATIENT, YOU'LL SEE WHAT MARVELOUS RESULTS YOU CAN PRODUCE.
PERSISTENCE, PAIN, AND EFFORT WILL PAY OFF IN THE END.
THIS APPLIES TO THOSE WHO ARE FEARFUL WHEN THEY BEGIN THEIR STUDIES.
LATER, AFTER THEY SET OUT TO ATTAIN MASTERY OVER THEMSELVES, AND PATIENTLY GIVE CONTINUAL ATTENTION TO THEIR STUDIES, WE SEE THEM PRODUCE THINGS OF MARVELOUS EFFECT.

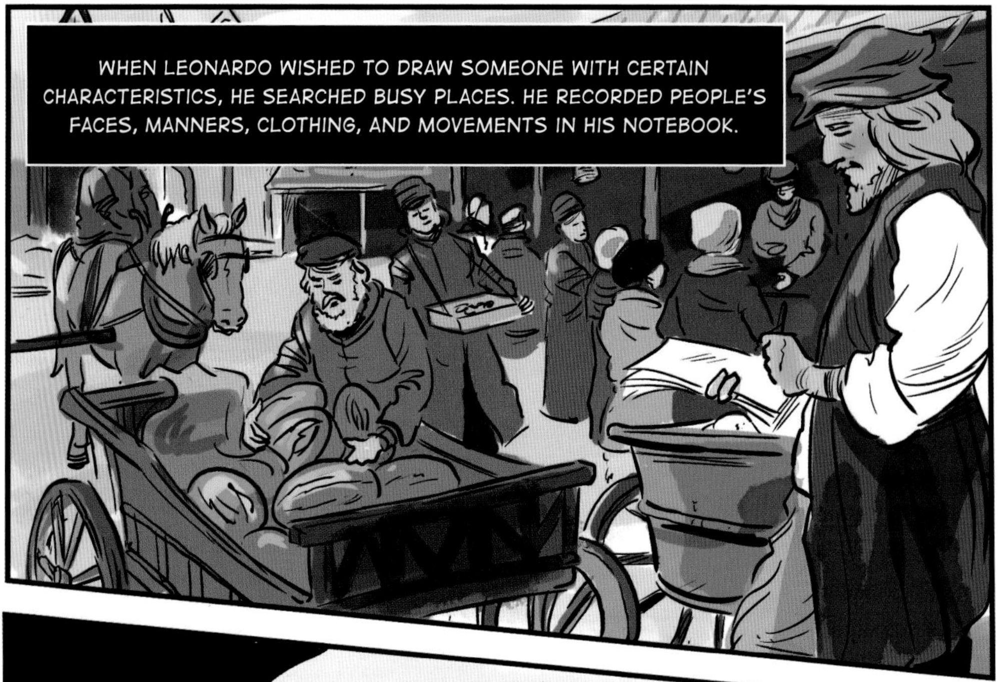
WHEN LEONARDO WISHED TO DRAW SOMEONE WITH CERTAIN CHARACTERISTICS, HE SEARCHED BUSY PLACES. HE RECORDED PEOPLE'S FACES, MANNERS, CLOTHING, AND MOVEMENTS IN HIS NOTEBOOK.

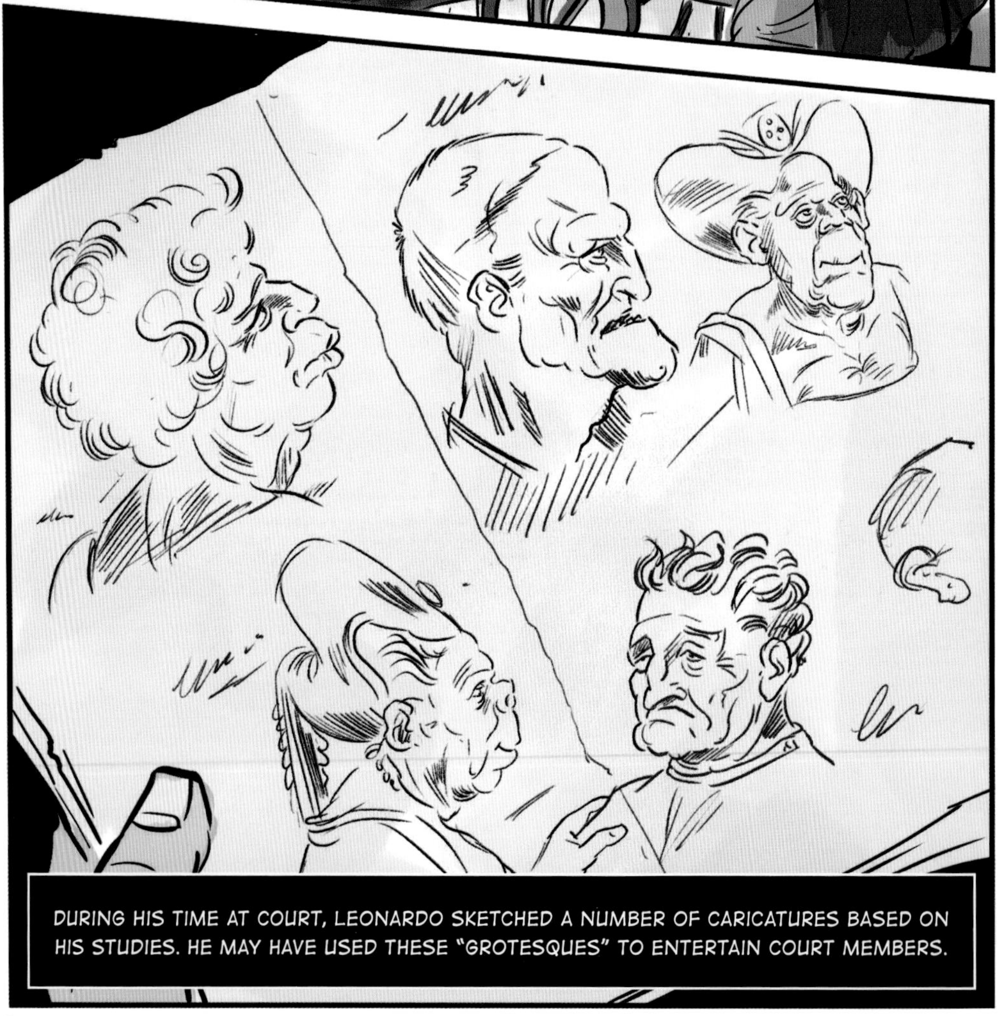
DURING HIS TIME AT COURT, LEONARDO SKETCHED A NUMBER OF CARICATURES BASED ON HIS STUDIES. HE MAY HAVE USED THESE "GROTESQUES" TO ENTERTAIN COURT MEMBERS.

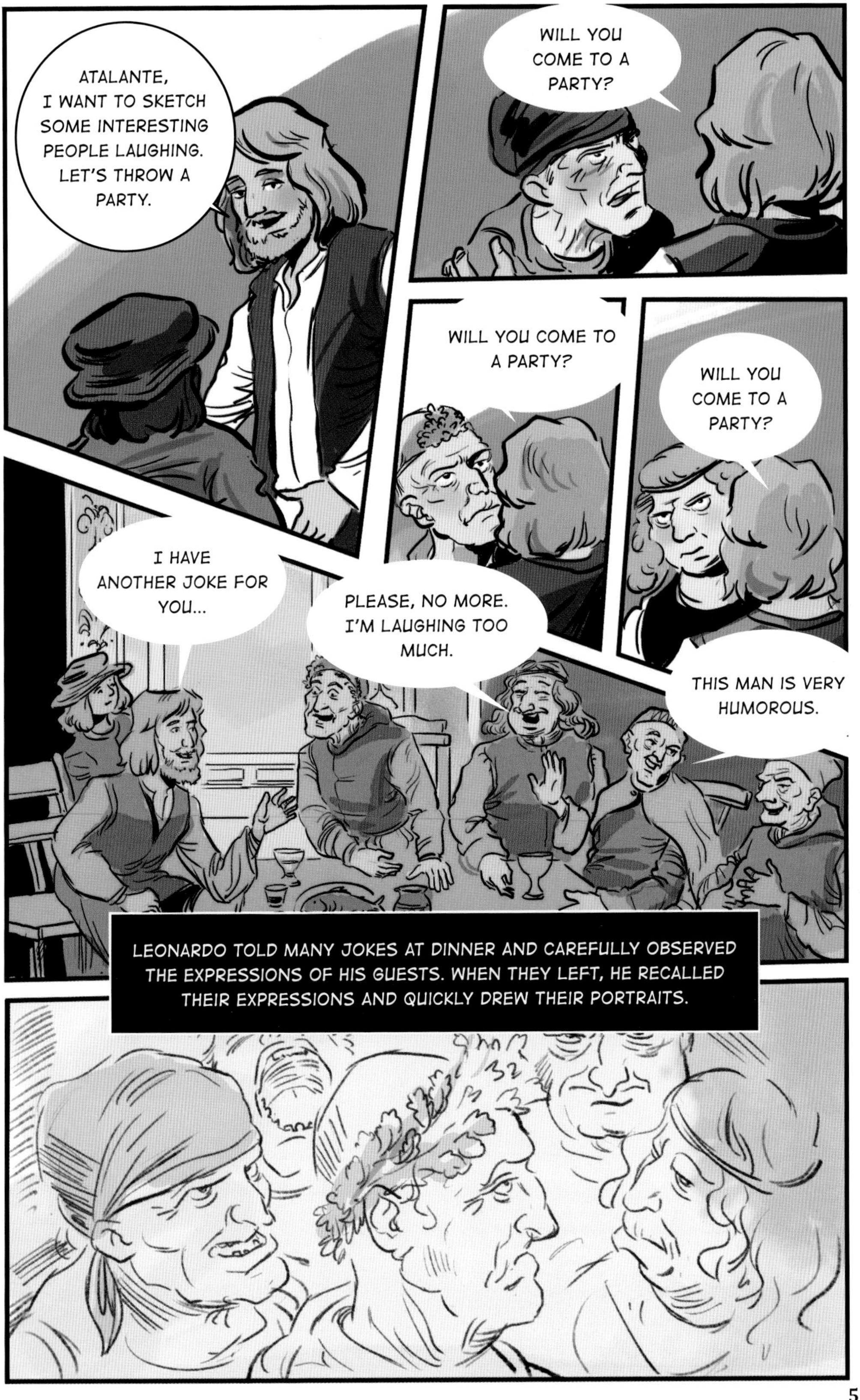
ATALANTE, I WANT TO SKETCH SOME INTERESTING PEOPLE LAUGHING. LET'S THROW A PARTY.
WILL YOU COME TO A PARTY?
WILL YOU COME TO A PARTY?
WILL YOU COME TO A PARTY?
I HAVE ANOTHER JOKE FOR YOU...
PLEASE, NO MORE. I'M LAUGHING TOO MUCH.
THIS MAN IS VERY HUMOROUS.
LEONARDO TOLD MANY JOKES AT DINNER AND CAREFULLY OBSERVED THE EXPRESSIONS OF HIS GUESTS. WHEN THEY LEFT, HE RECALLED THEIR EXPRESSIONS AND QUICKLY DREW THEIR PORTRAITS.

CHAPTER 5

THE PLAGUE AND LEONARDO'S "NEW CITIES"

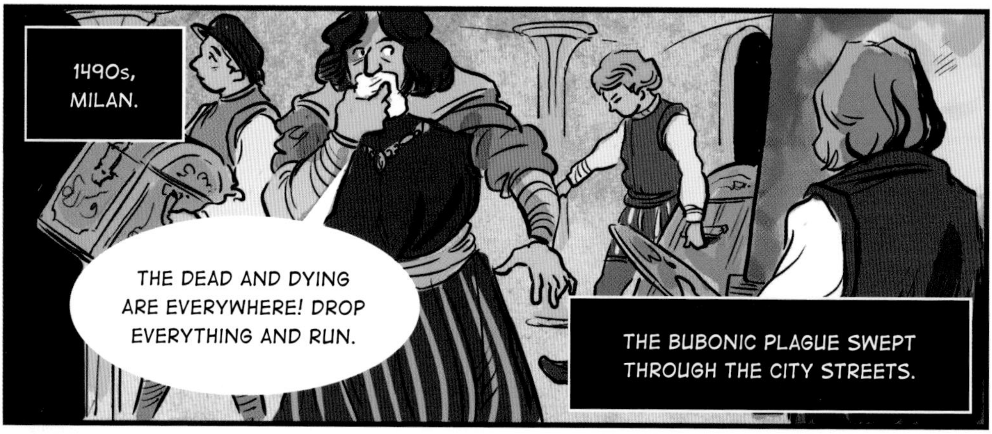
1490s, MILAN.
THE DEAD AND DYING ARE EVERYWHERE! DROP EVERYTHING AND RUN.
THE BUBONIC PLAGUE SWEPT THROUGH THE CITY STREETS.

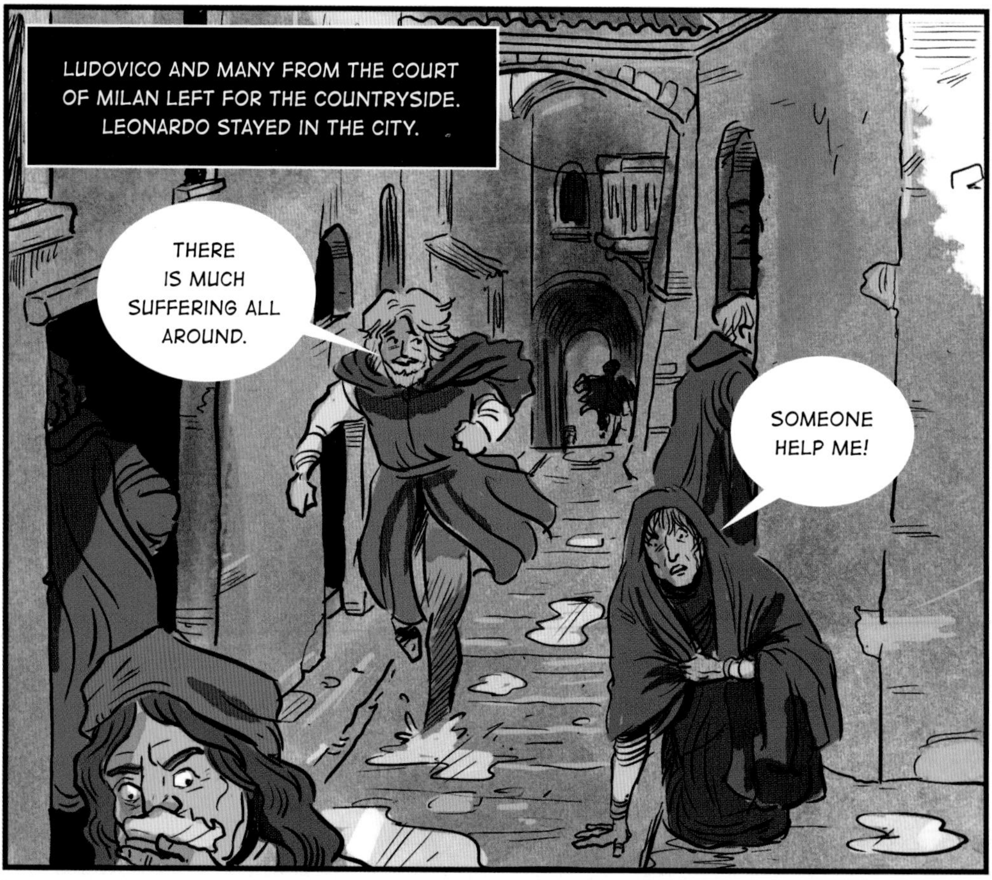
LUDOVICO AND MANY FROM THE COURT OF MILAN LEFT FOR THE COUNTRYSIDE. LEONARDO STAYED IN THE CITY.
THERE IS MUCH SUFFERING ALL AROUND.
SOMEONE HELP ME!

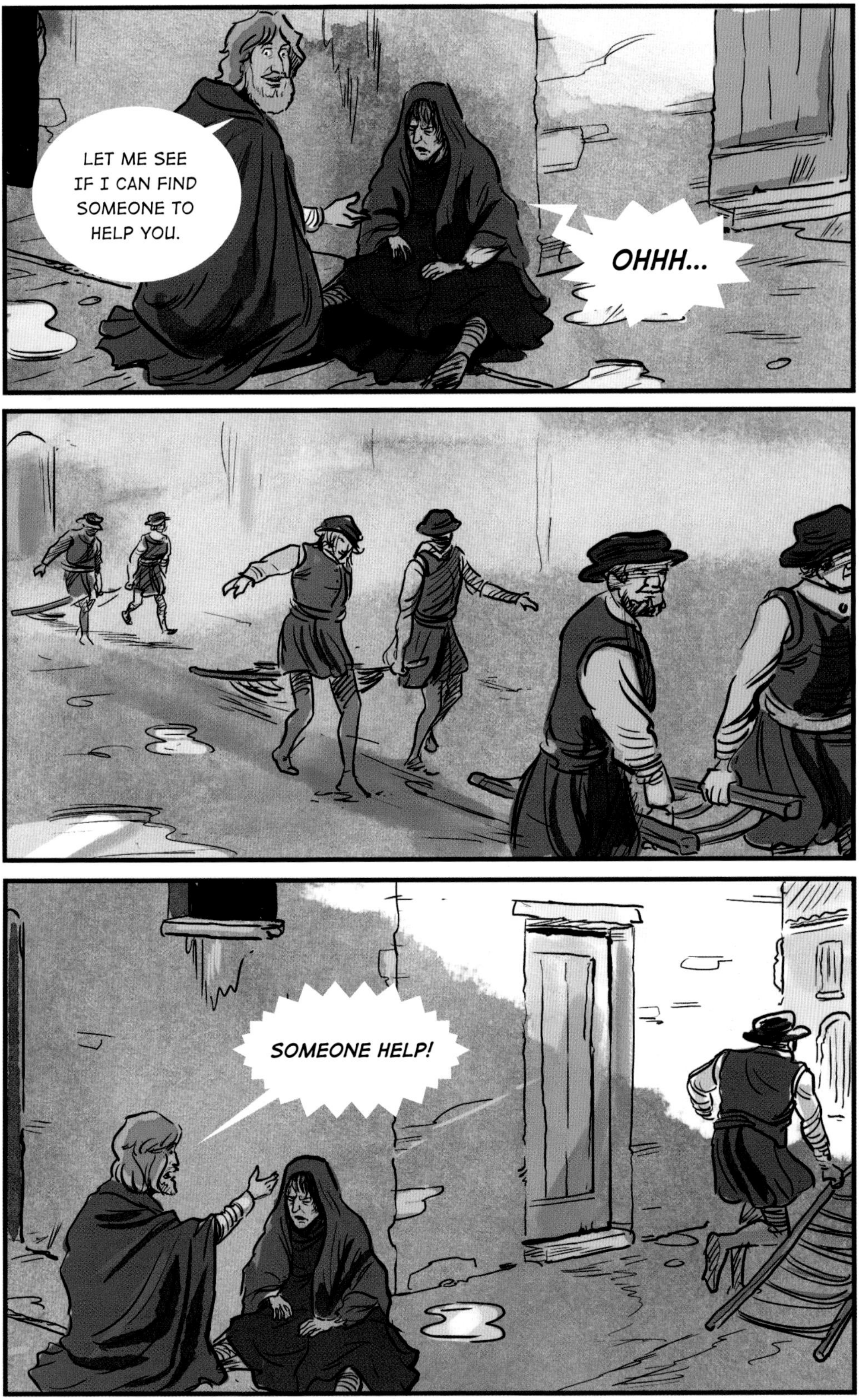
LET ME SEE IF I CAN FIND SOMEONE TO HELP YOU.
OHHH...
SOMEONE HELP!

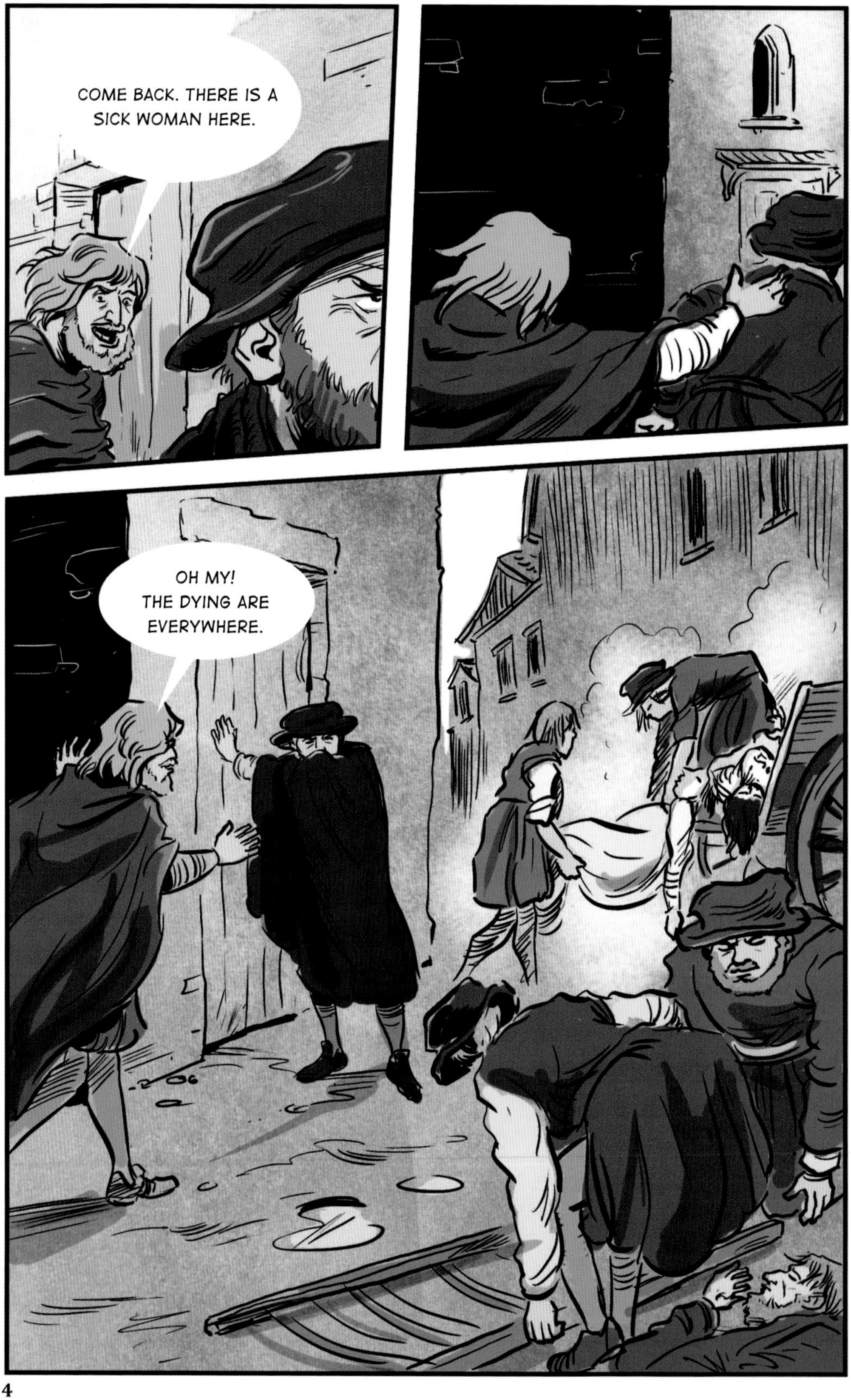

COME BACK. THERE IS A SICK WOMAN HERE.
OH MY! THE DYING ARE EVERYWHERE.

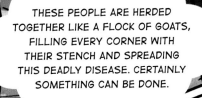

THESE PEOPLE ARE HERDED TOGETHER LIKE A FLOCK OF GOATS, FILLING EVERY CORNER WITH THEIR STENCH AND SPREADING THIS DEADLY DISEASE. CERTAINLY SOMETHING CAN BE DONE.

AFTER THREE YEARS OF PLAGUE, ROUGHLY ONE-THIRD OF THE TOWNSPEOPLE HAD DIED.

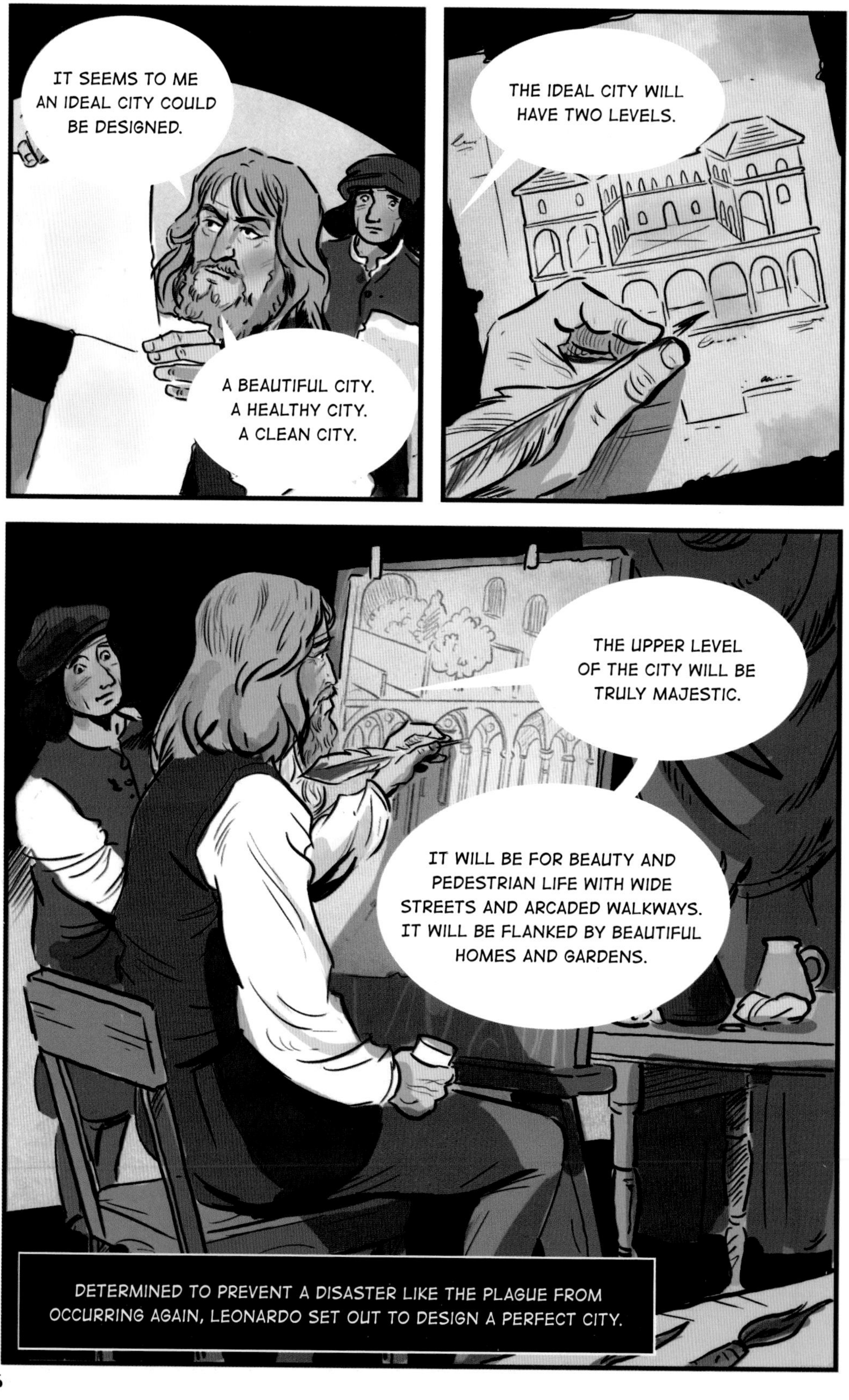
IT SEEMS TO ME AN IDEAL CITY COULD BE DESIGNED.
A BEAUTIFUL CITY. A HEALTHY CITY. A CLEAN CITY.
THE IDEAL CITY WILL HAVE TWO LEVELS.
THE UPPER LEVEL OF THE CITY WILL BE TRULY MAJESTIC.
IT WILL BE FOR BEAUTY AND PEDESTRIAN LIFE WITH WIDE STREETS AND ARCADED WALKWAYS. IT WILL BE FLANKED BY BEAUTIFUL HOMES AND GARDENS.
DETERMINED TO PREVENT A DISASTER LIKE THE PLAGUE FROM OCCURRING AGAIN, LEONARDO SET OUT TO DESIGN A PERFECT CITY.

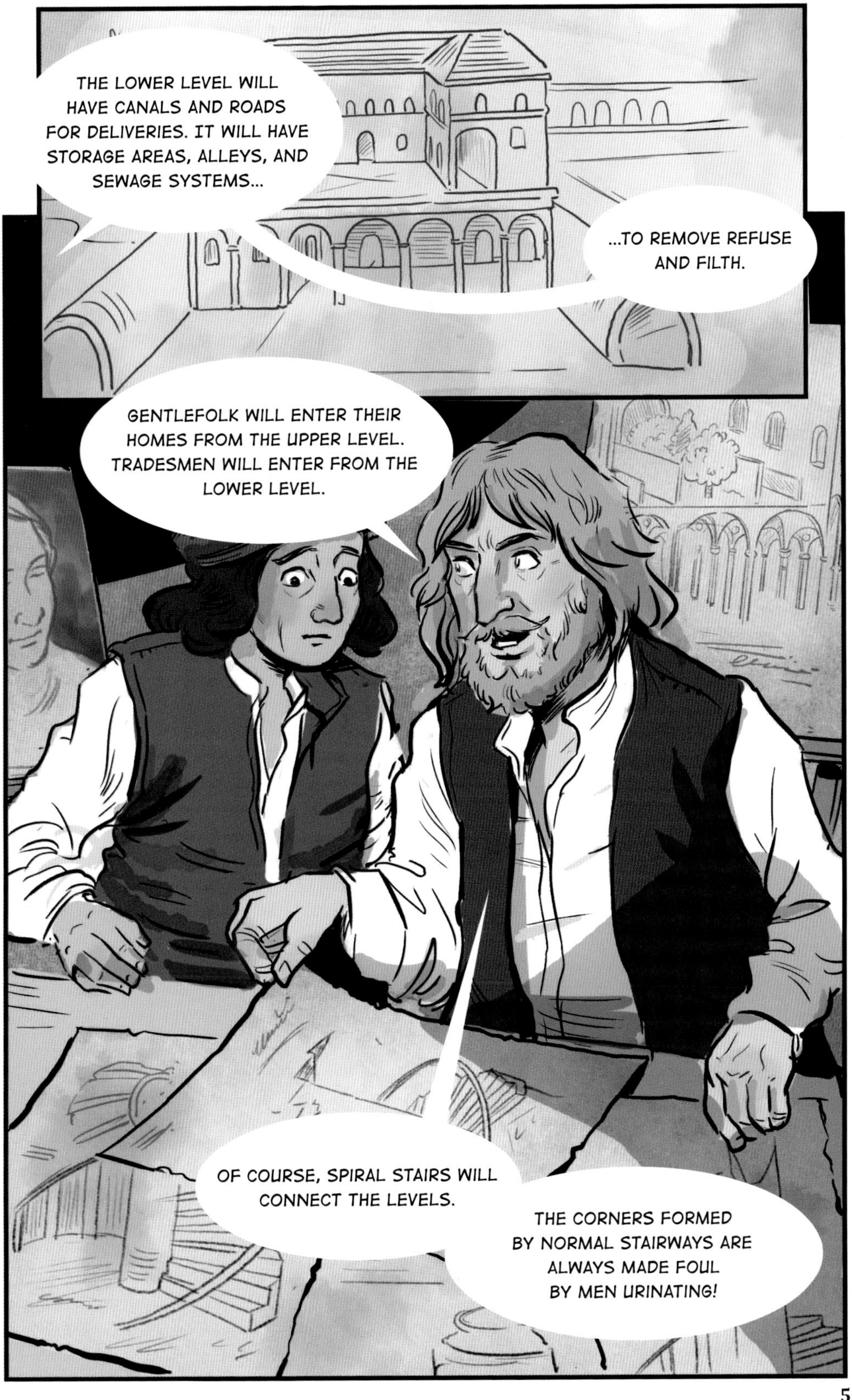

THE LOWER LEVEL WILL HAVE CANALS AND ROADS FOR DELIVERIES. IT WILL HAVE STORAGE AREAS, ALLEYS, AND SEWAGE SYSTEMS...
...TO REMOVE REFUSE AND FILTH.
GENTLEFOLK WILL ENTER THEIR HOMES FROM THE UPPER LEVEL. TRADESMEN WILL ENTER FROM THE LOWER LEVEL.
OF COURSE, SPIRAL STAIRS WILL CONNECT THE LEVELS.
THE CORNERS FORMED BY NORMAL STAIRWAYS ARE ALWAYS MADE FOUL BY MEN URINATING!

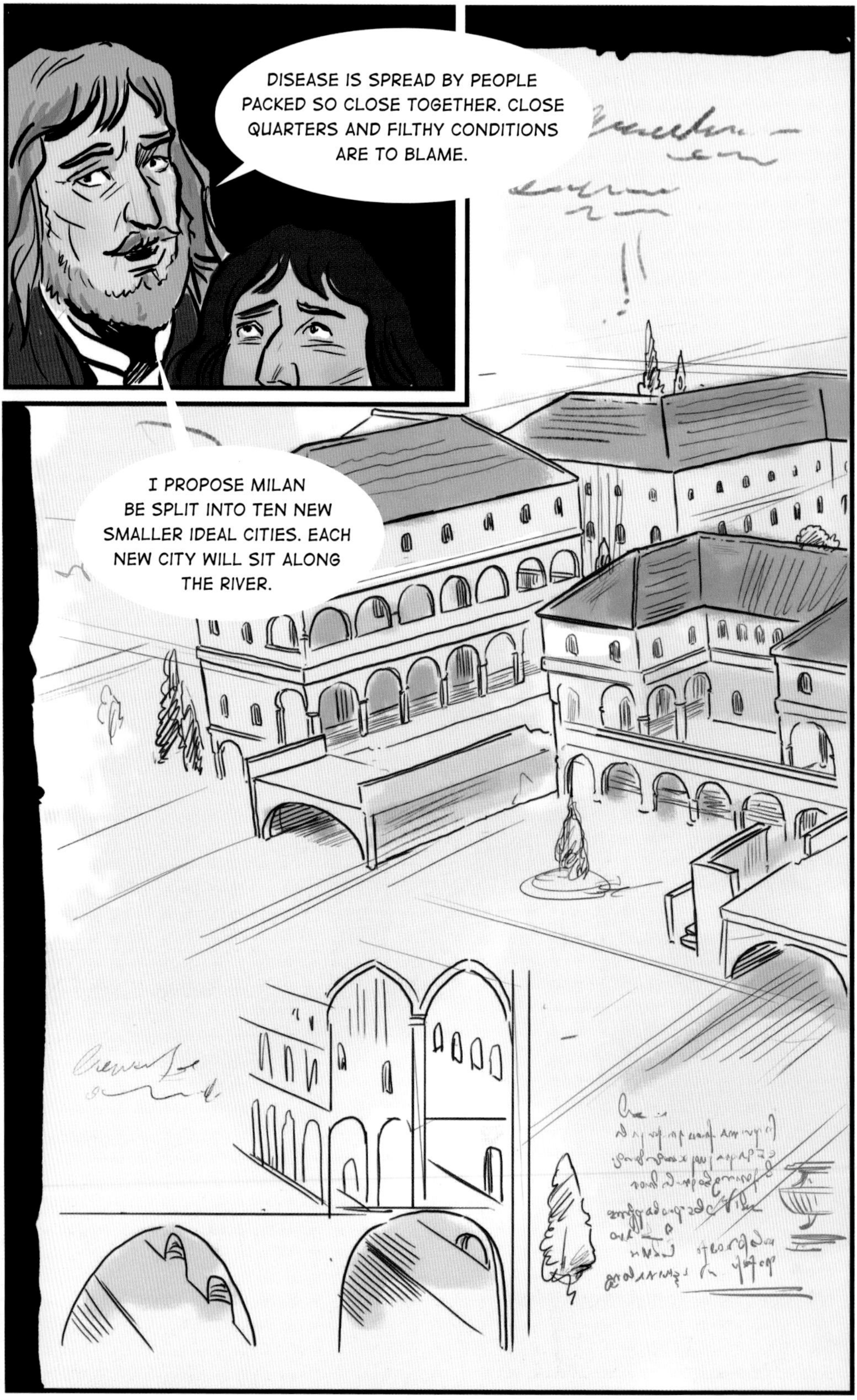
DISEASE IS SPREAD BY PEOPLE PACKED SO CLOSE TOGETHER. CLOSE QUARTERS AND FILTHY CONDITIONS ARE TO BLAME.
I PROPOSE MILAN BE SPLIT INTO TEN NEW SMALLER IDEAL CITIES. EACH NEW CITY WILL SIT ALONG THE RIVER.

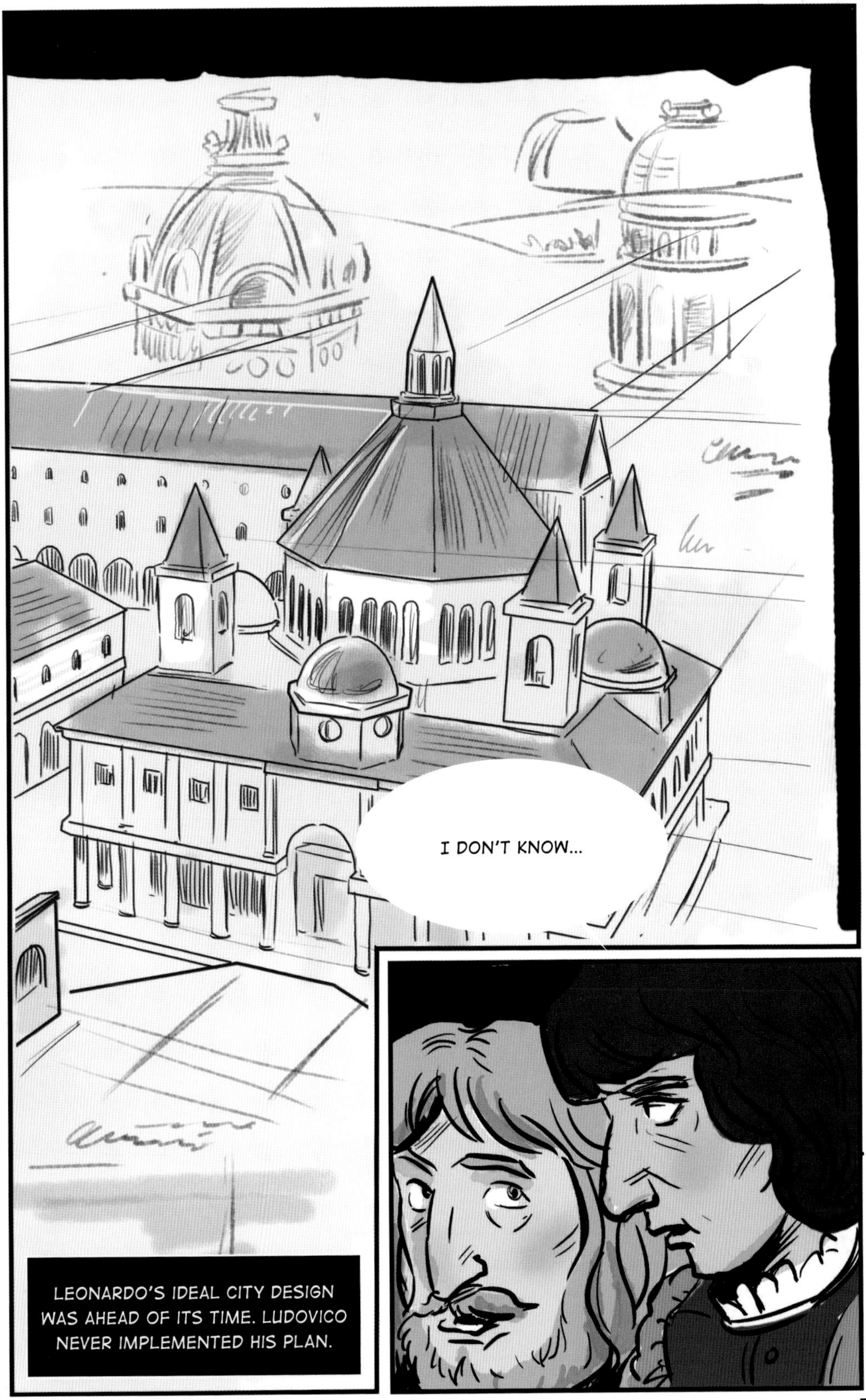
I DON'T KNOW...
LEONARDO'S IDEAL CITY DESIGN WAS AHEAD OF ITS TIME. LUDOVICO NEVER IMPLEMENTED HIS PLAN.

CHAPTER 6
INVENTIONS AND ART IN MILAN

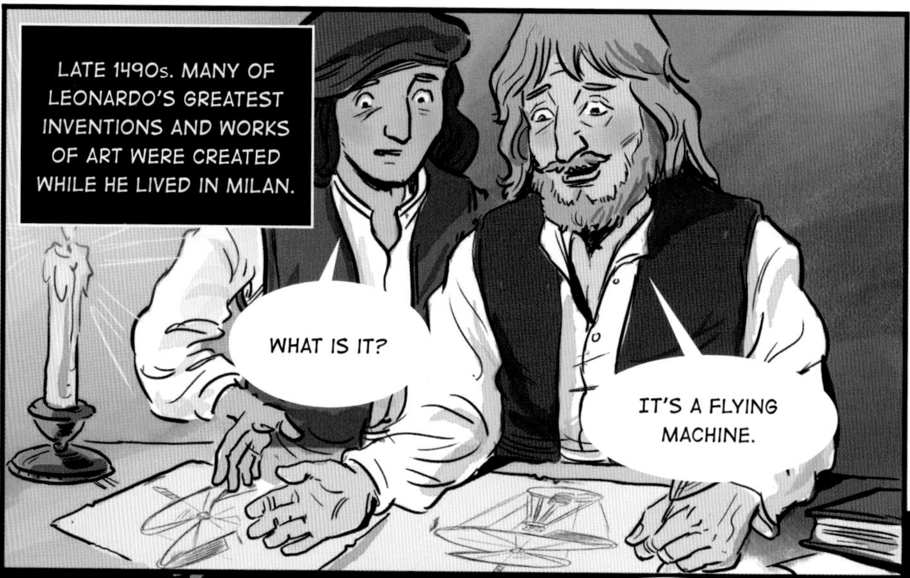

LATE 1490s. MANY OF LEONARDO'S GREATEST INVENTIONS AND WORKS OF ART WERE CREATED WHILE HE LIVED IN MILAN.
WHAT IS IT?
IT'S A FLYING MACHINE.

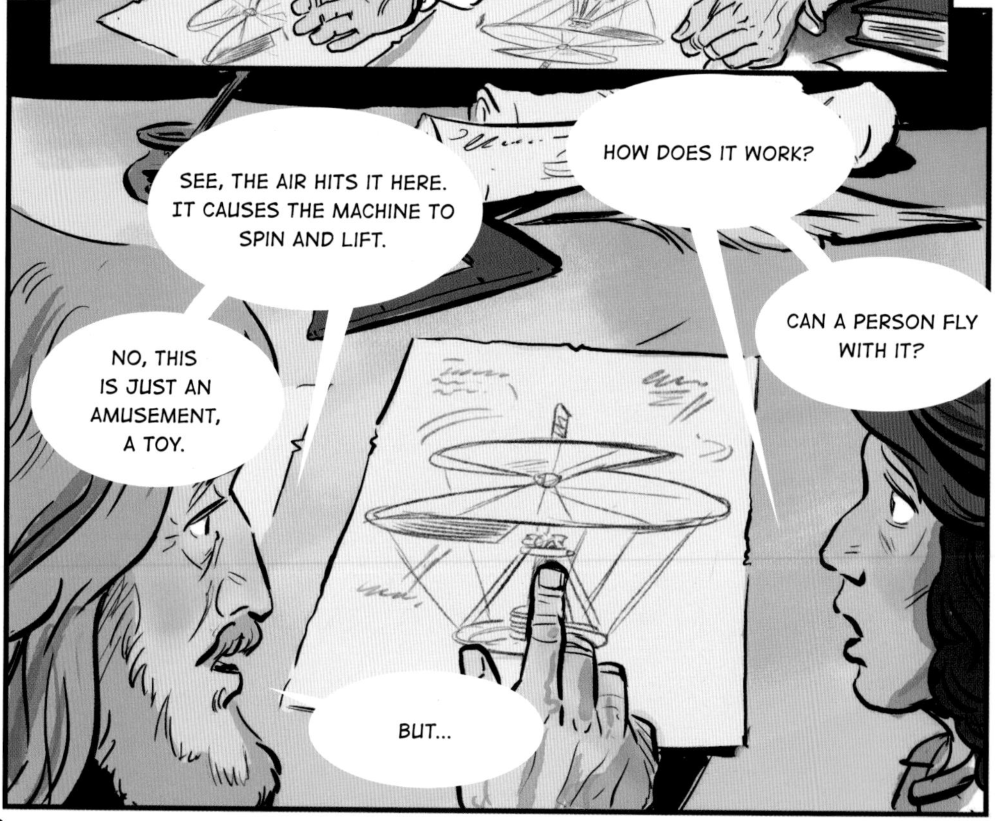

HOW DOES IT WORK?
SEE, THE AIR HITS IT HERE. IT CAUSES THE MACHINE TO SPIN AND LIFT.
CAN A PERSON FLY WITH IT?
NO, THIS IS JUST AN AMUSEMENT, A TOY.
BUT...

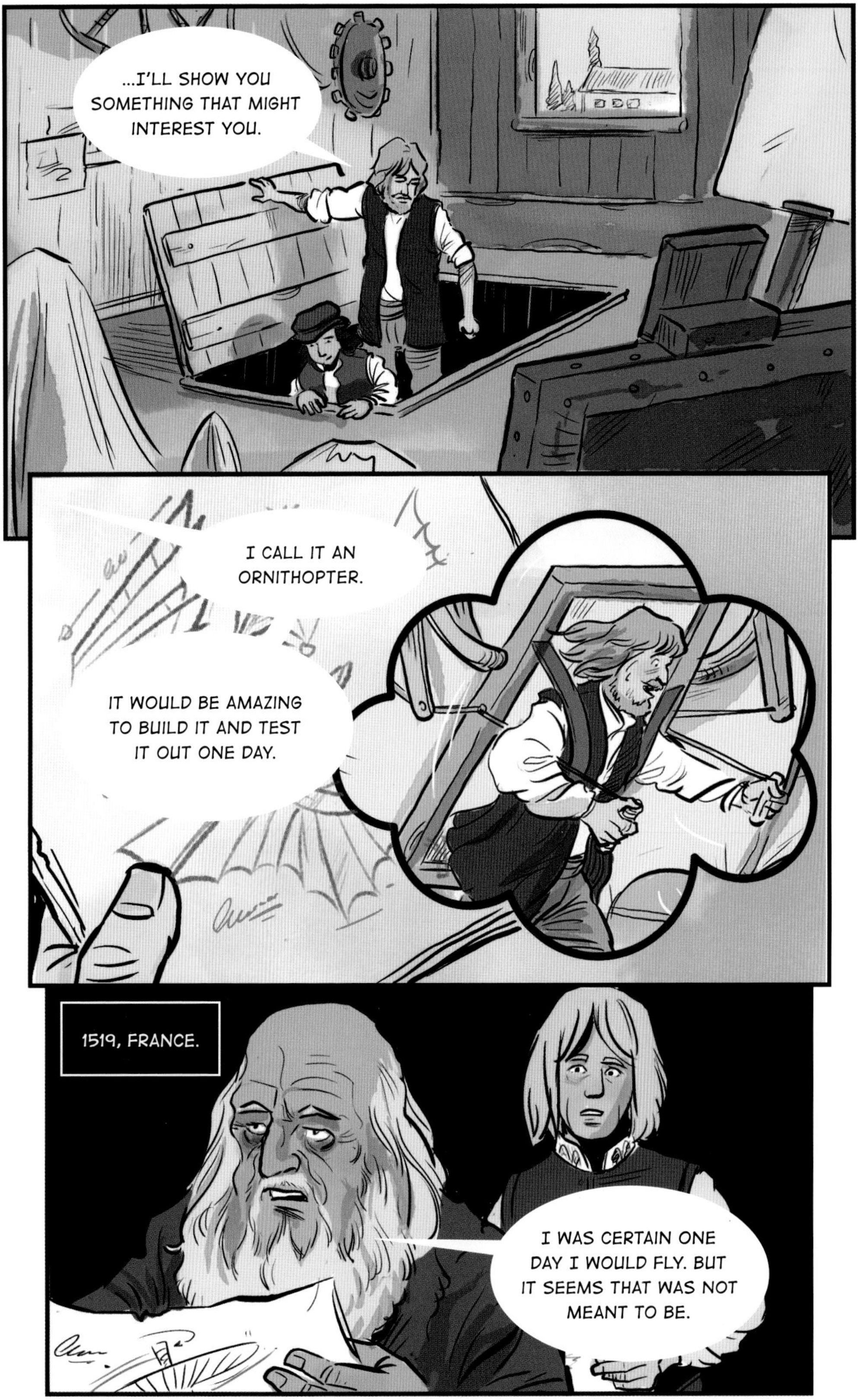
...I'LL SHOW YOU SOMETHING THAT MIGHT INTEREST YOU.
I CALL IT AN ORNITHOPTER.
IT WOULD BE AMAZING TO BUILD IT AND TEST IT OUT ONE DAY.
1519, FRANCE.
I WAS CERTAIN ONE DAY I WOULD FLY. BUT IT SEEMS THAT WAS NOT MEANT TO BE.

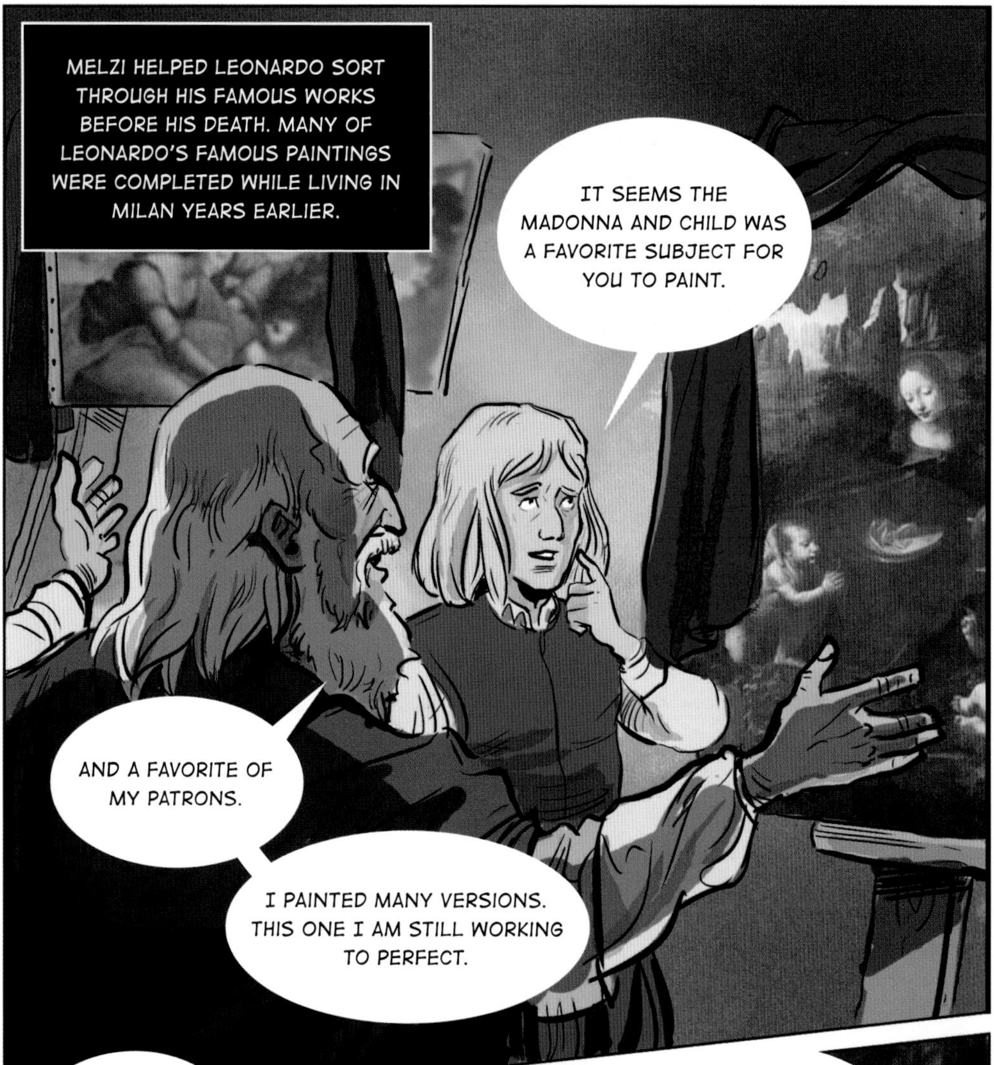
MELZI HELPED LEONARDO SORT THROUGH HIS FAMOUS WORKS BEFORE HIS DEATH. MANY OF LEONARDO'S FAMOUS PAINTINGS WERE COMPLETED WHILE LIVING IN MILAN YEARS EARLIER.
IT SEEMS THE MADONNA AND CHILD WAS A FAVORITE SUBJECT FOR YOU TO PAINT.
AND A FAVORITE OF MY PATRONS.
I PAINTED MANY VERSIONS. THIS ONE I AM STILL WORKING TO PERFECT.

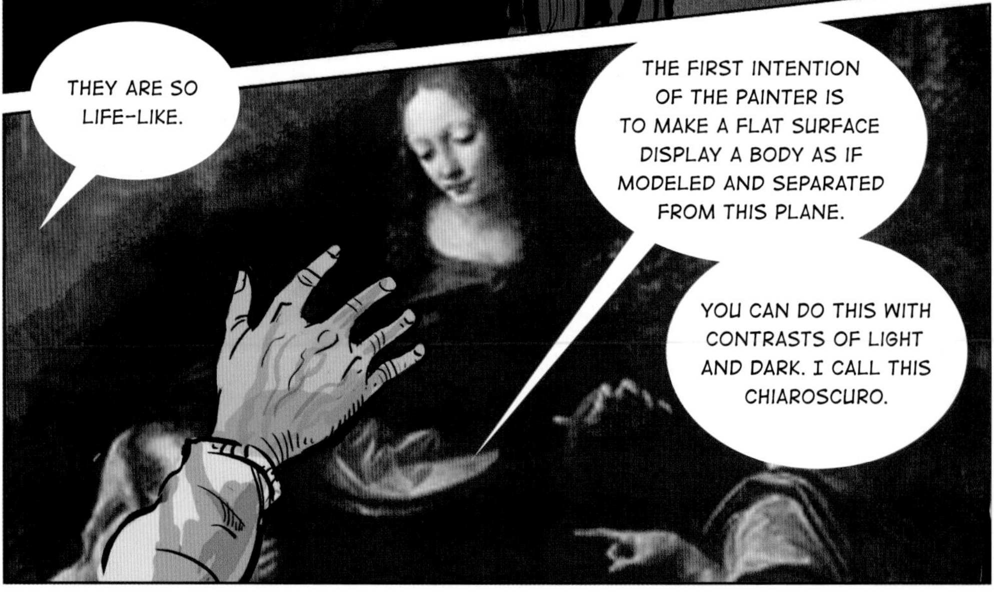
THEY ARE SO LIFE-LIKE.
THE FIRST INTENTION OF THE PAINTER IS TO MAKE A FLAT SURFACE DISPLAY A BODY AS IF MODELED AND SEPARATED FROM THIS PLANE.
YOU CAN DO THIS WITH CONTRASTS OF LIGHT AND DARK. I CALL THIS CHIAROSCURO.

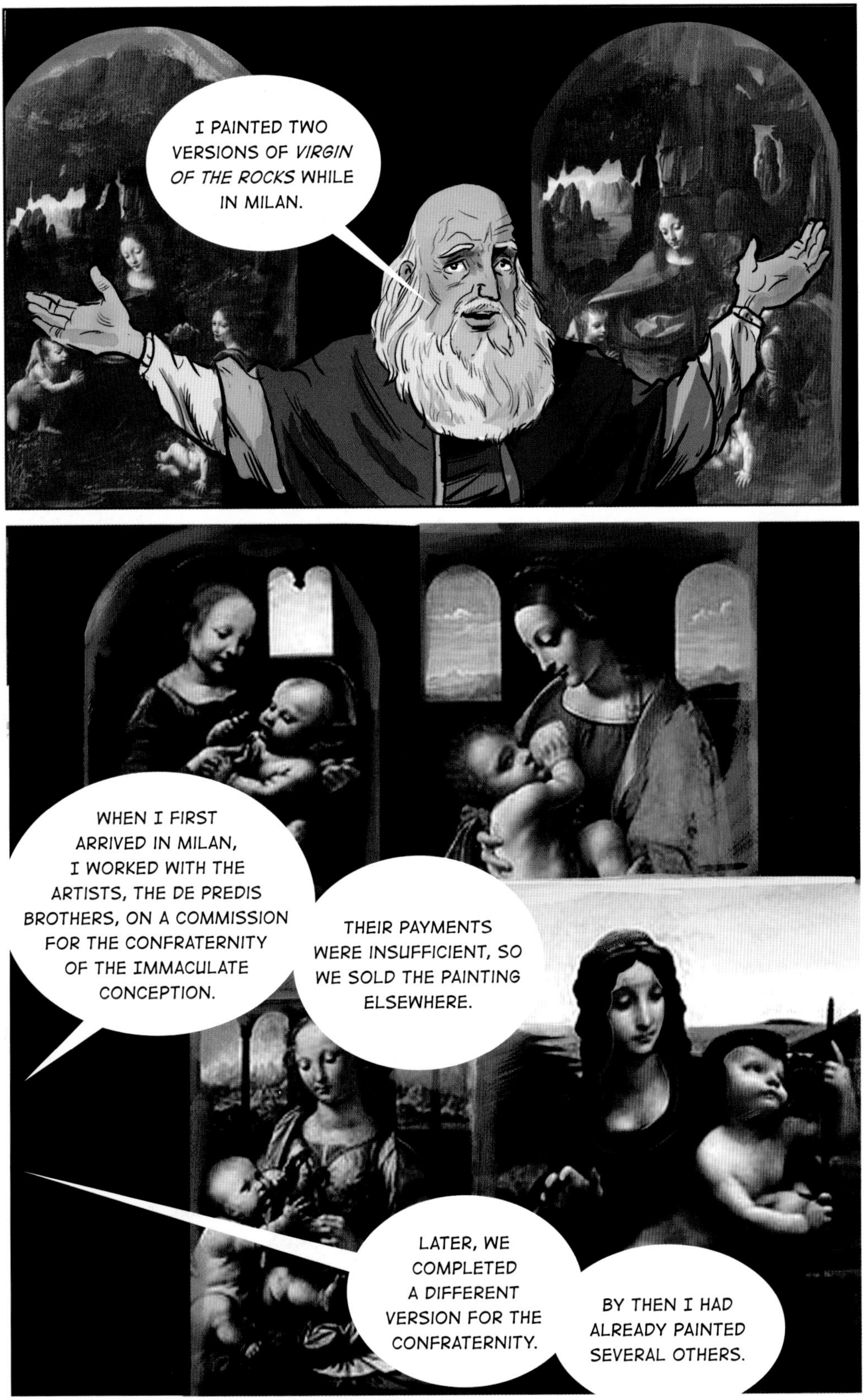
I PAINTED TWO VERSIONS OF *VIRGIN OF THE ROCKS* WHILE IN MILAN.
WHEN I FIRST ARRIVED IN MILAN, I WORKED WITH THE ARTISTS, THE DE PREDIS BROTHERS, ON A COMMISSION FOR THE CONFRATERNITY OF THE IMMACULATE CONCEPTION.
THEIR PAYMENTS WERE INSUFFICIENT, SO WE SOLD THE PAINTING ELSEWHERE.
LATER, WE COMPLETED A DIFFERENT VERSION FOR THE CONFRATERNITY.
BY THEN I HAD ALREADY PAINTED SEVERAL OTHERS.

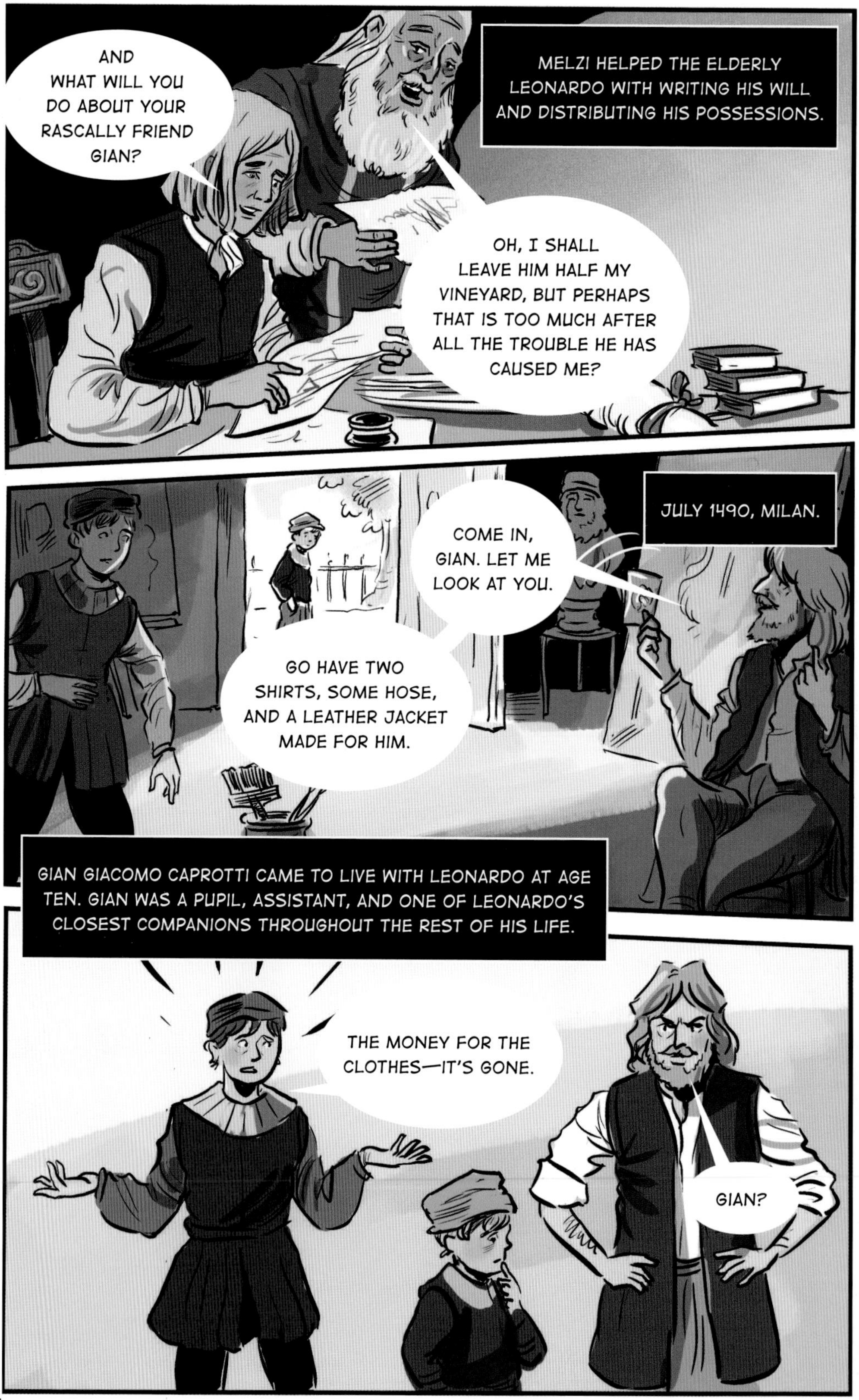
MELZI HELPED THE ELDERLY LEONARDO WITH WRITING HIS WILL AND DISTRIBUTING HIS POSSESSIONS.
AND WHAT WILL YOU DO ABOUT YOUR RASCALLY FRIEND GIAN?
OH, I SHALL LEAVE HIM HALF MY VINEYARD, BUT PERHAPS THAT IS TOO MUCH AFTER ALL THE TROUBLE HE HAS CAUSED ME?
JULY 1490, MILAN.
COME IN, GIAN. LET ME LOOK AT YOU.
GO HAVE TWO SHIRTS, SOME HOSE, AND A LEATHER JACKET MADE FOR HIM.
GIAN GIACOMO CAPROTTI CAME TO LIVE WITH LEONARDO AT AGE TEN. GIAN WAS A PUPIL, ASSISTANT, AND ONE OF LEONARDO'S CLOSEST COMPANIONS THROUGHOUT THE REST OF HIS LIFE.
THE MONEY FOR THE CLOTHES—IT'S GONE.
GIAN?

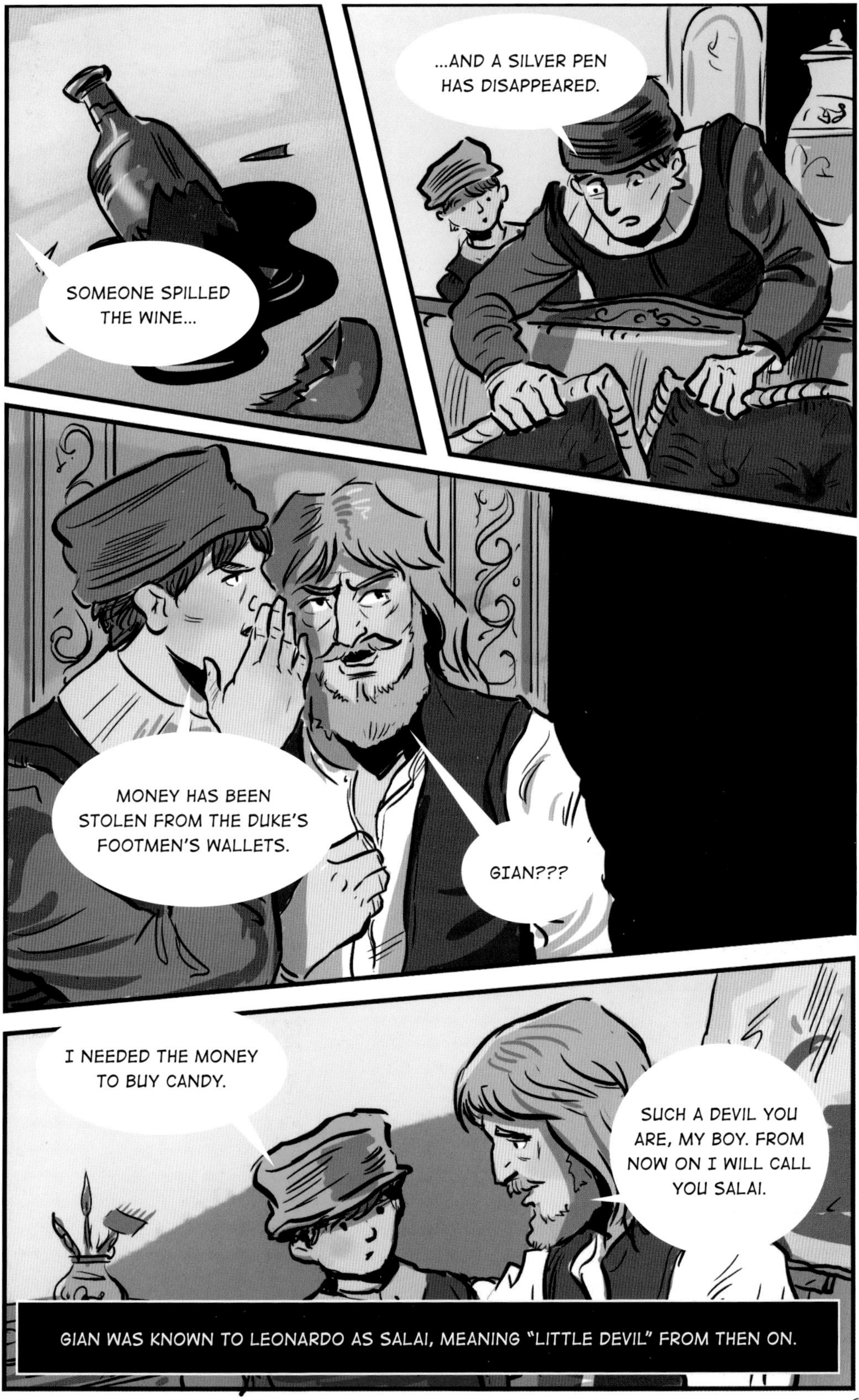
SOMEONE SPILLED THE WINE...
...AND A SILVER PEN HAS DISAPPEARED.
MONEY HAS BEEN STOLEN FROM THE DUKE'S FOOTMEN'S WALLETS.
GIAN???
I NEEDED THE MONEY TO BUY CANDY.
SUCH A DEVIL YOU ARE, MY BOY. FROM NOW ON I WILL CALL YOU SALAI.
GIAN WAS KNOWN TO LEONARDO AS SALAI, MEANING "LITTLE DEVIL" FROM THEN ON.

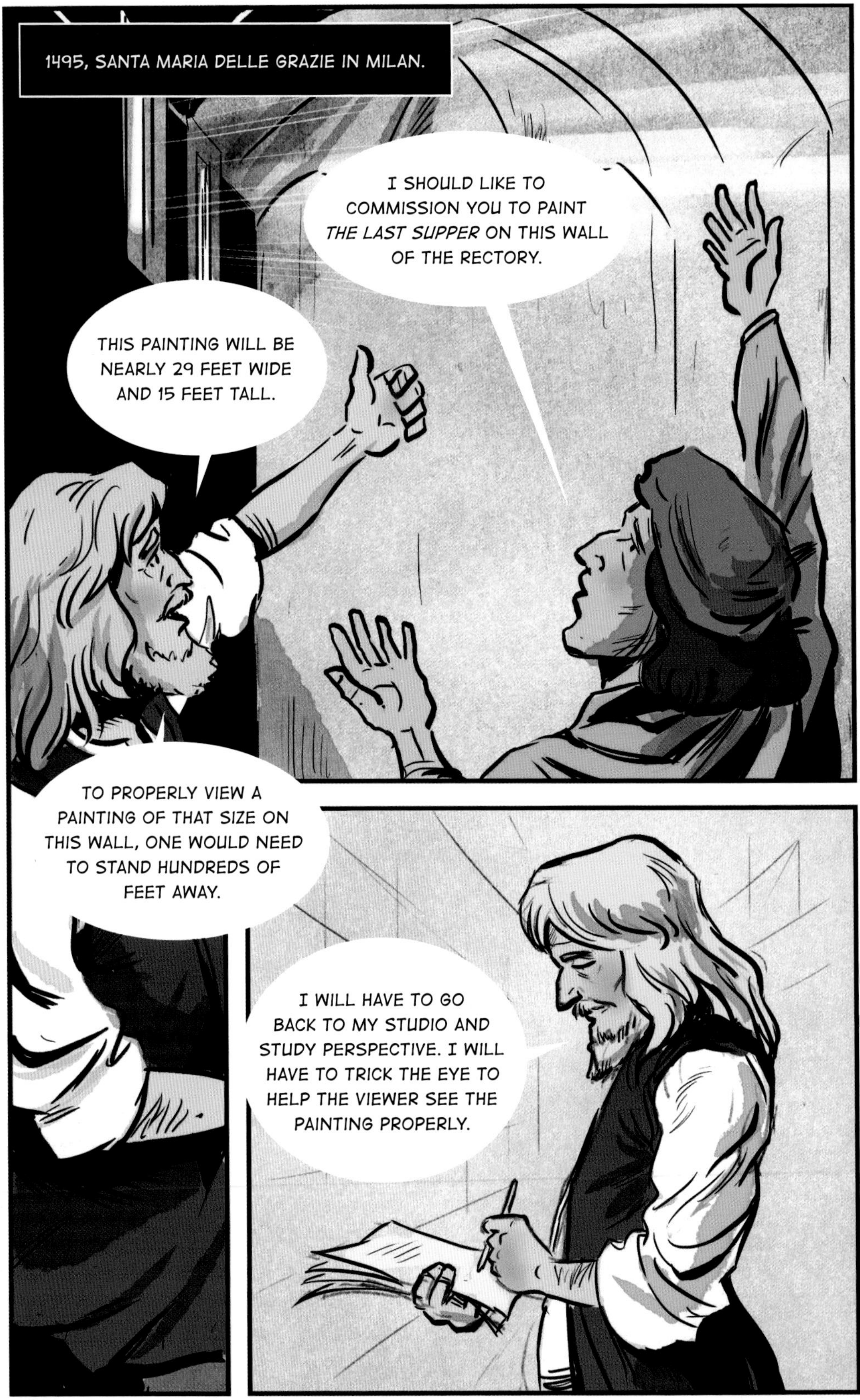
1495, SANTA MARIA DELLE GRAZIE IN MILAN.
I SHOULD LIKE TO COMMISSION YOU TO PAINT *THE LAST SUPPER* ON THIS WALL OF THE RECTORY.
THIS PAINTING WILL BE NEARLY 29 FEET WIDE AND 15 FEET TALL.
TO PROPERLY VIEW A PAINTING OF THAT SIZE ON THIS WALL, ONE WOULD NEED TO STAND HUNDREDS OF FEET AWAY.
I WILL HAVE TO GO BACK TO MY STUDIO AND STUDY PERSPECTIVE. I WILL HAVE TO TRICK THE EYE TO HELP THE VIEWER SEE THE PAINTING PROPERLY.

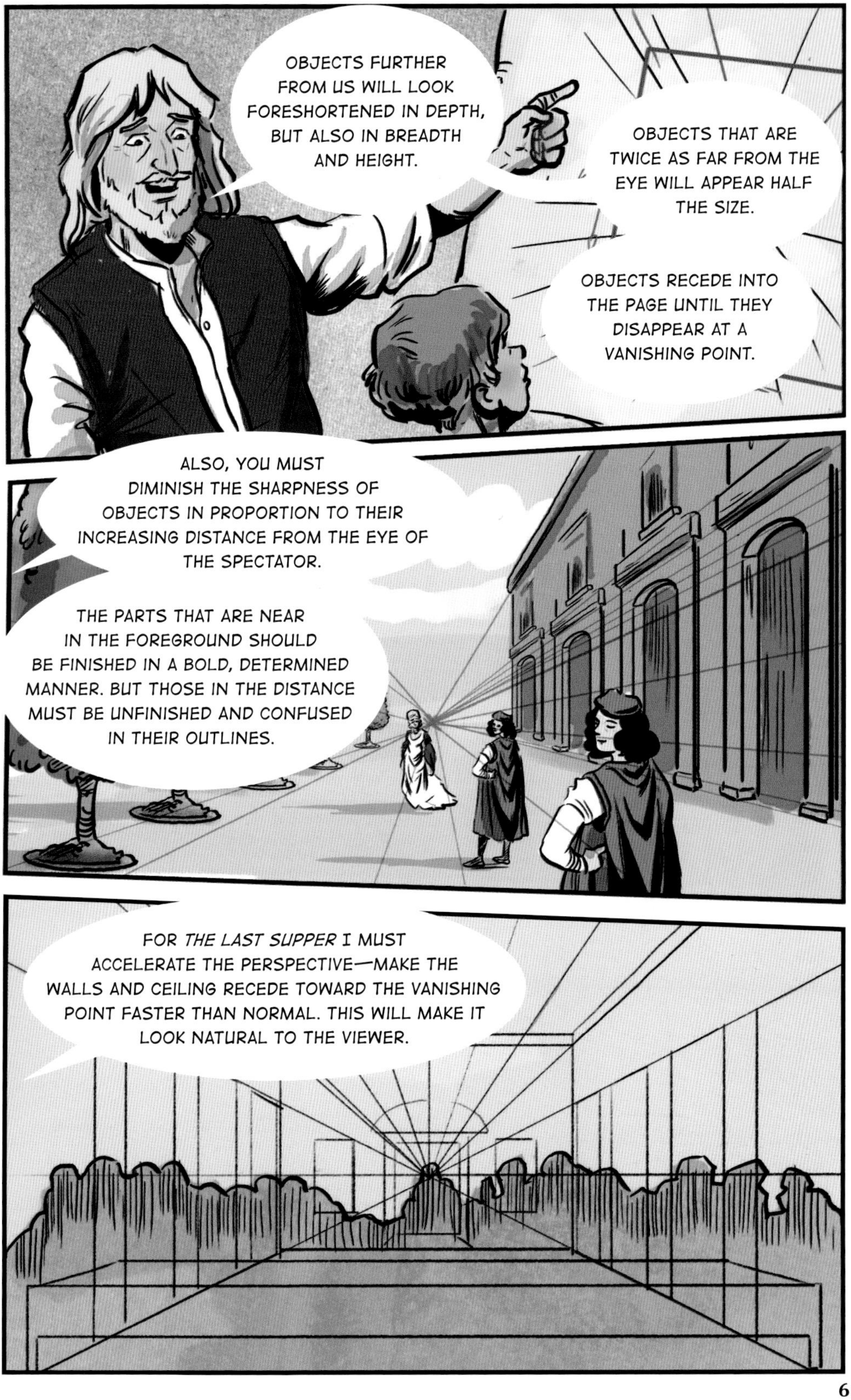
OBJECTS FURTHER FROM US WILL LOOK FORESHORTENED IN DEPTH, BUT ALSO IN BREADTH AND HEIGHT.
OBJECTS THAT ARE TWICE AS FAR FROM THE EYE WILL APPEAR HALF THE SIZE.
OBJECTS RECEDE INTO THE PAGE UNTIL THEY DISAPPEAR AT A VANISHING POINT.
ALSO, YOU MUST DIMINISH THE SHARPNESS OF OBJECTS IN PROPORTION TO THEIR INCREASING DISTANCE FROM THE EYE OF THE SPECTATOR.
THE PARTS THAT ARE NEAR IN THE FOREGROUND SHOULD BE FINISHED IN A BOLD, DETERMINED MANNER. BUT THOSE IN THE DISTANCE MUST BE UNFINISHED AND CONFUSED IN THEIR OUTLINES.
FOR *THE LAST SUPPER* I MUST ACCELERATE THE PERSPECTIVE—MAKE THE WALLS AND CEILING RECEDE TOWARD THE VANISHING POINT FASTER THAN NORMAL. THIS WILL MAKE IT LOOK NATURAL TO THE VIEWER.

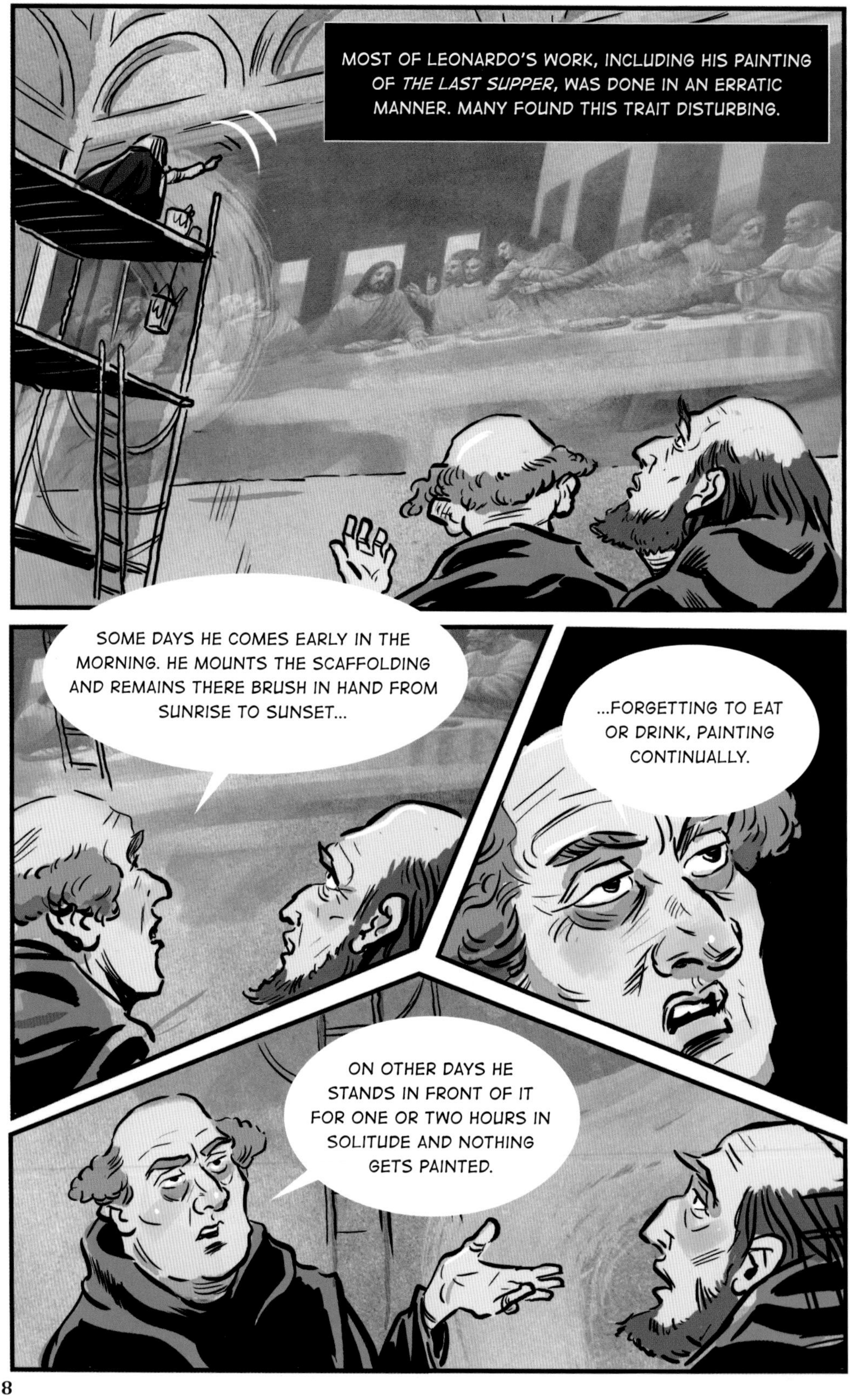
MOST OF LEONARDO'S WORK, INCLUDING HIS PAINTING OF *THE LAST SUPPER*, WAS DONE IN AN ERRATIC MANNER. MANY FOUND THIS TRAIT DISTURBING.
SOME DAYS HE COMES EARLY IN THE MORNING. HE MOUNTS THE SCAFFOLDING AND REMAINS THERE BRUSH IN HAND FROM SUNRISE TO SUNSET...
...FORGETTING TO EAT OR DRINK, PAINTING CONTINUALLY.
ON OTHER DAYS HE STANDS IN FRONT OF IT FOR ONE OR TWO HOURS IN SOLITUDE AND NOTHING GETS PAINTED.

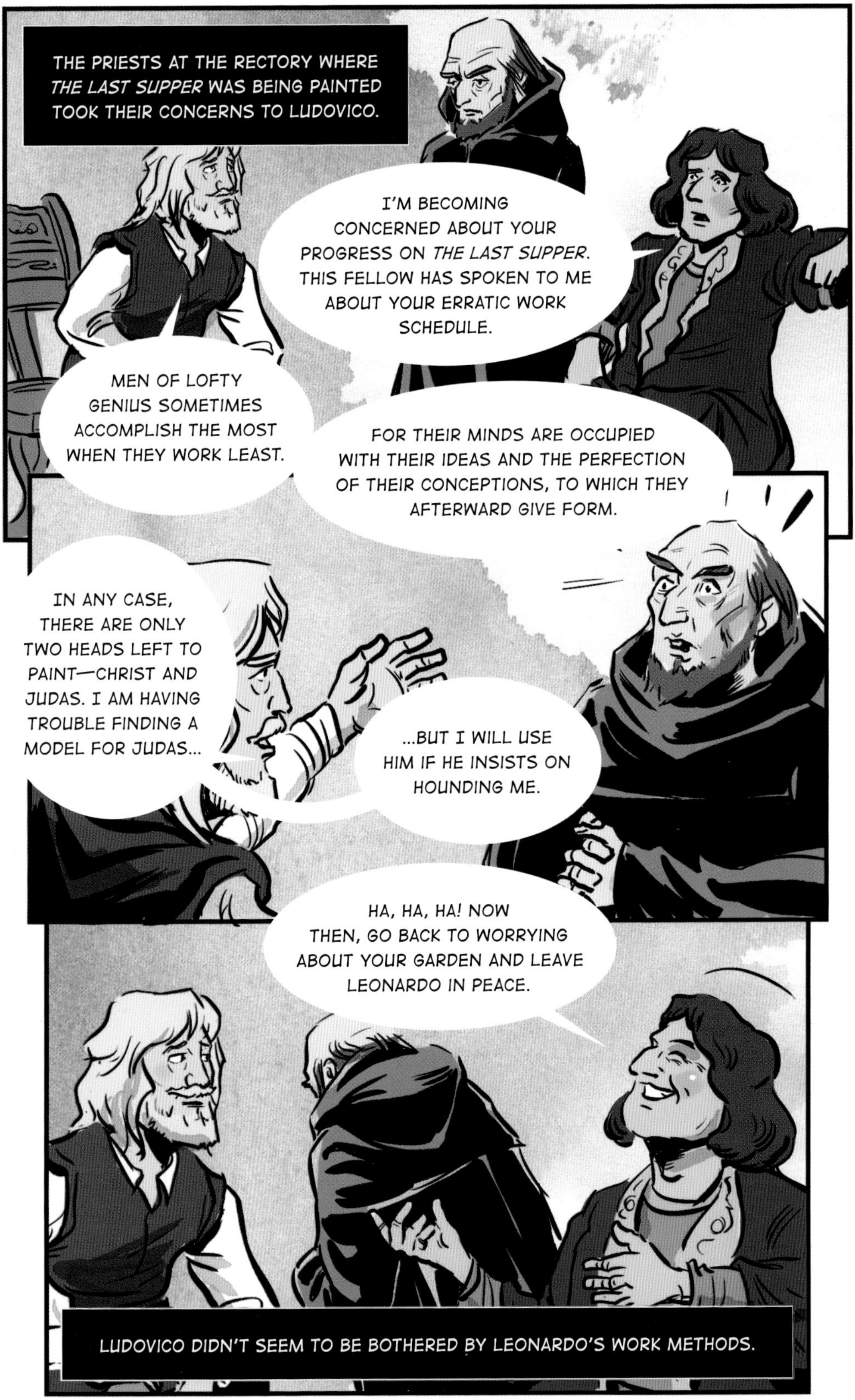
THE PRIESTS AT THE RECTORY WHERE *THE LAST SUPPER* WAS BEING PAINTED TOOK THEIR CONCERNS TO LUDOVICO.
I'M BECOMING CONCERNED ABOUT YOUR PROGRESS ON *THE LAST SUPPER*. THIS FELLOW HAS SPOKEN TO ME ABOUT YOUR ERRATIC WORK SCHEDULE.
MEN OF LOFTY GENIUS SOMETIMES ACCOMPLISH THE MOST WHEN THEY WORK LEAST.
FOR THEIR MINDS ARE OCCUPIED WITH THEIR IDEAS AND THE PERFECTION OF THEIR CONCEPTIONS, TO WHICH THEY AFTERWARD GIVE FORM.
IN ANY CASE, THERE ARE ONLY TWO HEADS LEFT TO PAINT—CHRIST AND JUDAS. I AM HAVING TROUBLE FINDING A MODEL FOR JUDAS...
...BUT I WILL USE HIM IF HE INSISTS ON HOUNDING ME.
HA, HA, HA! NOW THEN, GO BACK TO WORRYING ABOUT YOUR GARDEN AND LEAVE LEONARDO IN PEACE.
LUDOVICO DIDN'T SEEM TO BE BOTHERED BY LEONARDO'S WORK METHODS.

CHAPTER 7

THE GREAT BRONZE HORSE

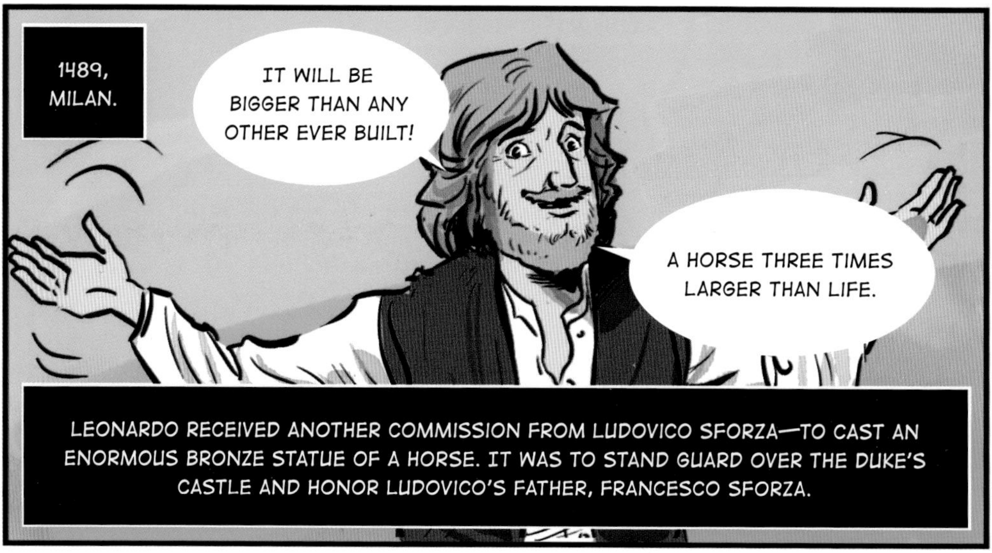
1489, MILAN.
IT WILL BE BIGGER THAN ANY OTHER EVER BUILT!
A HORSE THREE TIMES LARGER THAN LIFE.
LEONARDO RECEIVED ANOTHER COMMISSION FROM LUDOVICO SFORZA—TO CAST AN ENORMOUS BRONZE STATUE OF A HORSE. IT WAS TO STAND GUARD OVER THE DUKE'S CASTLE AND HONOR LUDOVICO'S FATHER, FRANCESCO SFORZA.

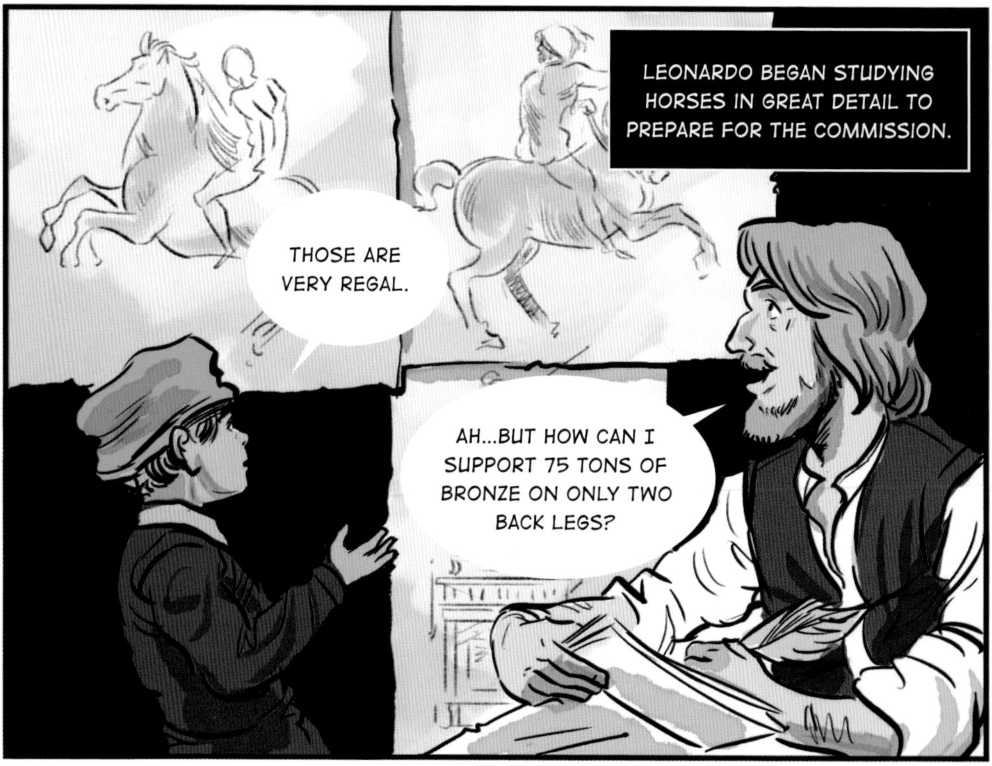
LEONARDO BEGAN STUDYING HORSES IN GREAT DETAIL TO PREPARE FOR THE COMMISSION.
THOSE ARE VERY REGAL.
AH...BUT HOW CAN I SUPPORT 75 TONS OF BRONZE ON ONLY TWO BACK LEGS?

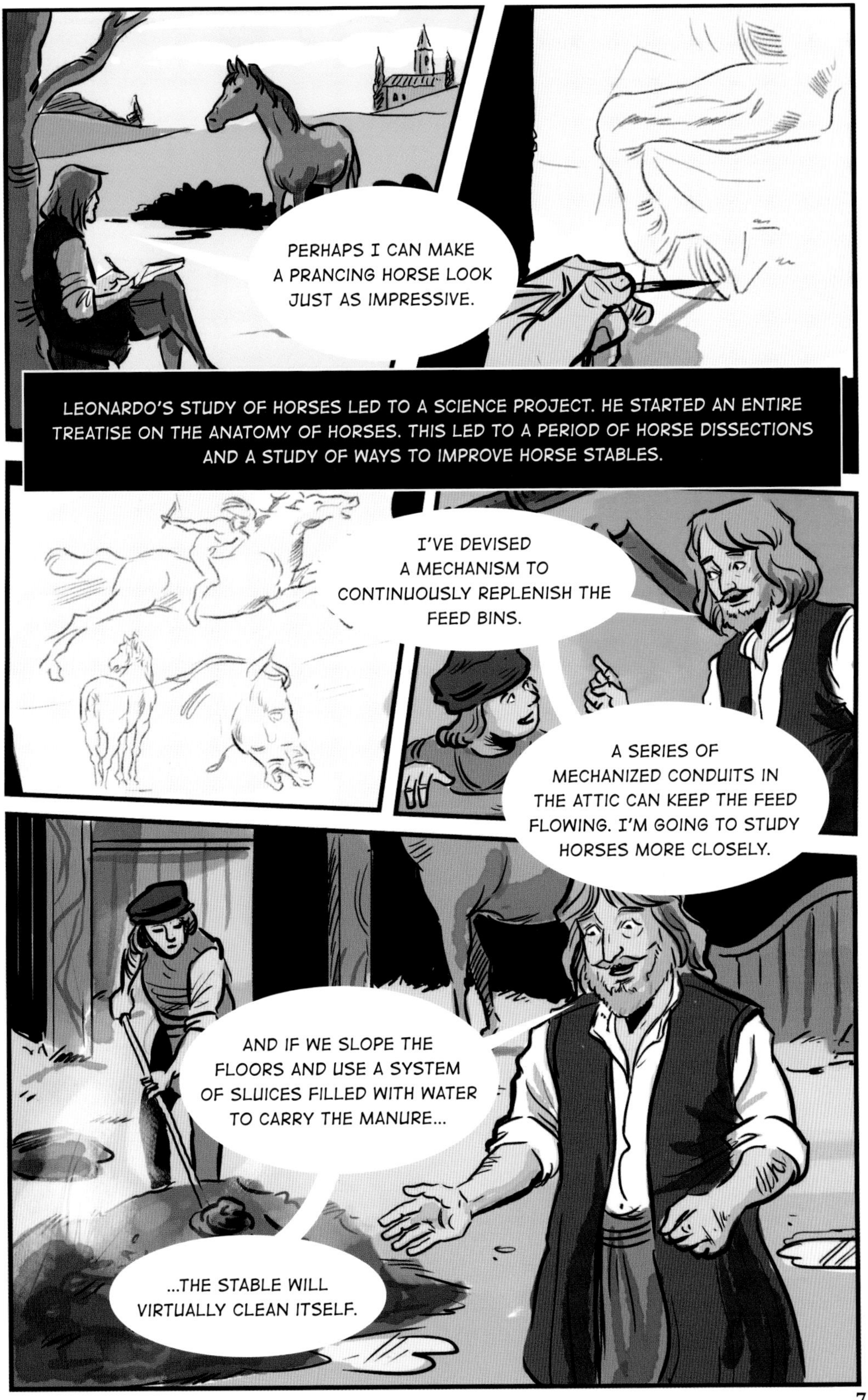
PERHAPS I CAN MAKE A PRANCING HORSE LOOK JUST AS IMPRESSIVE.
LEONARDO'S STUDY OF HORSES LED TO A SCIENCE PROJECT. HE STARTED AN ENTIRE TREATISE ON THE ANATOMY OF HORSES. THIS LED TO A PERIOD OF HORSE DISSECTIONS AND A STUDY OF WAYS TO IMPROVE HORSE STABLES.
I'VE DEVISED A MECHANISM TO CONTINUOUSLY REPLENISH THE FEED BINS.
A SERIES OF MECHANIZED CONDUITS IN THE ATTIC CAN KEEP THE FEED FLOWING. I'M GOING TO STUDY HORSES MORE CLOSELY.
AND IF WE SLOPE THE FLOORS AND USE A SYSTEM OF SLUICES FILLED WITH WATER TO CARRY THE MANURE...
...THE STABLE WILL VIRTUALLY CLEAN ITSELF.

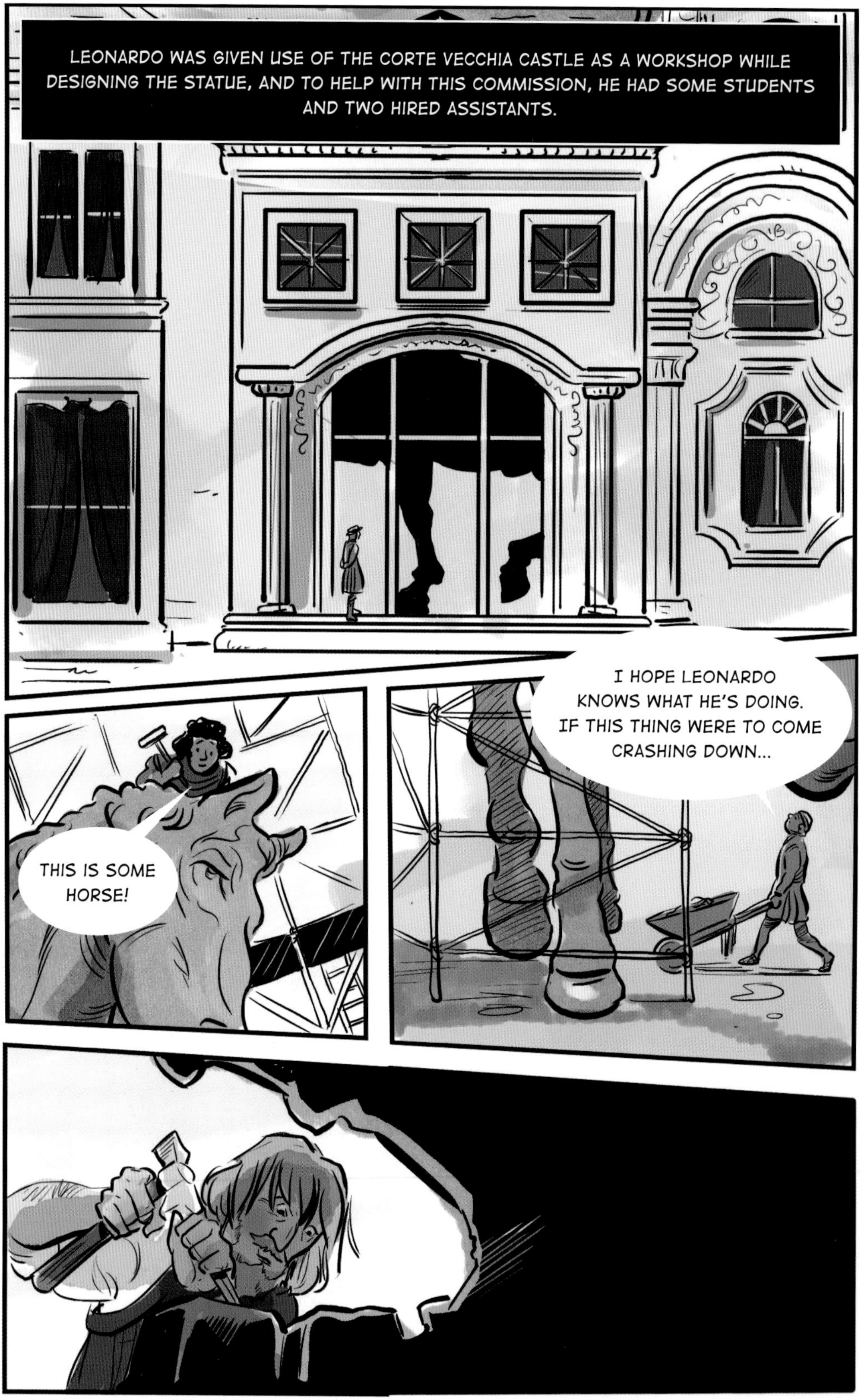
LEONARDO WAS GIVEN USE OF THE CORTE VECCHIA CASTLE AS A WORKSHOP WHILE DESIGNING THE STATUE, AND TO HELP WITH THIS COMMISSION, HE HAD SOME STUDENTS AND TWO HIRED ASSISTANTS.
THIS IS SOME HORSE!
I HOPE LEONARDO KNOWS WHAT HE'S DOING. IF THIS THING WERE TO COME CRASHING DOWN...

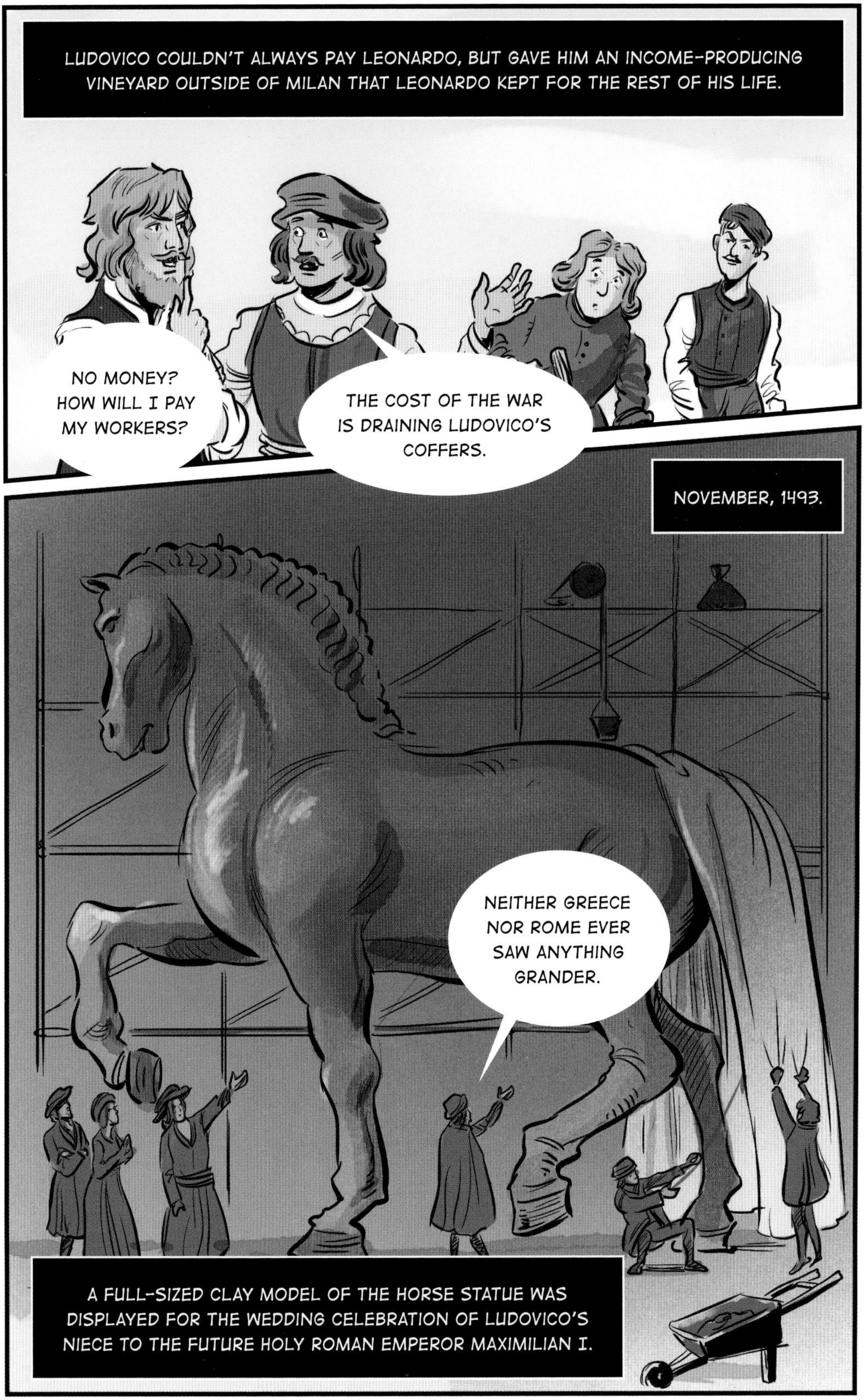
LUDOVICO COULDN'T ALWAYS PAY LEONARDO, BUT GAVE HIM AN INCOME-PRODUCING VINEYARD OUTSIDE OF MILAN THAT LEONARDO KEPT FOR THE REST OF HIS LIFE.
NO MONEY? HOW WILL I PAY MY WORKERS?
THE COST OF THE WAR IS DRAINING LUDOVICO'S COFFERS.
NOVEMBER, 1493.
NEITHER GREECE NOR ROME EVER SAW ANYTHING GRANDER.
A FULL-SIZED CLAY MODEL OF THE HORSE STATUE WAS DISPLAYED FOR THE WEDDING CELEBRATION OF LUDOVICO'S NIECE TO THE FUTURE HOLY ROMAN EMPEROR MAXIMILIAN I.

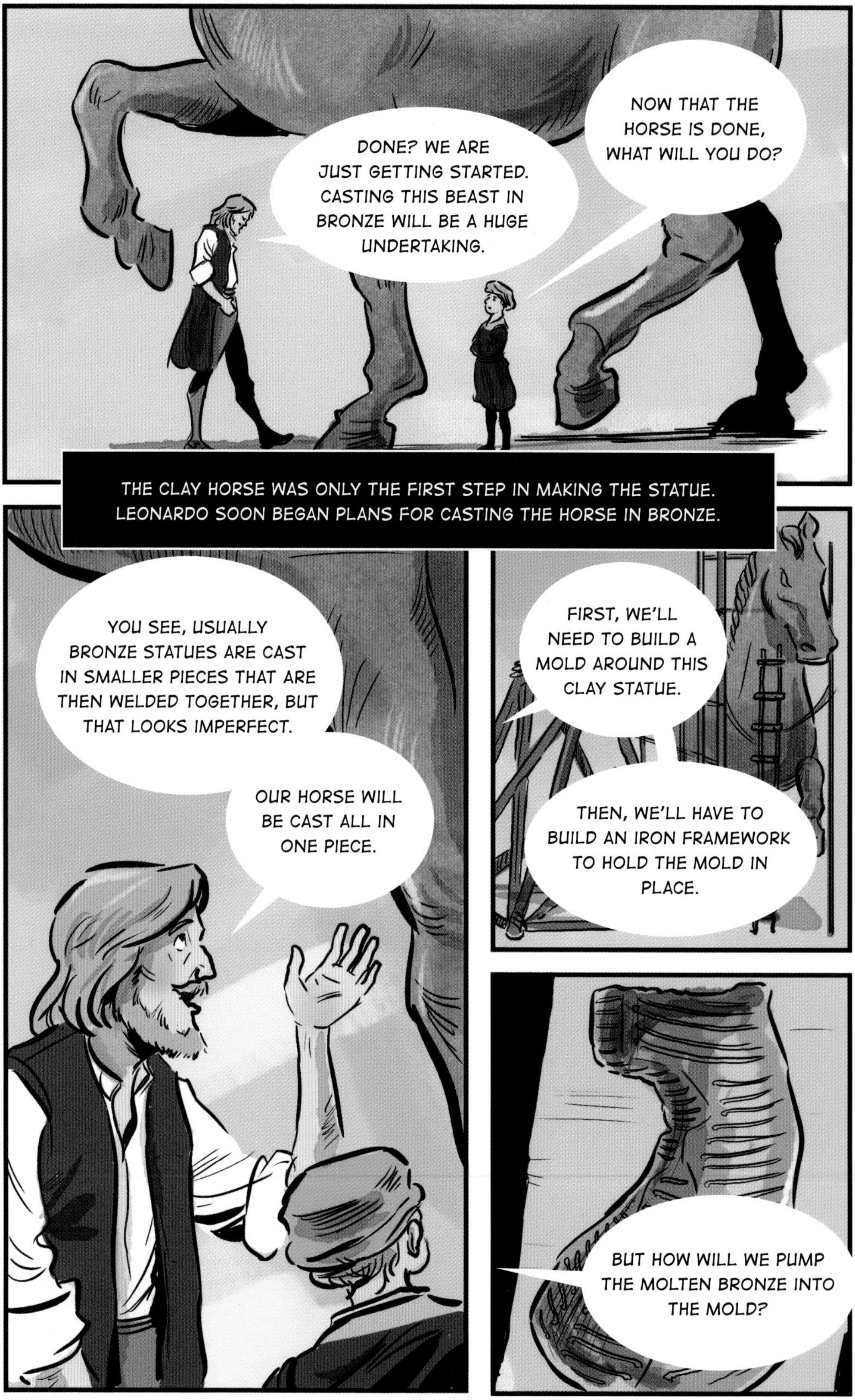
NOW THAT THE HORSE IS DONE, WHAT WILL YOU DO?
DONE? WE ARE JUST GETTING STARTED. CASTING THIS BEAST IN BRONZE WILL BE A HUGE UNDERTAKING.
THE CLAY HORSE WAS ONLY THE FIRST STEP IN MAKING THE STATUE. LEONARDO SOON BEGAN PLANS FOR CASTING THE HORSE IN BRONZE.
YOU SEE, USUALLY BRONZE STATUES ARE CAST IN SMALLER PIECES THAT ARE THEN WELDED TOGETHER, BUT THAT LOOKS IMPERFECT.
OUR HORSE WILL BE CAST ALL IN ONE PIECE.
FIRST, WE'LL NEED TO BUILD A MOLD AROUND THIS CLAY STATUE.
THEN, WE'LL HAVE TO BUILD AN IRON FRAMEWORK TO HOLD THE MOLD IN PLACE.
BUT HOW WILL WE PUMP THE MOLTEN BRONZE INTO THE MOLD?

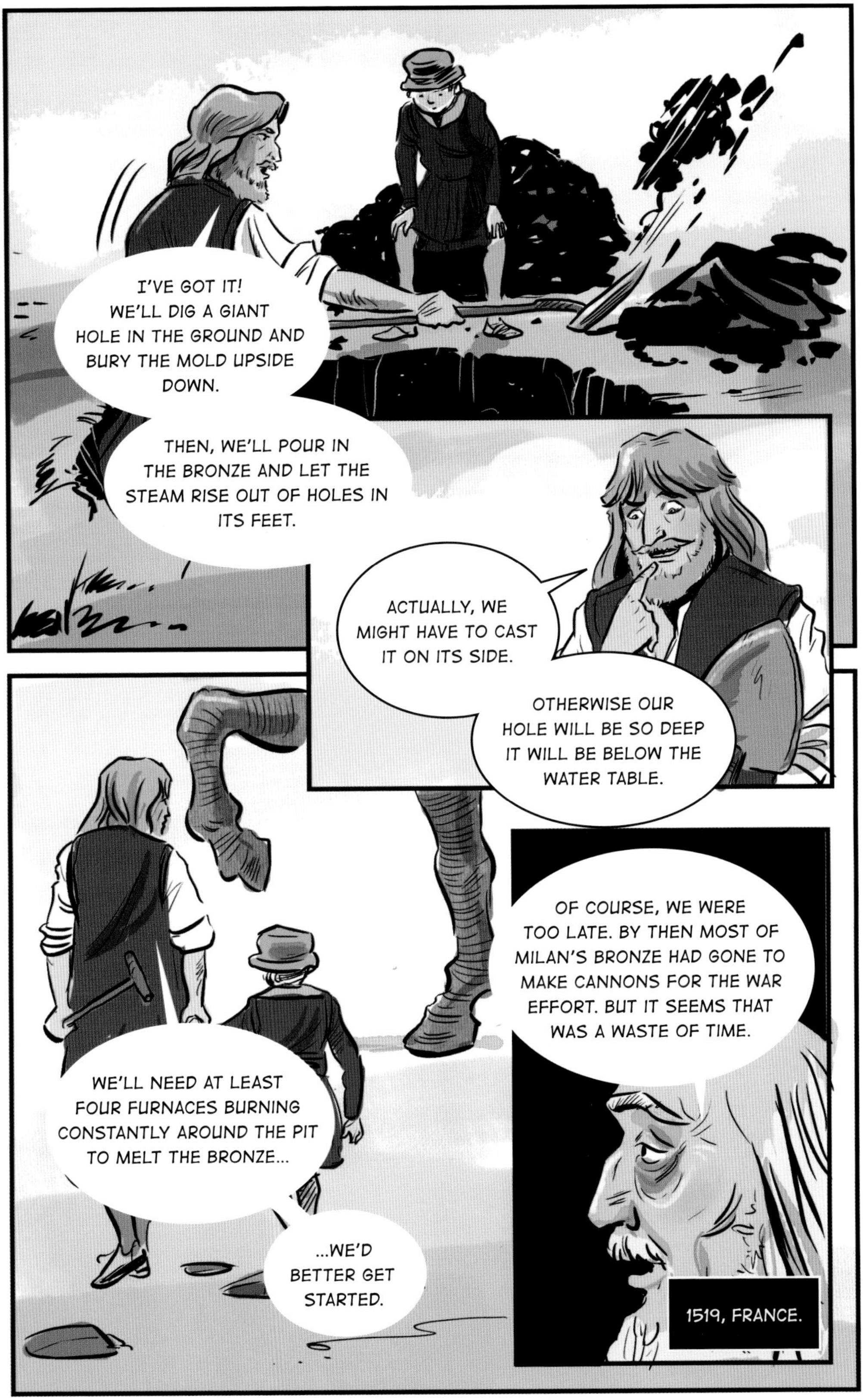
I'VE GOT IT! WE'LL DIG A GIANT HOLE IN THE GROUND AND BURY THE MOLD UPSIDE DOWN.
THEN, WE'LL POUR IN THE BRONZE AND LET THE STEAM RISE OUT OF HOLES IN ITS FEET.
ACTUALLY, WE MIGHT HAVE TO CAST IT ON ITS SIDE.
OTHERWISE OUR HOLE WILL BE SO DEEP IT WILL BE BELOW THE WATER TABLE.
WE'LL NEED AT LEAST FOUR FURNACES BURNING CONSTANTLY AROUND THE PIT TO MELT THE BRONZE...
...WE'D BETTER GET STARTED.
OF COURSE, WE WERE TOO LATE. BY THEN MOST OF MILAN'S BRONZE HAD GONE TO MAKE CANNONS FOR THE WAR EFFORT. BUT IT SEEMS THAT WAS A WASTE OF TIME.
1519, FRANCE.

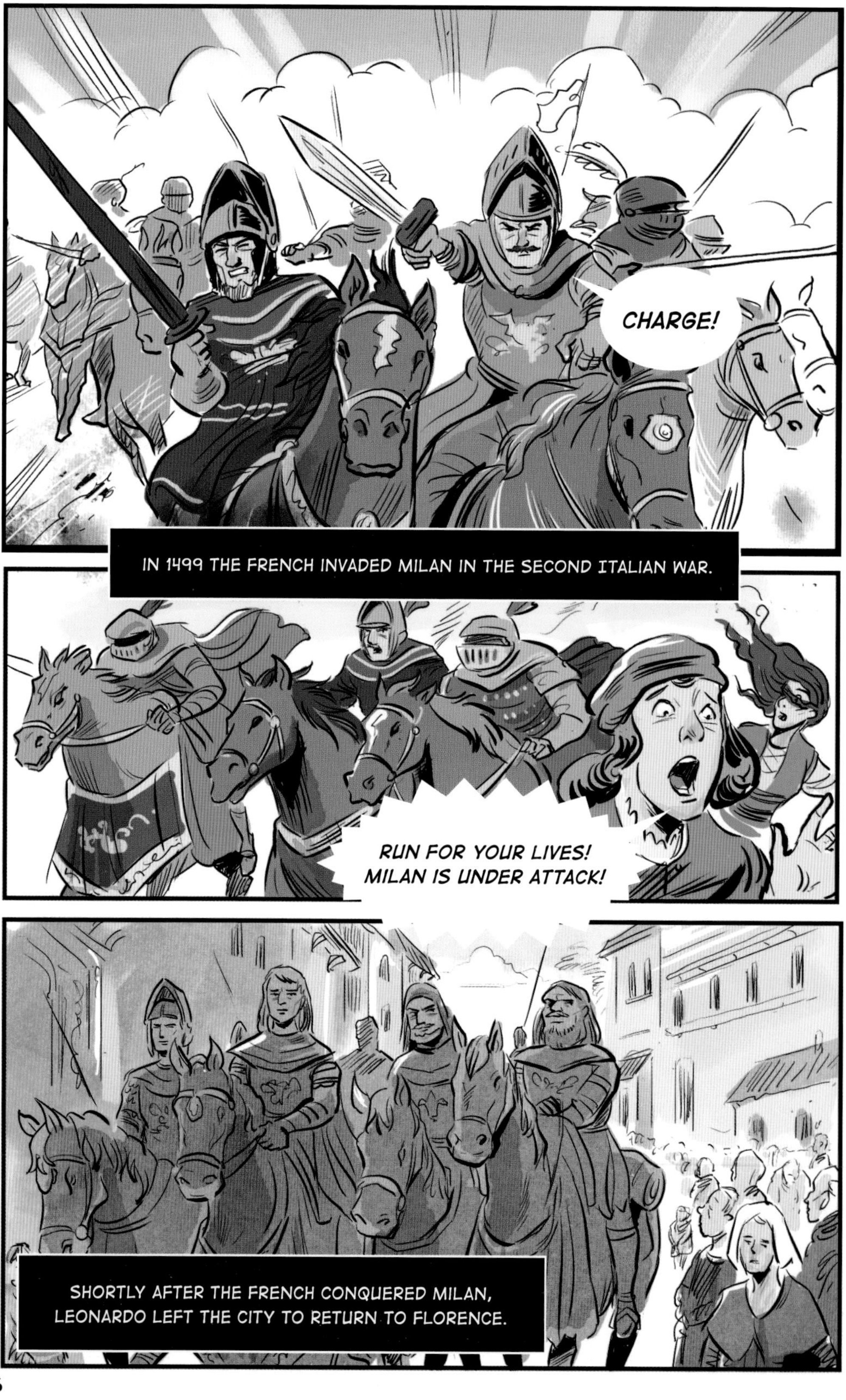
CHARGE!
IN 1499 THE FRENCH INVADED MILAN IN THE SECOND ITALIAN WAR.
RUN FOR YOUR LIVES! MILAN IS UNDER ATTACK!
SHORTLY AFTER THE FRENCH CONQUERED MILAN, LEONARDO LEFT THE CITY TO RETURN TO FLORENCE.

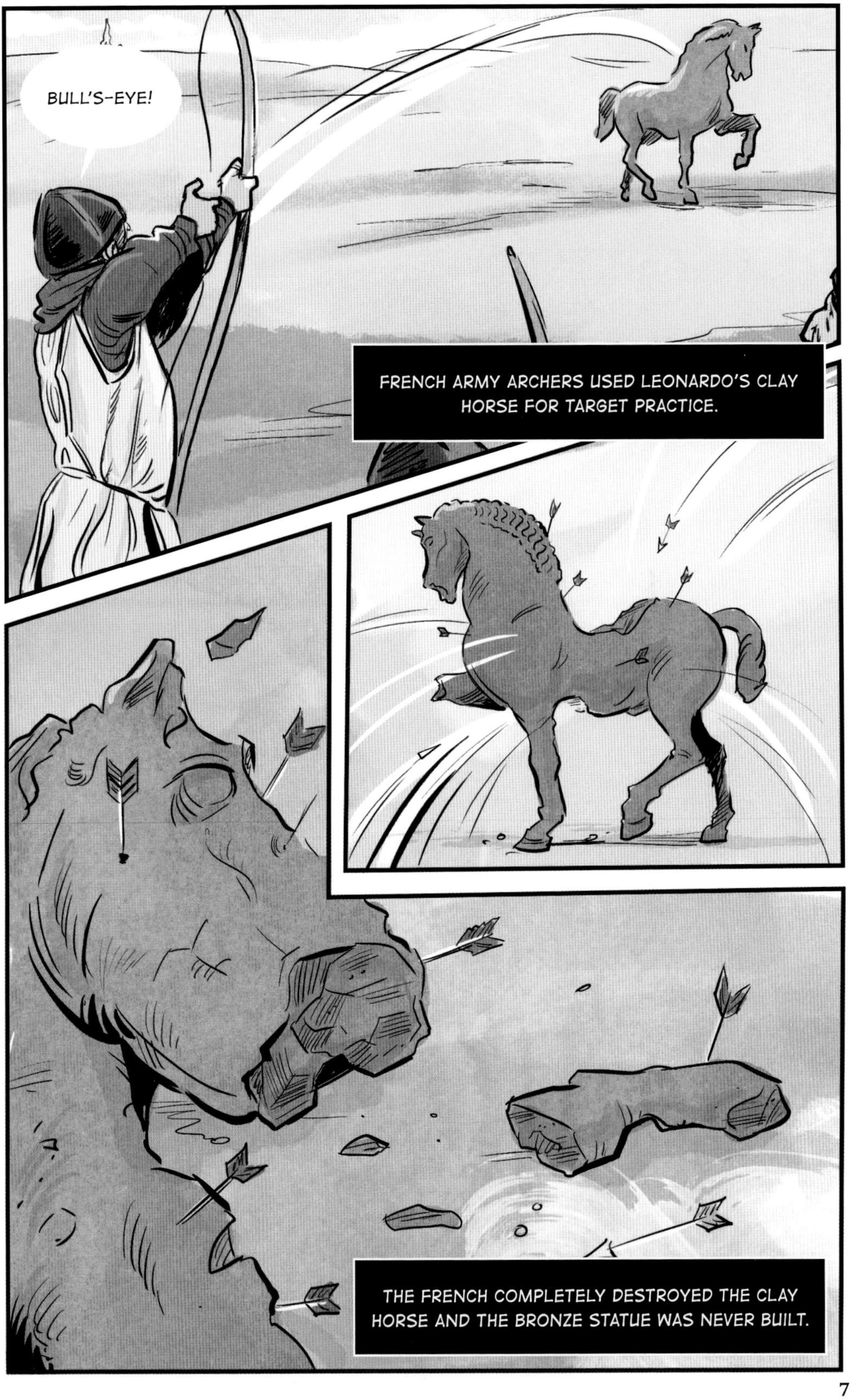
BULL'S-EYE!
FRENCH ARMY ARCHERS USED LEONARDO'S CLAY HORSE FOR TARGET PRACTICE.
THE FRENCH COMPLETELY DESTROYED THE CLAY HORSE AND THE BRONZE STATUE WAS NEVER BUILT.

CHAPTER 8

LEONARDO AIDS THE MILITARY

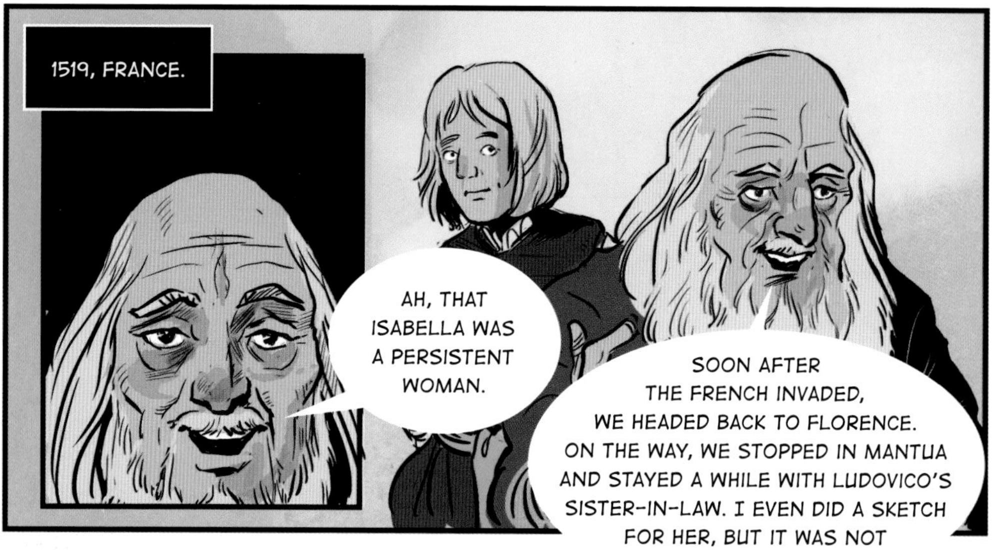
1519, FRANCE.
AH, THAT ISABELLA WAS A PERSISTENT WOMAN.
SOON AFTER THE FRENCH INVADED, WE HEADED BACK TO FLORENCE. ON THE WAY, WE STOPPED IN MANTUA AND STAYED A WHILE WITH LUDOVICO'S SISTER-IN-LAW. I EVEN DID A SKETCH FOR HER, BUT IT WAS NOT ENOUGH.

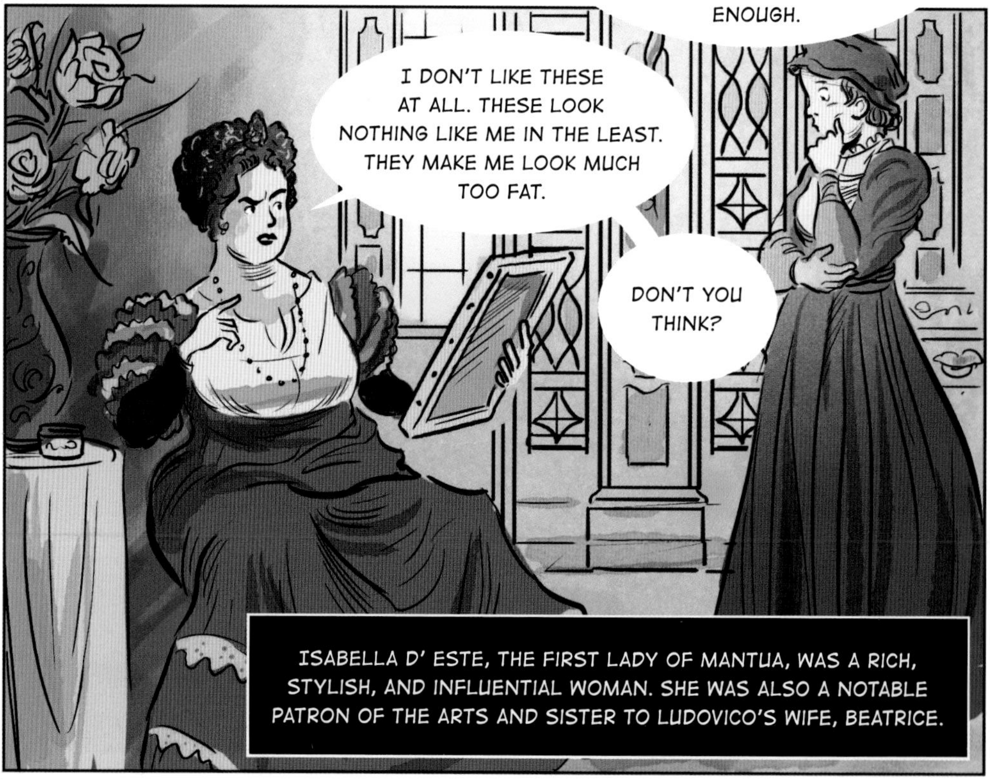
I DON'T LIKE THESE AT ALL. THESE LOOK NOTHING LIKE ME IN THE LEAST. THEY MAKE ME LOOK MUCH TOO FAT.
DON'T YOU THINK?
ISABELLA D' ESTE, THE FIRST LADY OF MANTUA, WAS A RICH, STYLISH, AND INFLUENTIAL WOMAN. SHE WAS ALSO A NOTABLE PATRON OF THE ARTS AND SISTER TO LUDOVICO'S WIFE, BEATRICE.

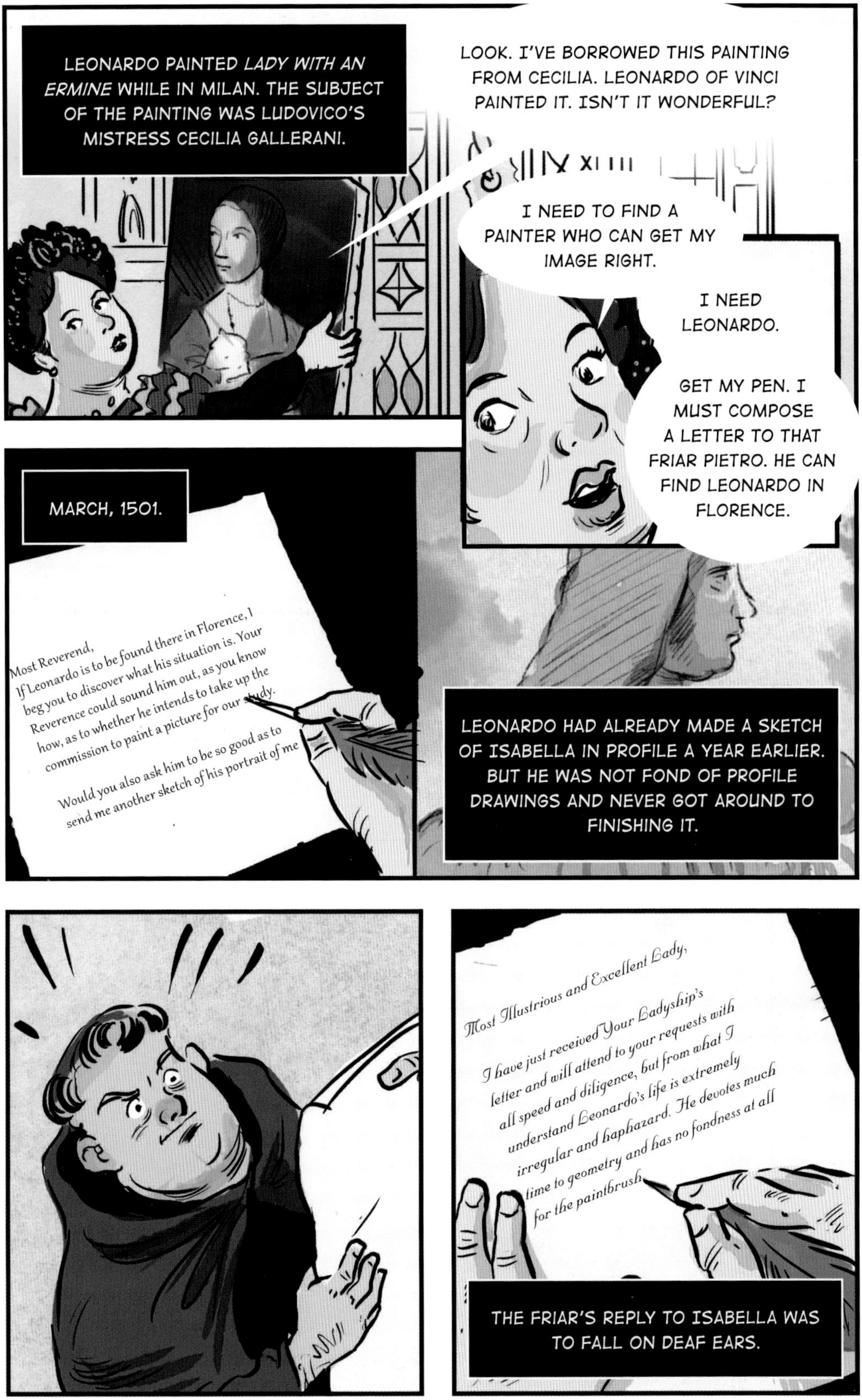
LEONARDO PAINTED *LADY WITH AN ERMINE* WHILE IN MILAN. THE SUBJECT OF THE PAINTING WAS LUDOVICO'S MISTRESS CECILIA GALLERANI.
LOOK. I'VE BORROWED THIS PAINTING FROM CECILIA. LEONARDO OF VINCI PAINTED IT. ISN'T IT WONDERFUL?
I NEED TO FIND A PAINTER WHO CAN GET MY IMAGE RIGHT.
I NEED LEONARDO.
GET MY PEN. I MUST COMPOSE A LETTER TO THAT FRIAR PIETRO. HE CAN FIND LEONARDO IN FLORENCE.
MARCH, 1501.
Most Reverend,
If Leonardo is to be found there in Florence, I beg you to discover what his situation is. Your Reverence could sound him out, as you know how, as to whether he intends to take up the commission to paint a picture for our study.
Would you also ask him to be so good as to send me another sketch of his portrait of me
LEONARDO HAD ALREADY MADE A SKETCH OF ISABELLA IN PROFILE A YEAR EARLIER. BUT HE WAS NOT FOND OF PROFILE DRAWINGS AND NEVER GOT AROUND TO FINISHING IT.
Most Illustrious and Excellent Lady,
I have just received Your Ladyship's letter and will attend to your requests with all speed and diligence, but from what I understand Leonardo's life is extremely irregular and haphazard. He devotes much time to geometry and has no fondness at all for the paintbrush
THE FRIAR'S REPLY TO ISABELLA WAS TO FALL ON DEAF EARS.

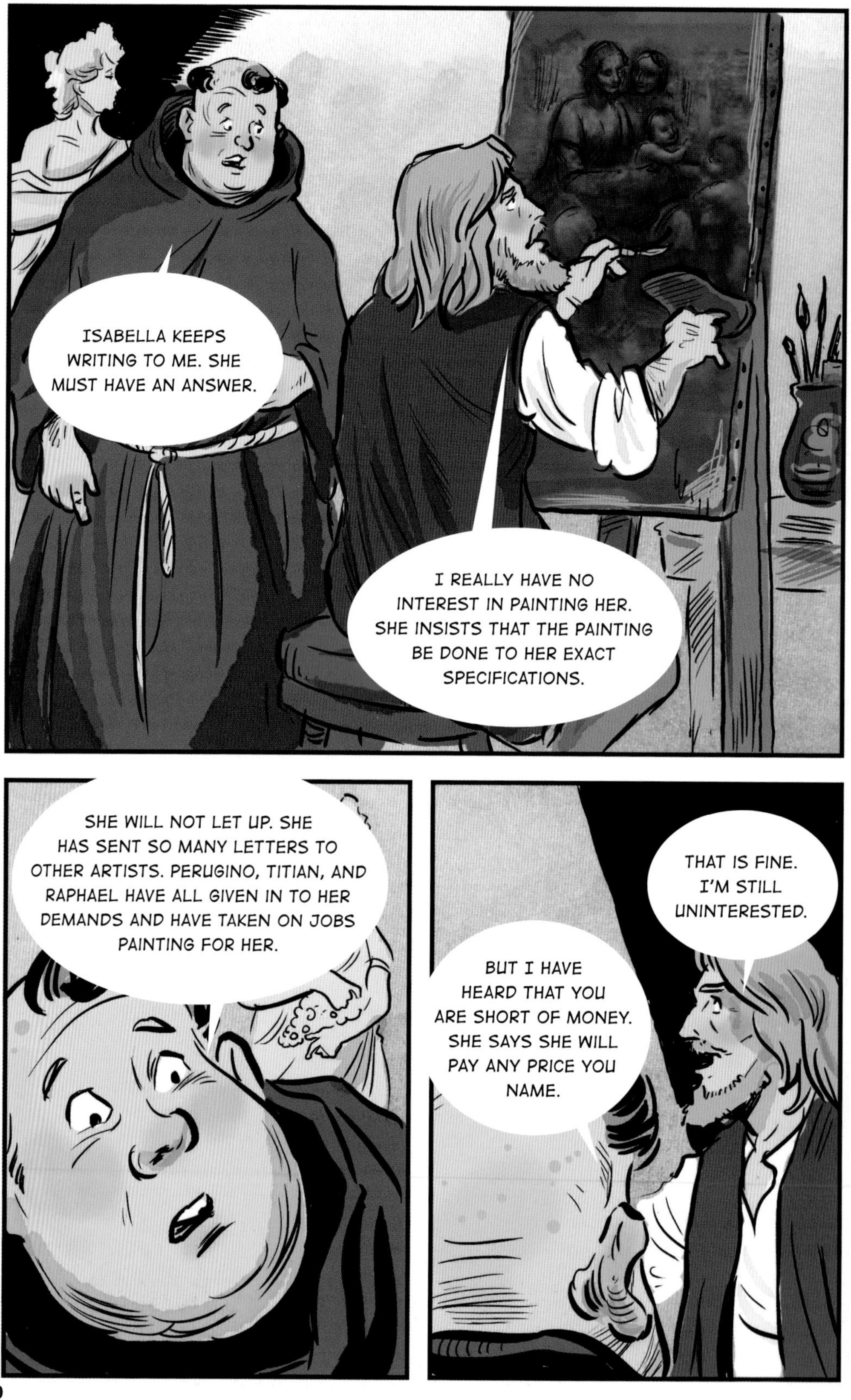
ISABELLA KEEPS WRITING TO ME. SHE MUST HAVE AN ANSWER.
I REALLY HAVE NO INTEREST IN PAINTING HER. SHE INSISTS THAT THE PAINTING BE DONE TO HER EXACT SPECIFICATIONS.
SHE WILL NOT LET UP. SHE HAS SENT SO MANY LETTERS TO OTHER ARTISTS. PERUGINO, TITIAN, AND RAPHAEL HAVE ALL GIVEN IN TO HER DEMANDS AND HAVE TAKEN ON JOBS PAINTING FOR HER.
BUT I HAVE HEARD THAT YOU ARE SHORT OF MONEY. SHE SAYS SHE WILL PAY ANY PRICE YOU NAME.
THAT IS FINE. I'M STILL UNINTERESTED.

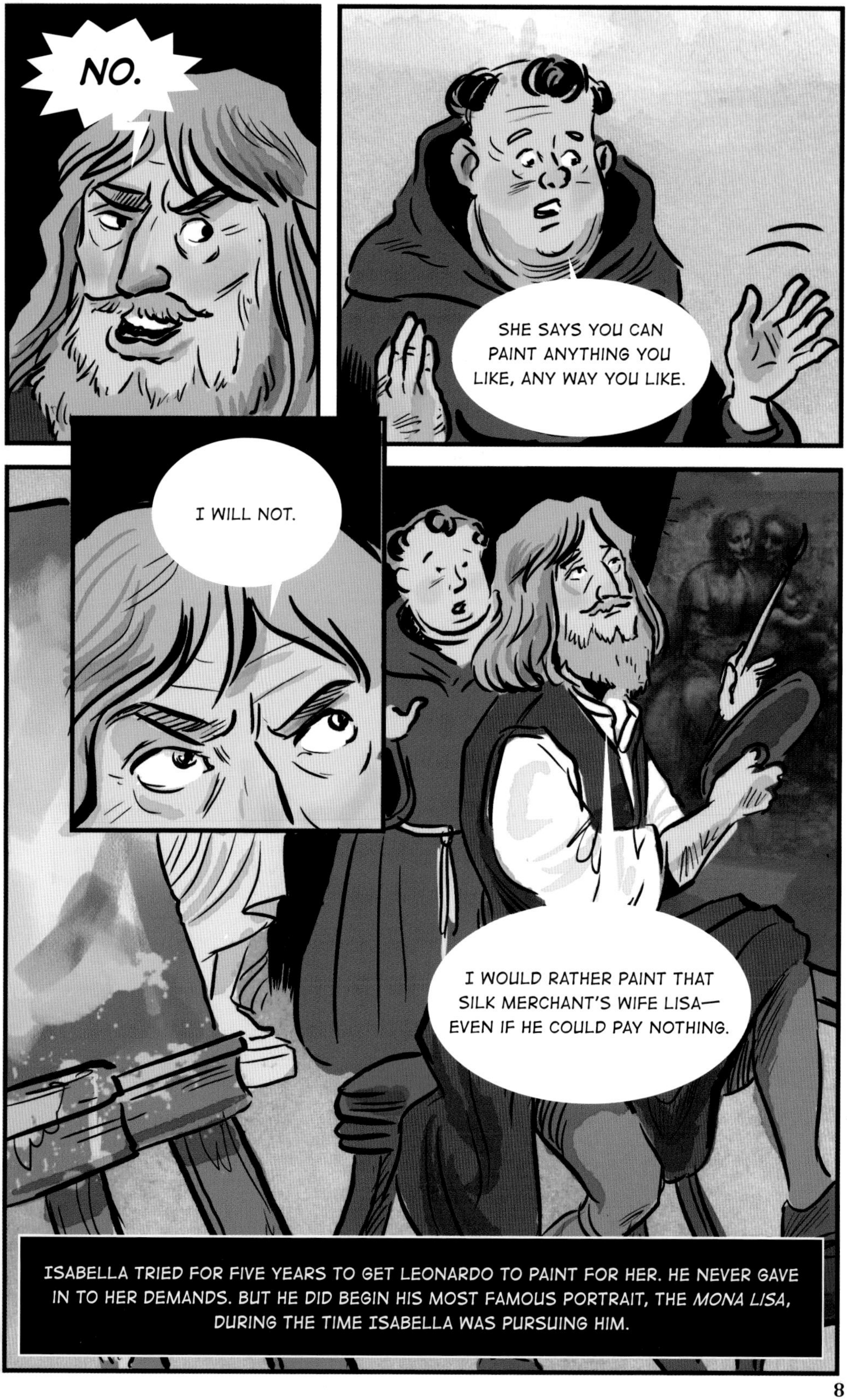
NO.
SHE SAYS YOU CAN PAINT ANYTHING YOU LIKE, ANY WAY YOU LIKE.
I WILL NOT.
I WOULD RATHER PAINT THAT SILK MERCHANT'S WIFE LISA— EVEN IF HE COULD PAY NOTHING.
ISABELLA TRIED FOR FIVE YEARS TO GET LEONARDO TO PAINT FOR HER. HE NEVER GAVE IN TO HER DEMANDS. BUT HE DID BEGIN HIS MOST FAMOUS PORTRAIT, THE *MONA LISA*, DURING THE TIME ISABELLA WAS PURSUING HIM.

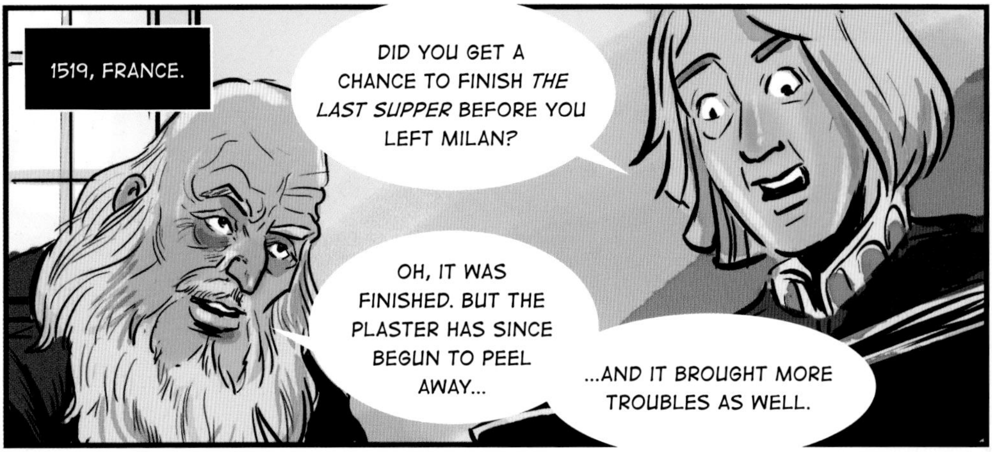
1519, FRANCE.
DID YOU GET A CHANCE TO FINISH *THE LAST SUPPER* BEFORE YOU LEFT MILAN?
OH, IT WAS FINISHED. BUT THE PLASTER HAS SINCE BEGUN TO PEEL AWAY...
...AND IT BROUGHT MORE TROUBLES AS WELL.

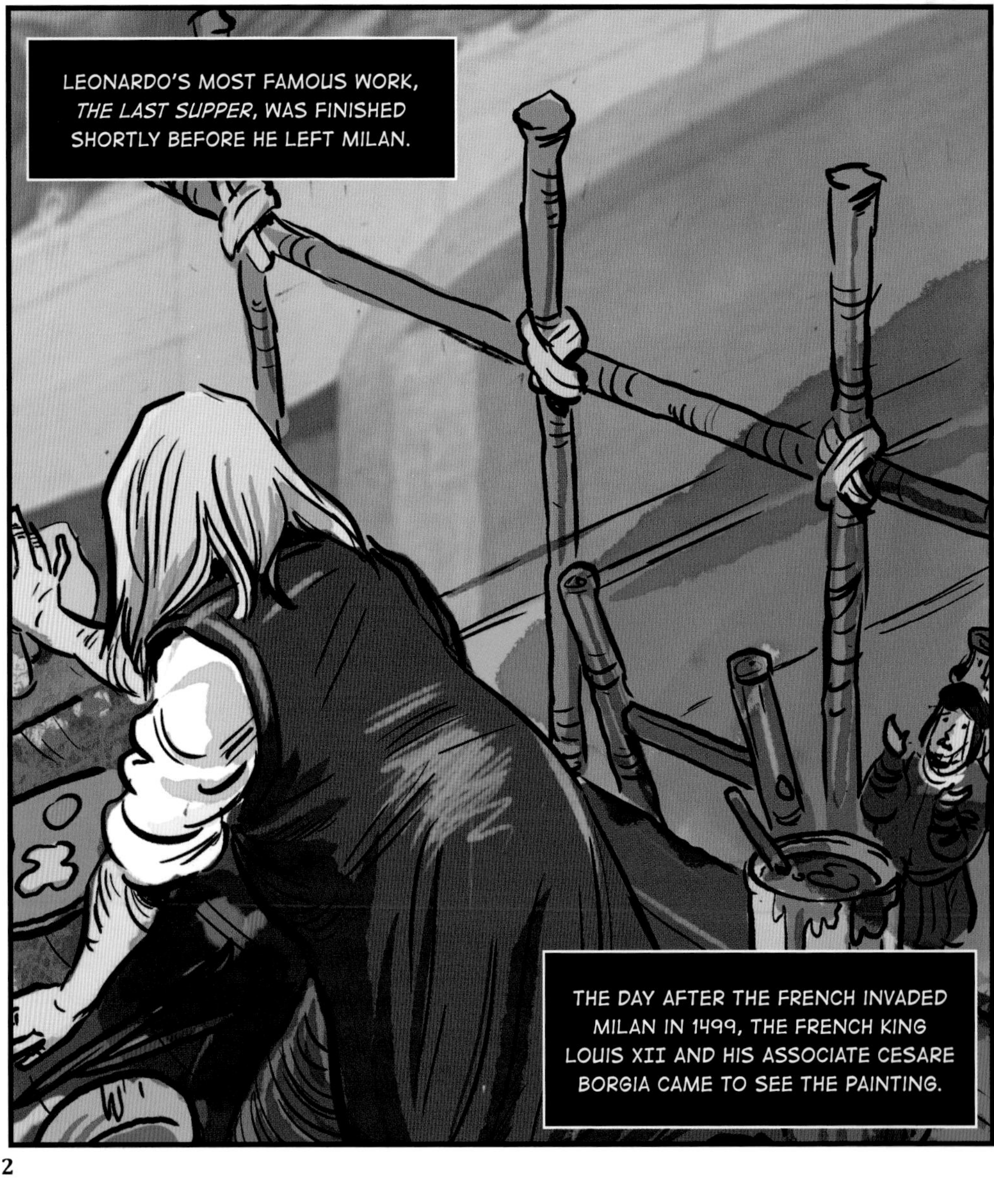
LEONARDO'S MOST FAMOUS WORK, *THE LAST SUPPER*, WAS FINISHED SHORTLY BEFORE HE LEFT MILAN.
THE DAY AFTER THE FRENCH INVADED MILAN IN 1499, THE FRENCH KING LOUIS XII AND HIS ASSOCIATE CESARE BORGIA CAME TO SEE THE PAINTING.

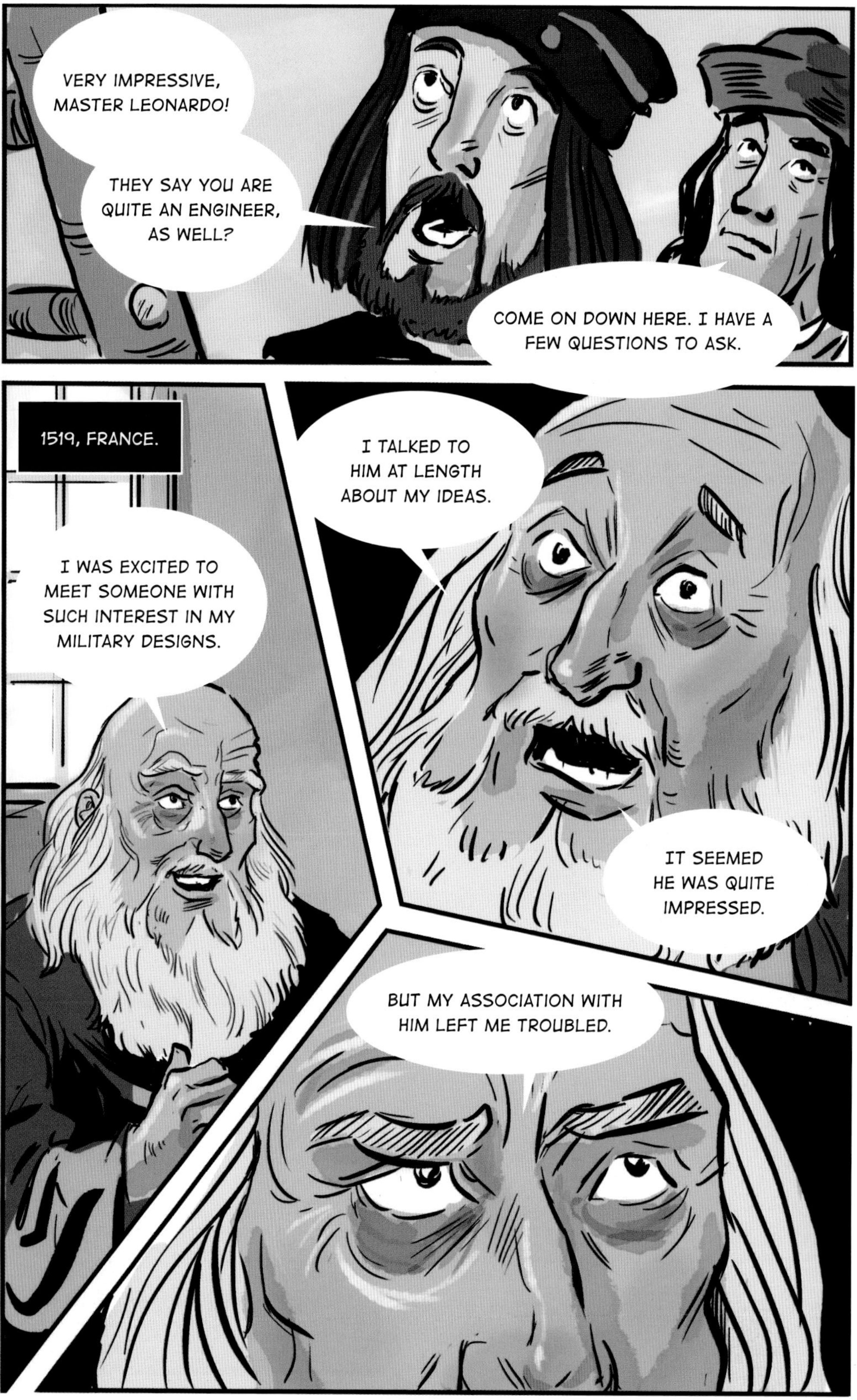
VERY IMPRESSIVE, MASTER LEONARDO!
THEY SAY YOU ARE QUITE AN ENGINEER, AS WELL?
COME ON DOWN HERE. I HAVE A FEW QUESTIONS TO ASK.
1519, FRANCE.
I WAS EXCITED TO MEET SOMEONE WITH SUCH INTEREST IN MY MILITARY DESIGNS.
I TALKED TO HIM AT LENGTH ABOUT MY IDEAS.
IT SEEMED HE WAS QUITE IMPRESSED.
BUT MY ASSOCIATION WITH HIM LEFT ME TROUBLED.

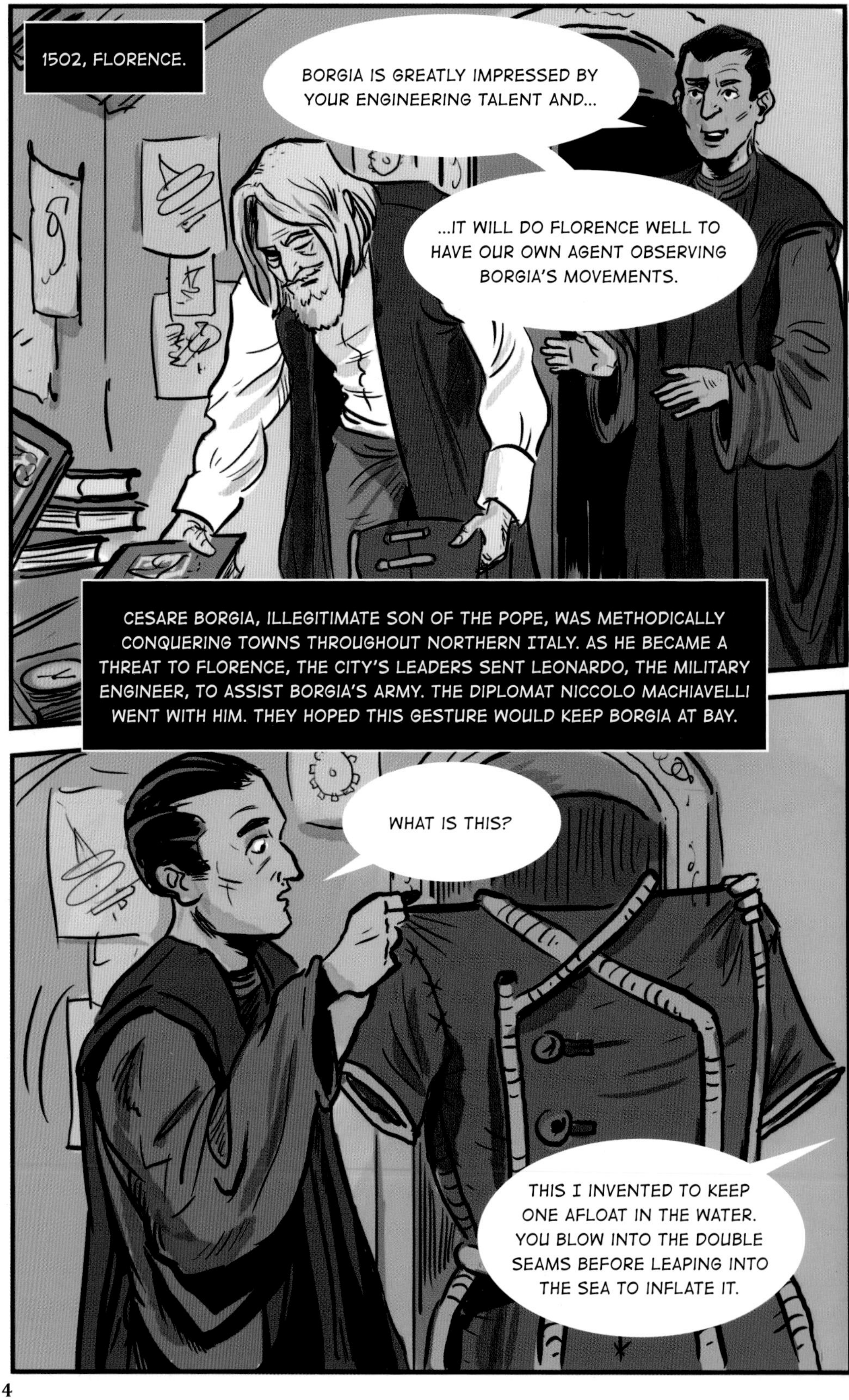
1502, FLORENCE.
BORGIA IS GREATLY IMPRESSED BY YOUR ENGINEERING TALENT AND...
...IT WILL DO FLORENCE WELL TO HAVE OUR OWN AGENT OBSERVING BORGIA'S MOVEMENTS.
CESARE BORGIA, ILLEGITIMATE SON OF THE POPE, WAS METHODICALLY CONQUERING TOWNS THROUGHOUT NORTHERN ITALY. AS HE BECAME A THREAT TO FLORENCE, THE CITY'S LEADERS SENT LEONARDO, THE MILITARY ENGINEER, TO ASSIST BORGIA'S ARMY. THE DIPLOMAT NICCOLO MACHIAVELLI WENT WITH HIM. THEY HOPED THIS GESTURE WOULD KEEP BORGIA AT BAY.
WHAT IS THIS?
THIS I INVENTED TO KEEP ONE AFLOAT IN THE WATER. YOU BLOW INTO THE DOUBLE SEAMS BEFORE LEAPING INTO THE SEA TO INFLATE IT.

AT FIFTY YEARS OF AGE, IT WILL BE GOOD, FINALLY, TO DO WORK AS A MILITARY ENGINEER.

PIOMBINO, ITALY.

LEONARDO'S FIRST ASSIGNMENT WAS TO INSPECT THE FORTS UNDER BORGIA'S CONTROL.

HE ALSO TRAVELED ACROSS ITALY GATHERING DATA FOR MAPS. HE LOOKED FOR WAYS TO DRAIN MARSHES AND SKETCHED BRIDGES AND LANDSCAPES.

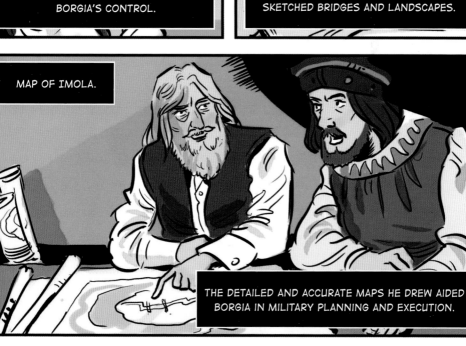

MAP OF IMOLA.

THE DETAILED AND ACCURATE MAPS HE DREW AIDED BORGIA IN MILITARY PLANNING AND EXECUTION.

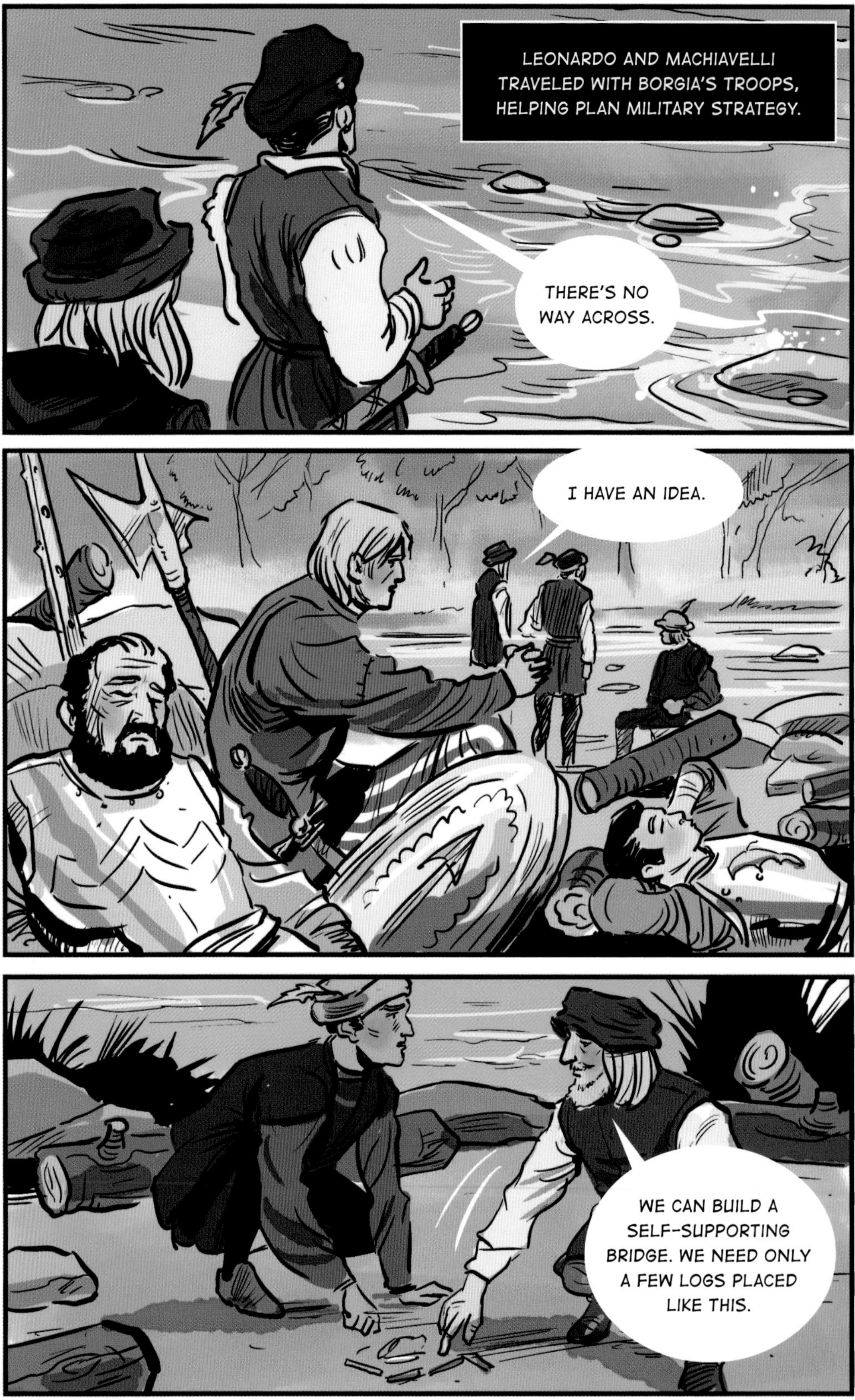
LEONARDO AND MACHIAVELLI TRAVELED WITH BORGIA'S TROOPS, HELPING PLAN MILITARY STRATEGY.
THERE'S NO WAY ACROSS.
I HAVE AN IDEA.
WE CAN BUILD A SELF-SUPPORTING BRIDGE. WE NEED ONLY A FEW LOGS PLACED LIKE THIS.

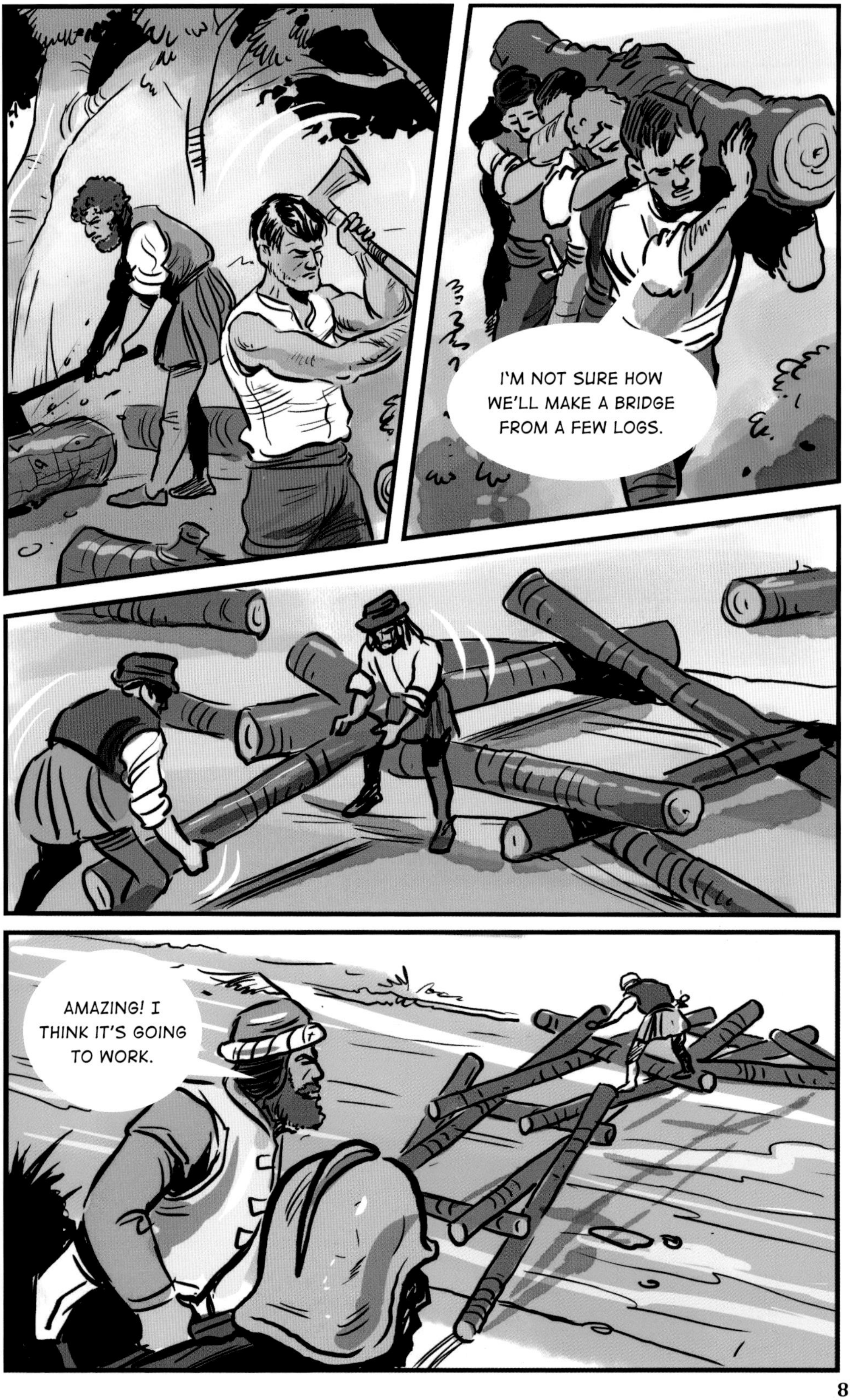
I'M NOT SURE HOW WE'LL MAKE A BRIDGE FROM A FEW LOGS.
AMAZING! I THINK IT'S GOING TO WORK.

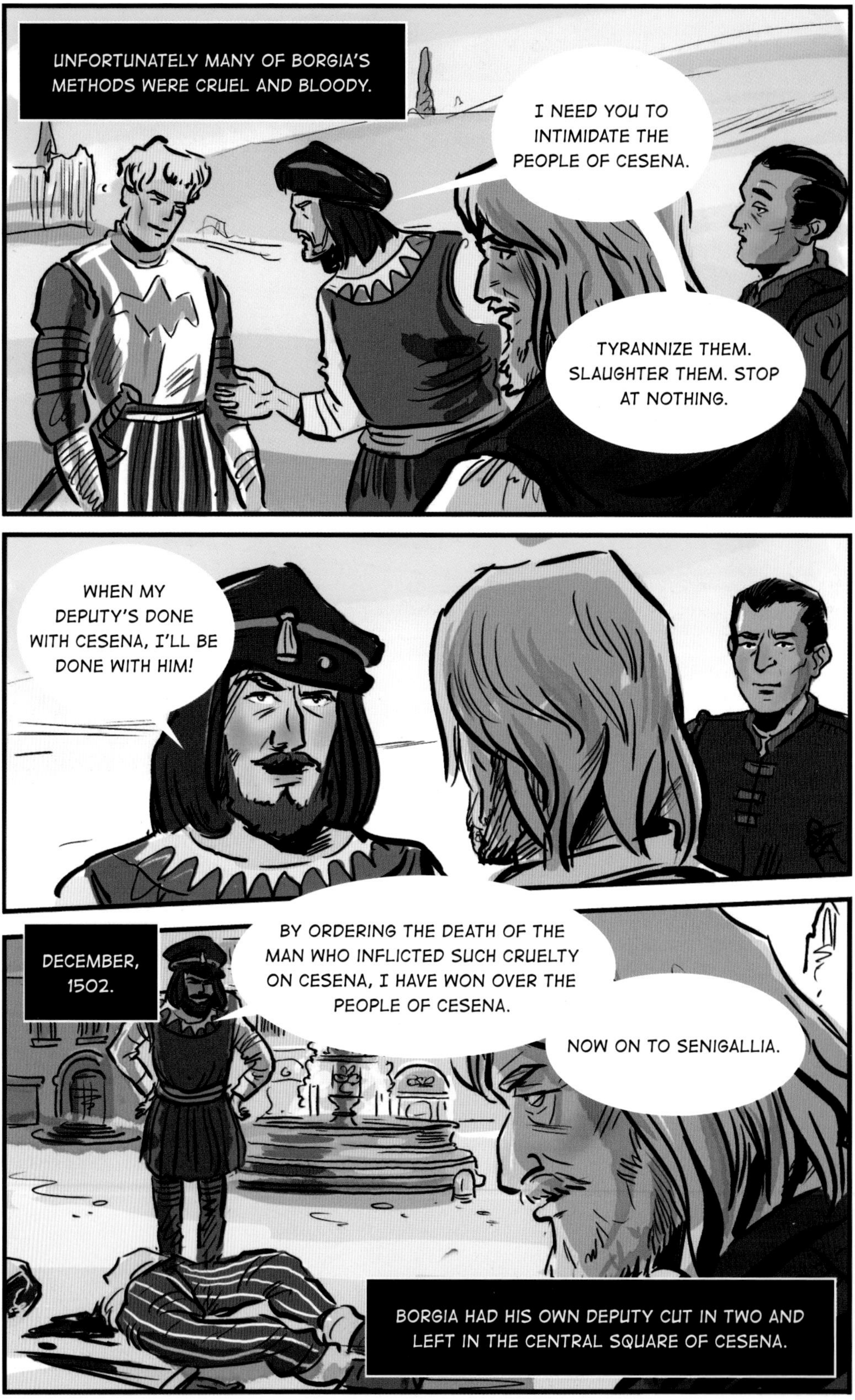
UNFORTUNATELY MANY OF BORGIA'S METHODS WERE CRUEL AND BLOODY.
I NEED YOU TO INTIMIDATE THE PEOPLE OF CESENA.
TYRANNIZE THEM. SLAUGHTER THEM. STOP AT NOTHING.
WHEN MY DEPUTY'S DONE WITH CESENA, I'LL BE DONE WITH HIM!
DECEMBER, 1502.
BY ORDERING THE DEATH OF THE MAN WHO INFLICTED SUCH CRUELTY ON CESENA, I HAVE WON OVER THE PEOPLE OF CESENA.
NOW ON TO SENIGALLIA.
BORGIA HAD HIS OWN DEPUTY CUT IN TWO AND LEFT IN THE CENTRAL SQUARE OF CESENA.

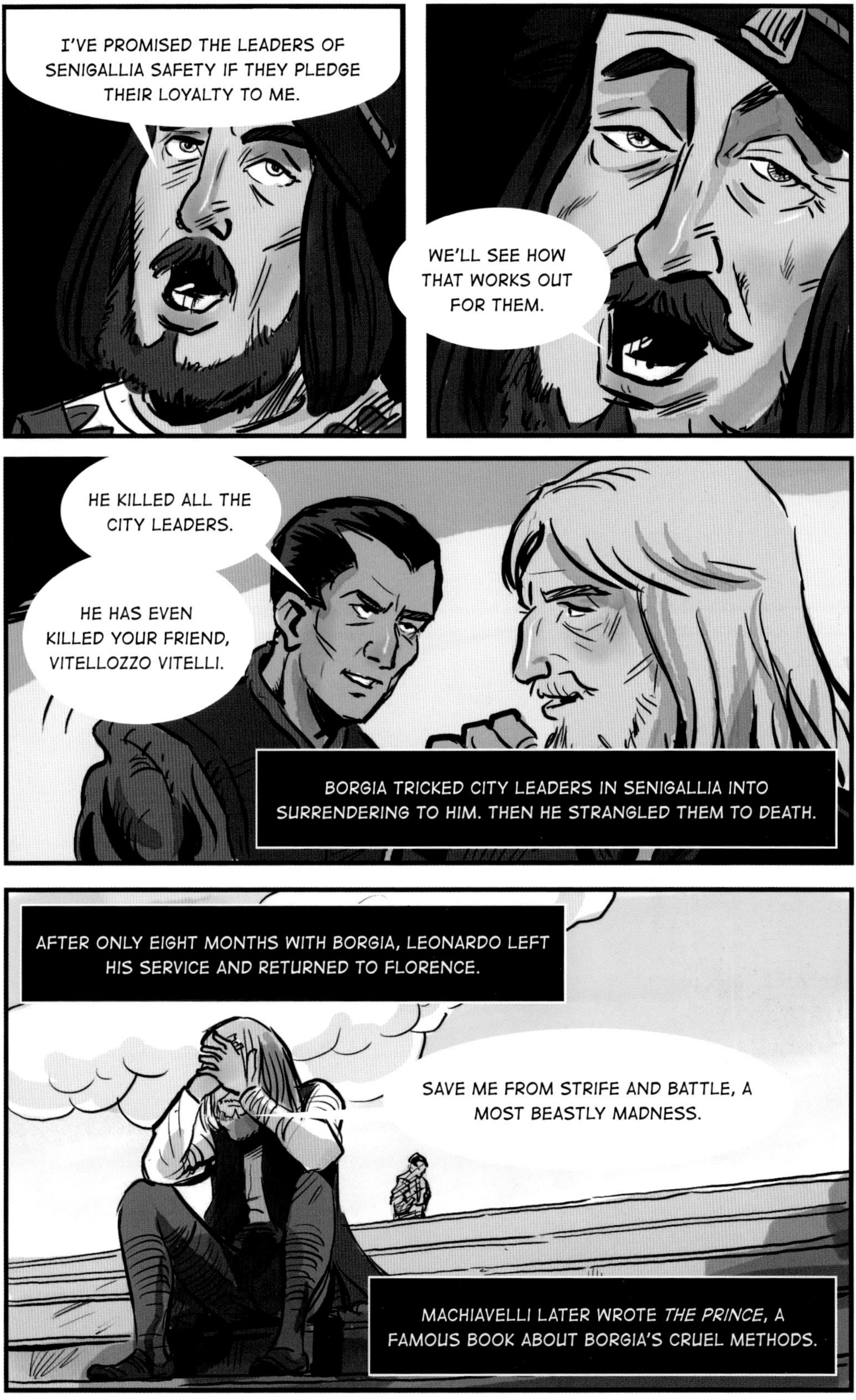
I'VE PROMISED THE LEADERS OF SENIGALLIA SAFETY IF THEY PLEDGE THEIR LOYALTY TO ME.
WE'LL SEE HOW THAT WORKS OUT FOR THEM.
HE KILLED ALL THE CITY LEADERS.
HE HAS EVEN KILLED YOUR FRIEND, VITELLOZZO VITELLI.
BORGIA TRICKED CITY LEADERS IN SENIGALLIA INTO SURRENDERING TO HIM. THEN HE STRANGLED THEM TO DEATH.
AFTER ONLY EIGHT MONTHS WITH BORGIA, LEONARDO LEFT HIS SERVICE AND RETURNED TO FLORENCE.
SAVE ME FROM STRIFE AND BATTLE, A MOST BEASTLY MADNESS.
MACHIAVELLI LATER WROTE *THE PRINCE*, A FAMOUS BOOK ABOUT BORGIA'S CRUEL METHODS.

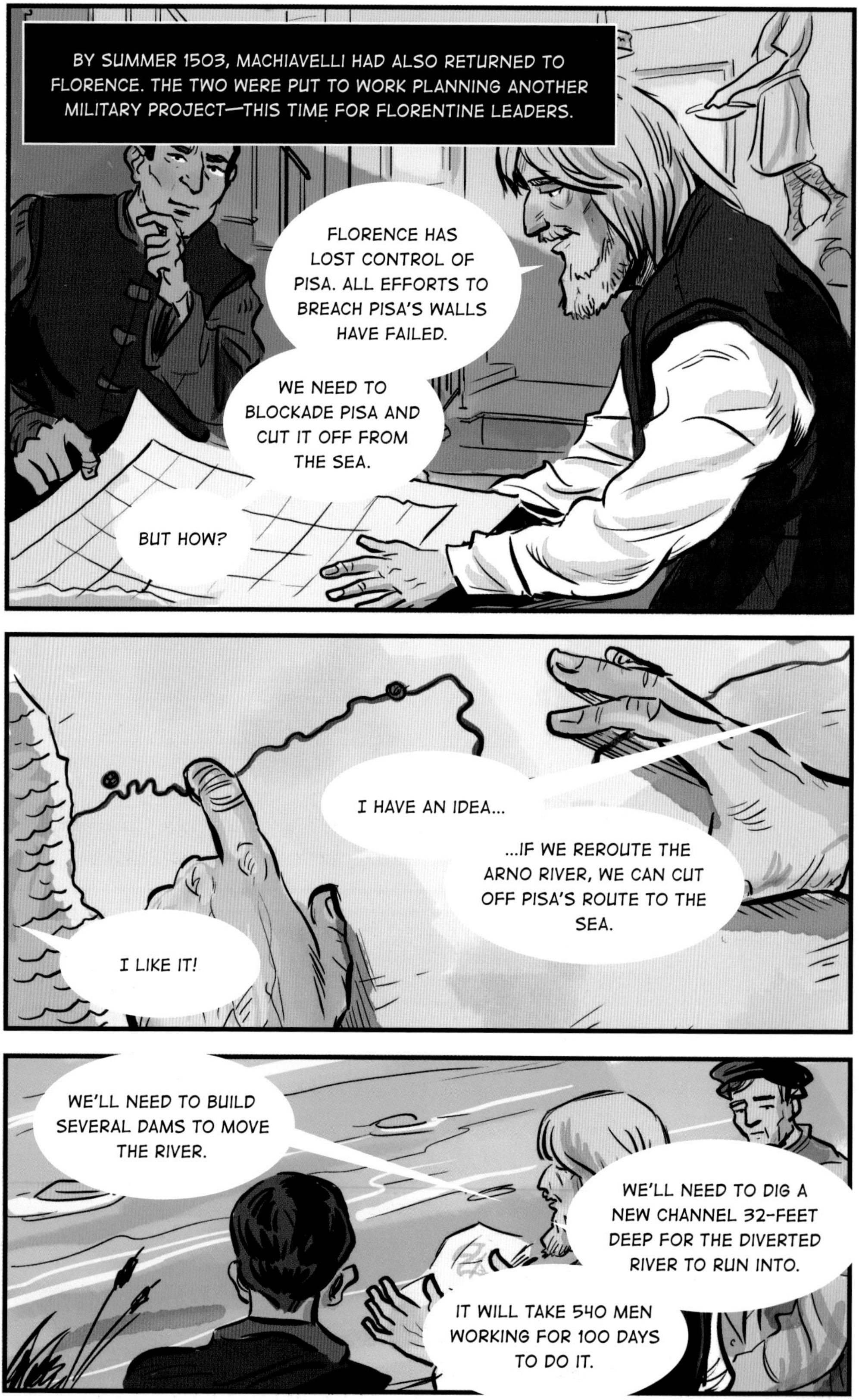
BY SUMMER 1503, MACHIAVELLI HAD ALSO RETURNED TO FLORENCE. THE TWO WERE PUT TO WORK PLANNING ANOTHER MILITARY PROJECT—THIS TIME FOR FLORENTINE LEADERS.
FLORENCE HAS LOST CONTROL OF PISA. ALL EFFORTS TO BREACH PISA'S WALLS HAVE FAILED.
WE NEED TO BLOCKADE PISA AND CUT IT OFF FROM THE SEA.
BUT HOW?
I HAVE AN IDEA...
...IF WE REROUTE THE ARNO RIVER, WE CAN CUT OFF PISA'S ROUTE TO THE SEA.
I LIKE IT!
WE'LL NEED TO BUILD SEVERAL DAMS TO MOVE THE RIVER.
WE'LL NEED TO DIG A NEW CHANNEL 32-FEET DEEP FOR THE DIVERTED RIVER TO RUN INTO.
IT WILL TAKE 540 MEN WORKING FOR 100 DAYS TO DO IT.

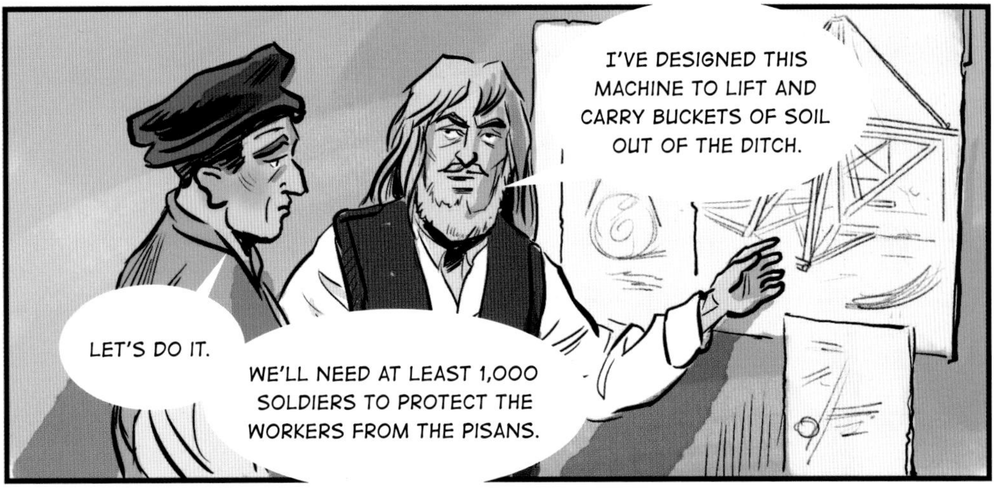
I'VE DESIGNED THIS MACHINE TO LIFT AND CARRY BUCKETS OF SOIL OUT OF THE DITCH.
LET'S DO IT.
WE'LL NEED AT LEAST 1,000 SOLDIERS TO PROTECT THE WORKERS FROM THE PISANS.

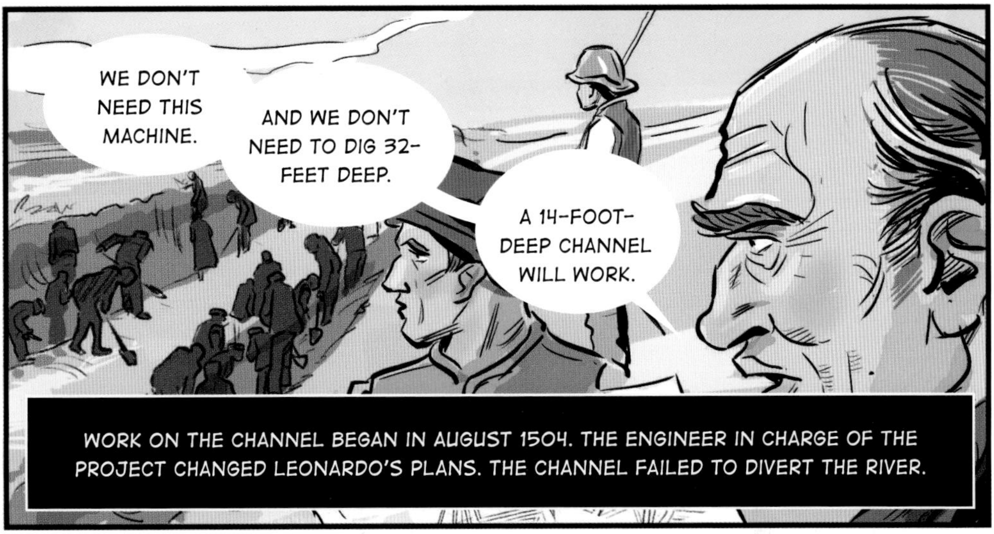
WE DON'T NEED THIS MACHINE.
AND WE DON'T NEED TO DIG 32-FEET DEEP.
A 14-FOOT-DEEP CHANNEL WILL WORK.
WORK ON THE CHANNEL BEGAN IN AUGUST 1504. THE ENGINEER IN CHARGE OF THE PROJECT CHANGED LEONARDO'S PLANS. THE CHANNEL FAILED TO DIVERT THE RIVER.

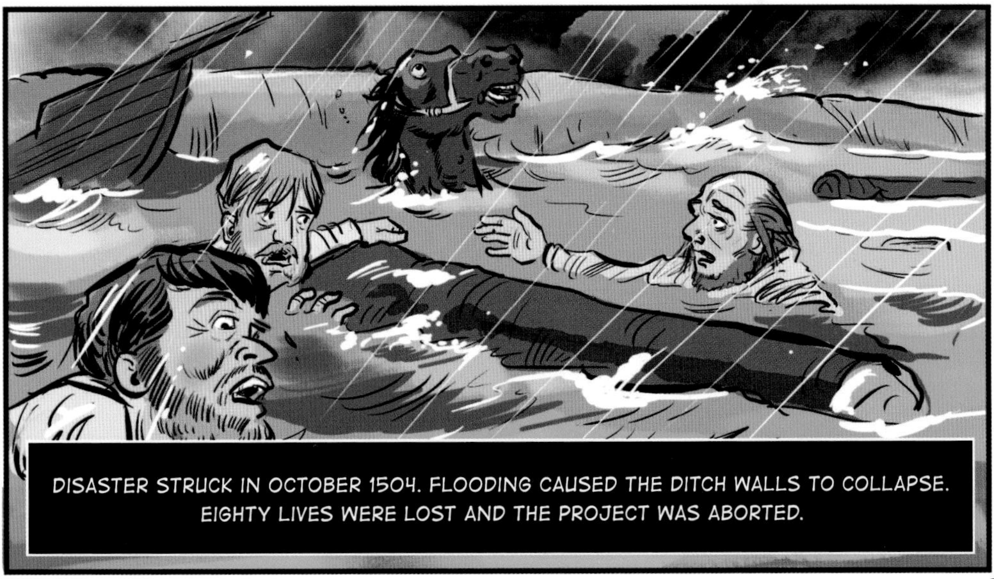
DISASTER STRUCK IN OCTOBER 1504. FLOODING CAUSED THE DITCH WALLS TO COLLAPSE. EIGHTY LIVES WERE LOST AND THE PROJECT WAS ABORTED.

CHAPTER 9

THE RIVALRY WITH MICHELANGELO

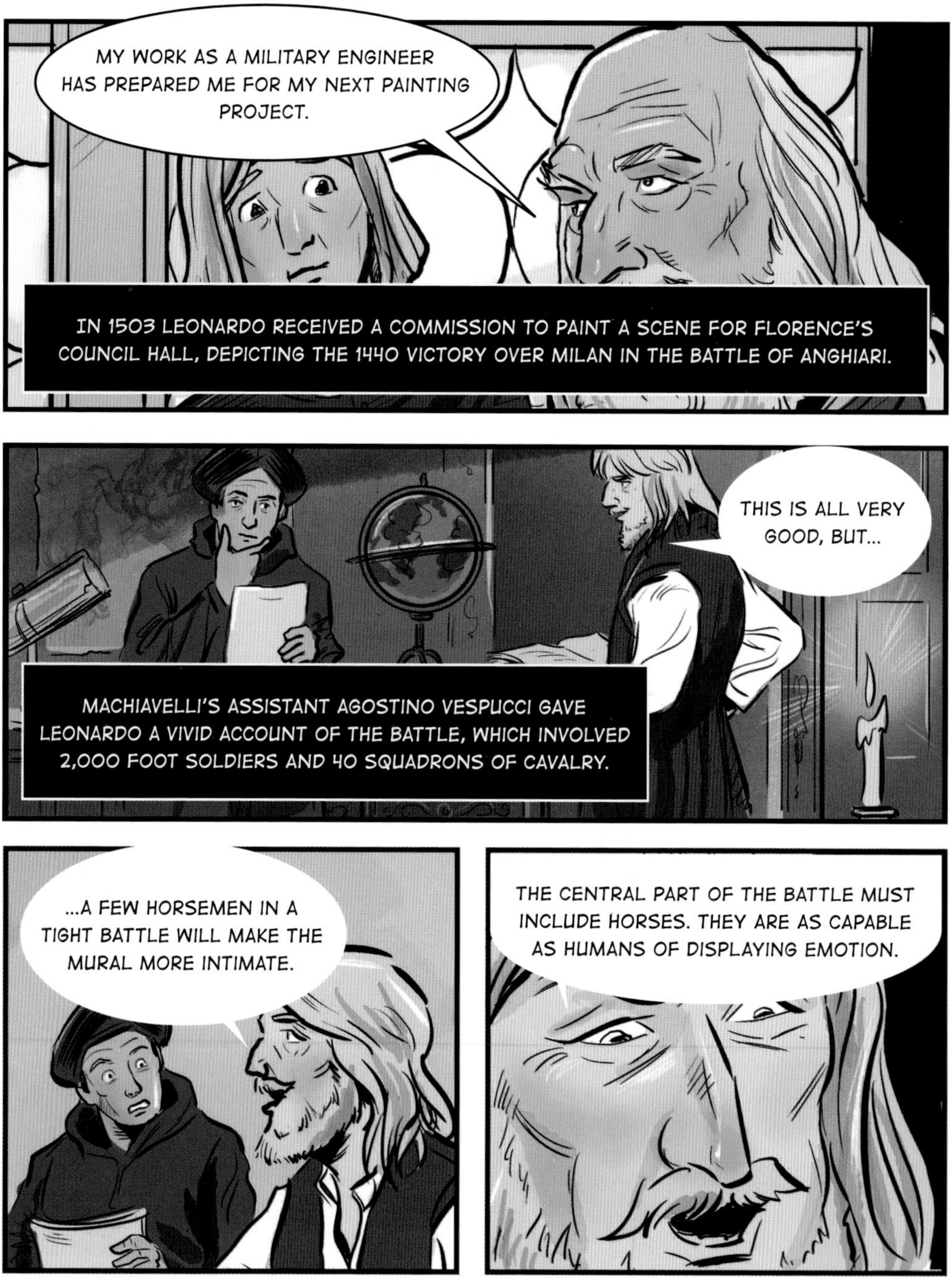
MY WORK AS A MILITARY ENGINEER HAS PREPARED ME FOR MY NEXT PAINTING PROJECT.
IN 1503 LEONARDO RECEIVED A COMMISSION TO PAINT A SCENE FOR FLORENCE'S COUNCIL HALL, DEPICTING THE 1440 VICTORY OVER MILAN IN THE BATTLE OF ANGHIARI.
THIS IS ALL VERY GOOD, BUT...
MACHIAVELLI'S ASSISTANT AGOSTINO VESPUCCI GAVE LEONARDO A VIVID ACCOUNT OF THE BATTLE, WHICH INVOLVED 2,000 FOOT SOLDIERS AND 40 SQUADRONS OF CAVALRY.
...A FEW HORSEMEN IN A TIGHT BATTLE WILL MAKE THE MURAL MORE INTIMATE.
THE CENTRAL PART OF THE BATTLE MUST INCLUDE HORSES. THEY ARE AS CAPABLE AS HUMANS OF DISPLAYING EMOTION.

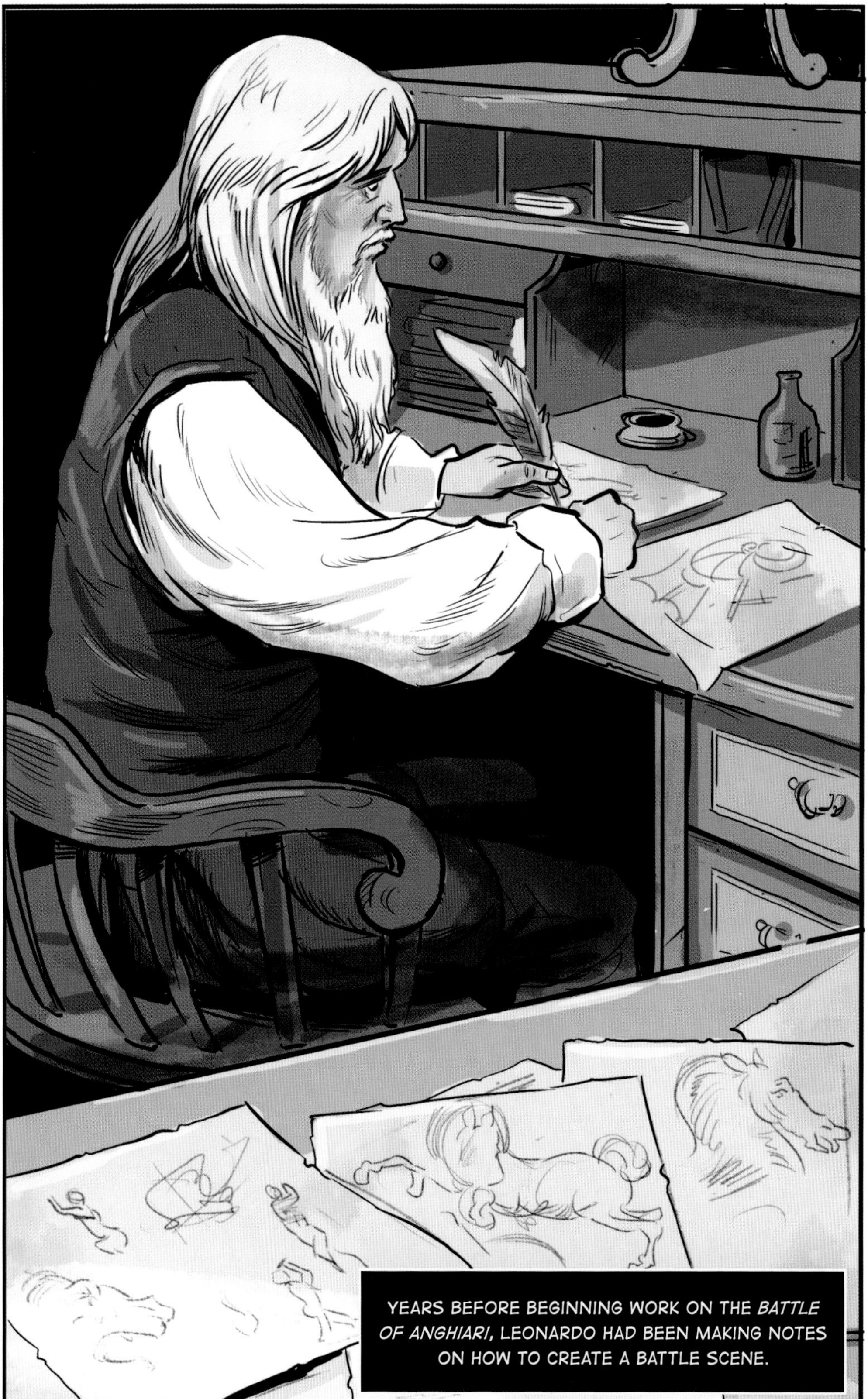
YEARS BEFORE BEGINNING WORK ON THE *BATTLE OF ANGHIARI*, LEONARDO HAD BEEN MAKING NOTES ON HOW TO CREATE A BATTLE SCENE.

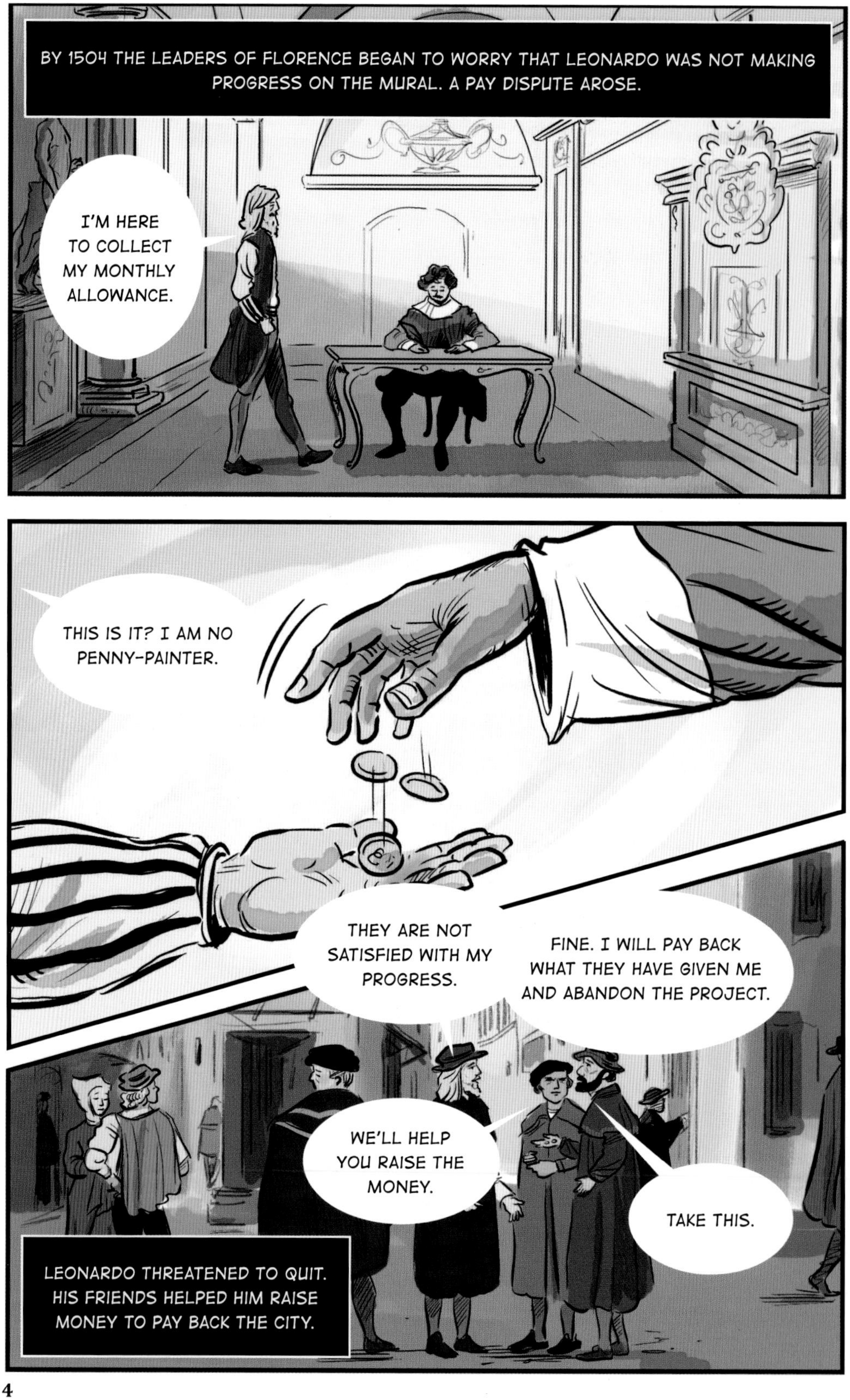
BY 1504 THE LEADERS OF FLORENCE BEGAN TO WORRY THAT LEONARDO WAS NOT MAKING PROGRESS ON THE MURAL. A PAY DISPUTE AROSE.
I'M HERE TO COLLECT MY MONTHLY ALLOWANCE.
THIS IS IT? I AM NO PENNY-PAINTER.
THEY ARE NOT SATISFIED WITH MY PROGRESS.
FINE. I WILL PAY BACK WHAT THEY HAVE GIVEN ME AND ABANDON THE PROJECT.
WE'LL HELP YOU RAISE THE MONEY.
TAKE THIS.
LEONARDO THREATENED TO QUIT. HIS FRIENDS HELPED HIM RAISE MONEY TO PAY BACK THE CITY.

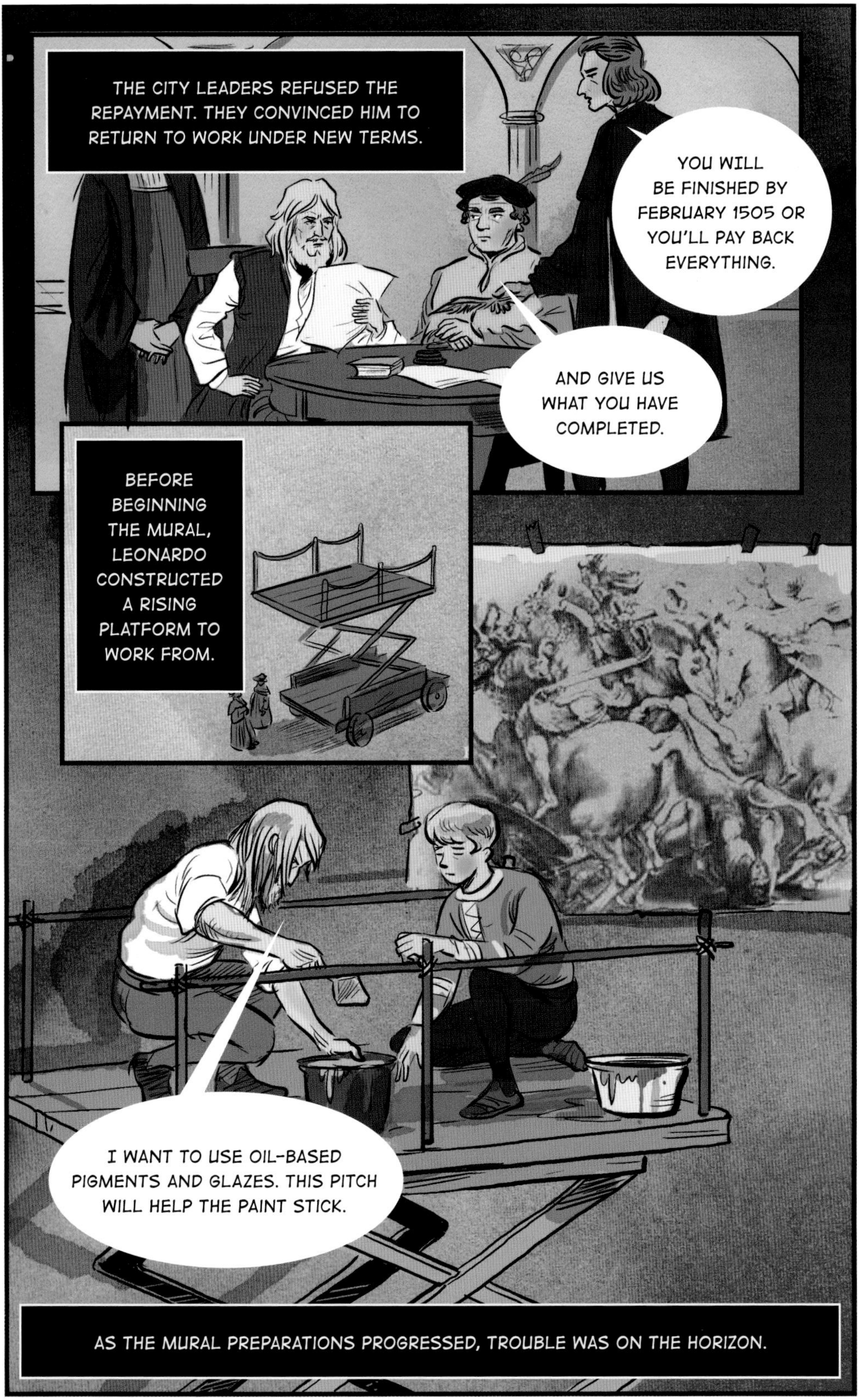
THE CITY LEADERS REFUSED THE REPAYMENT. THEY CONVINCED HIM TO RETURN TO WORK UNDER NEW TERMS.
YOU WILL BE FINISHED BY FEBRUARY 1505 OR YOU'LL PAY BACK EVERYTHING.
AND GIVE US WHAT YOU HAVE COMPLETED.
BEFORE BEGINNING THE MURAL, LEONARDO CONSTRUCTED A RISING PLATFORM TO WORK FROM.
I WANT TO USE OIL-BASED PIGMENTS AND GLAZES. THIS PITCH WILL HELP THE PAINT STICK.
AS THE MURAL PREPARATIONS PROGRESSED, TROUBLE WAS ON THE HORIZON.

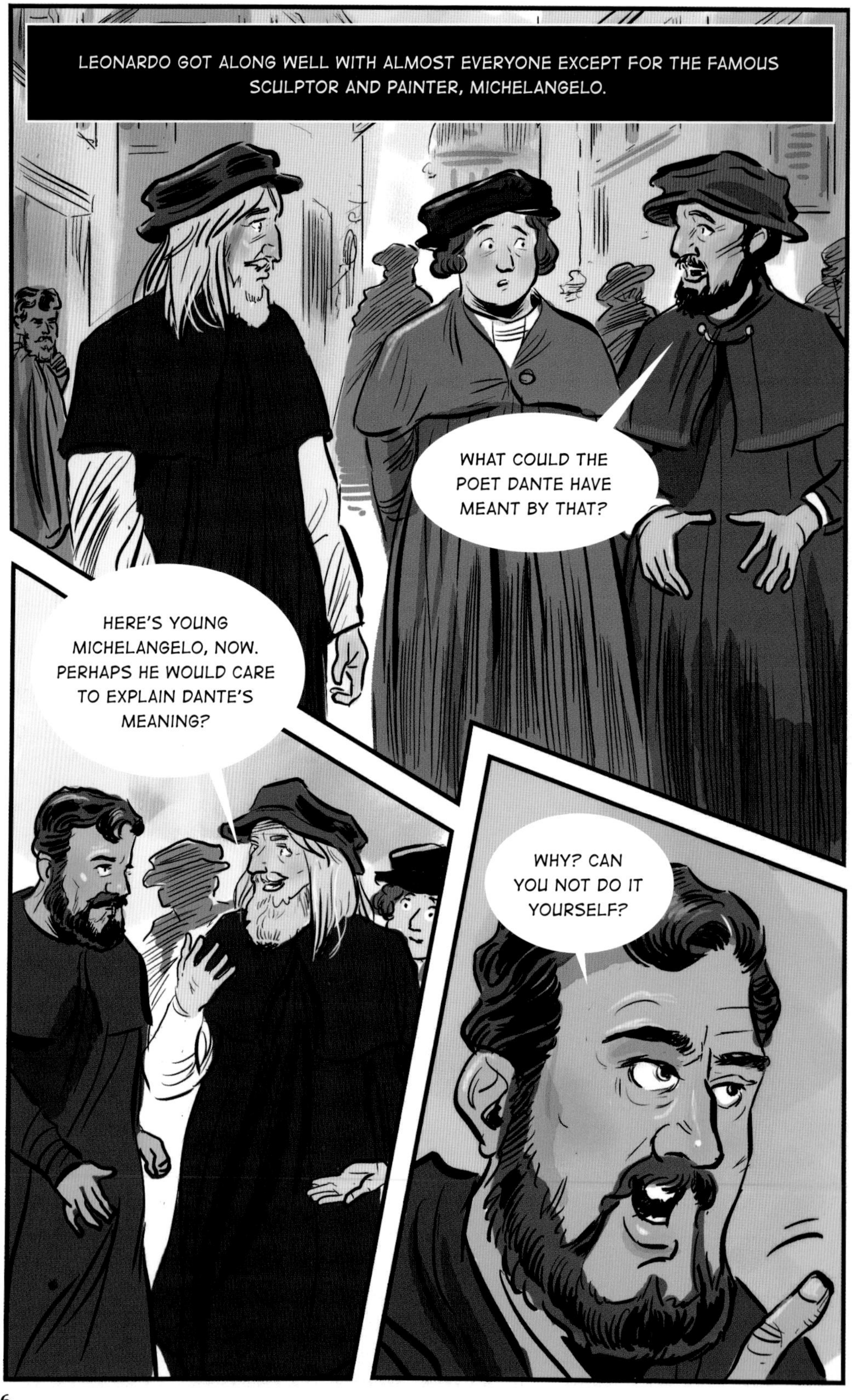
LEONARDO GOT ALONG WELL WITH ALMOST EVERYONE EXCEPT FOR THE FAMOUS SCULPTOR AND PAINTER, MICHELANGELO.
WHAT COULD THE POET DANTE HAVE MEANT BY THAT?
HERE'S YOUNG MICHELANGELO, NOW. PERHAPS HE WOULD CARE TO EXPLAIN DANTE'S MEANING?
WHY? CAN YOU NOT DO IT YOURSELF?

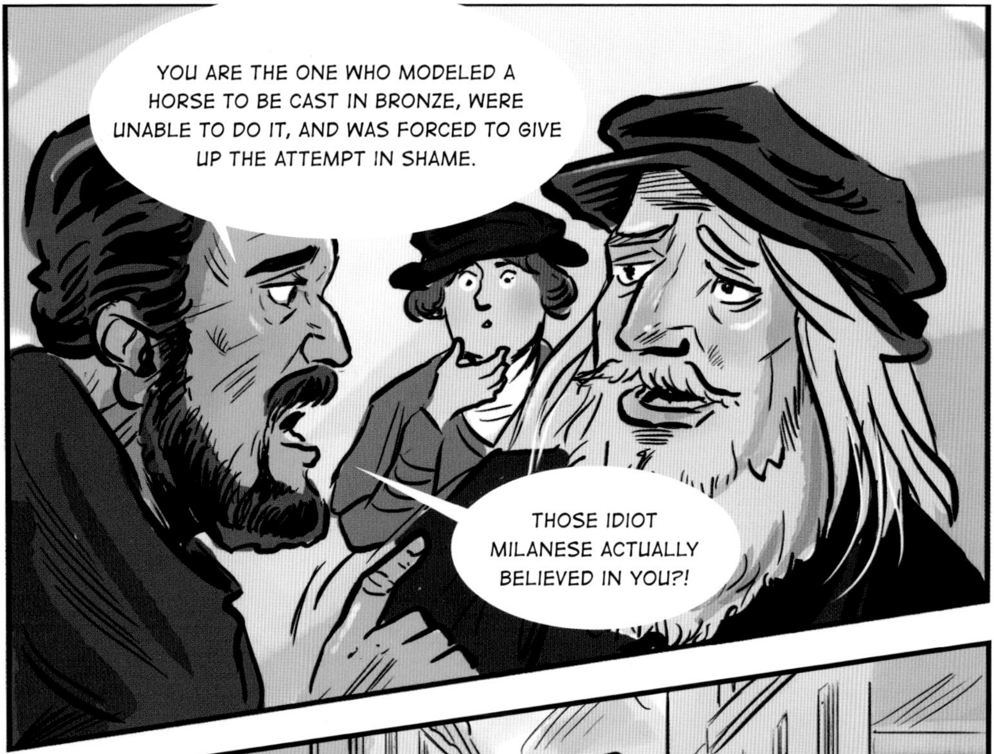
YOU ARE THE ONE WHO MODELED A HORSE TO BE CAST IN BRONZE, WERE UNABLE TO DO IT, AND WAS FORCED TO GIVE UP THE ATTEMPT IN SHAME.
THOSE IDIOT MILANESE ACTUALLY BELIEVED IN YOU?!

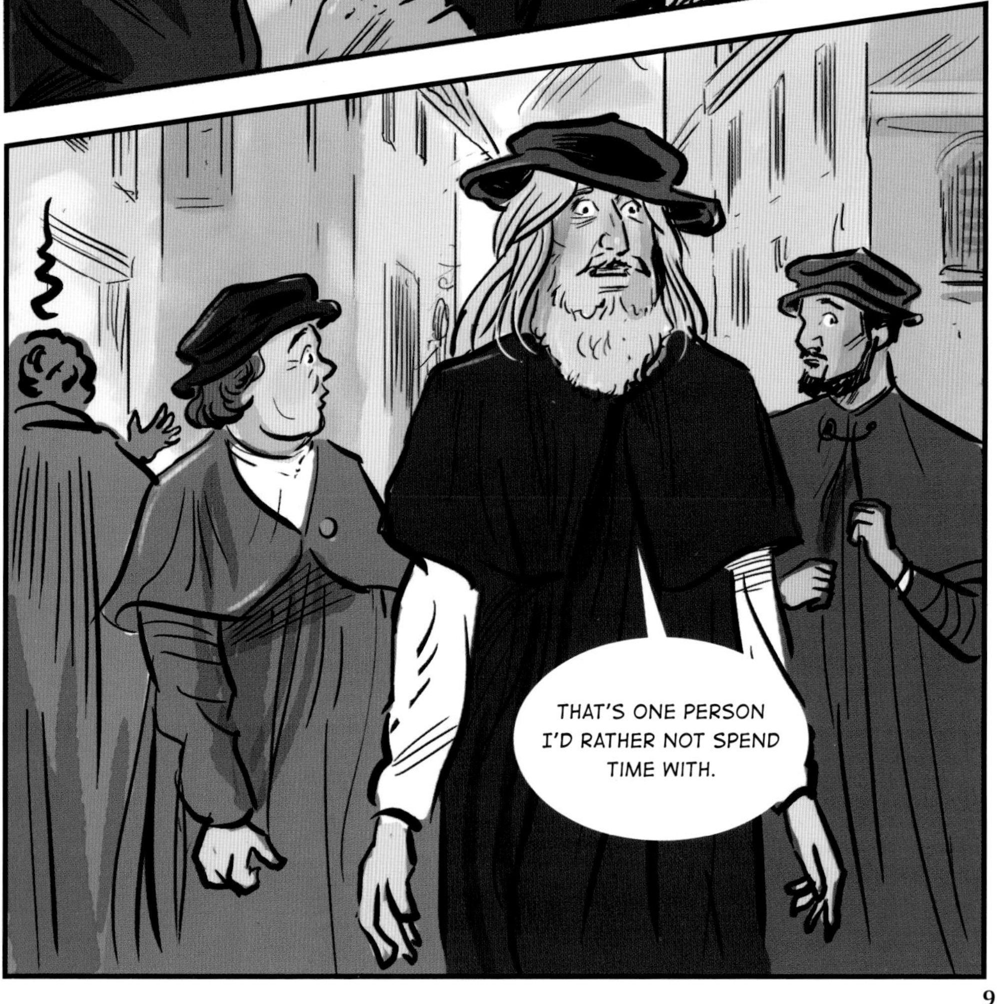
THAT'S ONE PERSON I'D RATHER NOT SPEND TIME WITH.

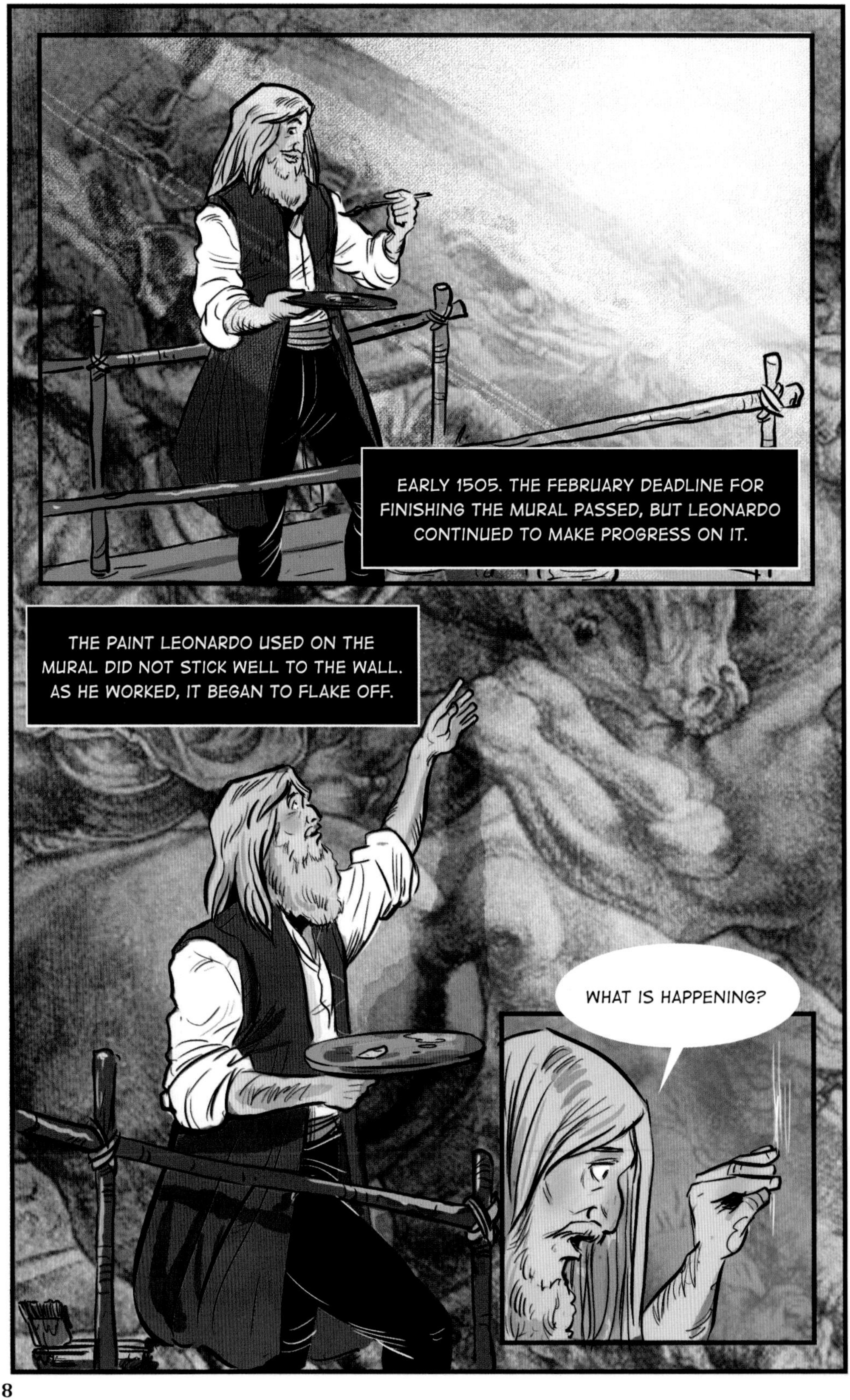
EARLY 1505. THE FEBRUARY DEADLINE FOR FINISHING THE MURAL PASSED, BUT LEONARDO CONTINUED TO MAKE PROGRESS ON IT.
THE PAINT LEONARDO USED ON THE MURAL DID NOT STICK WELL TO THE WALL. AS HE WORKED, IT BEGAN TO FLAKE OFF.
WHAT IS HAPPENING?

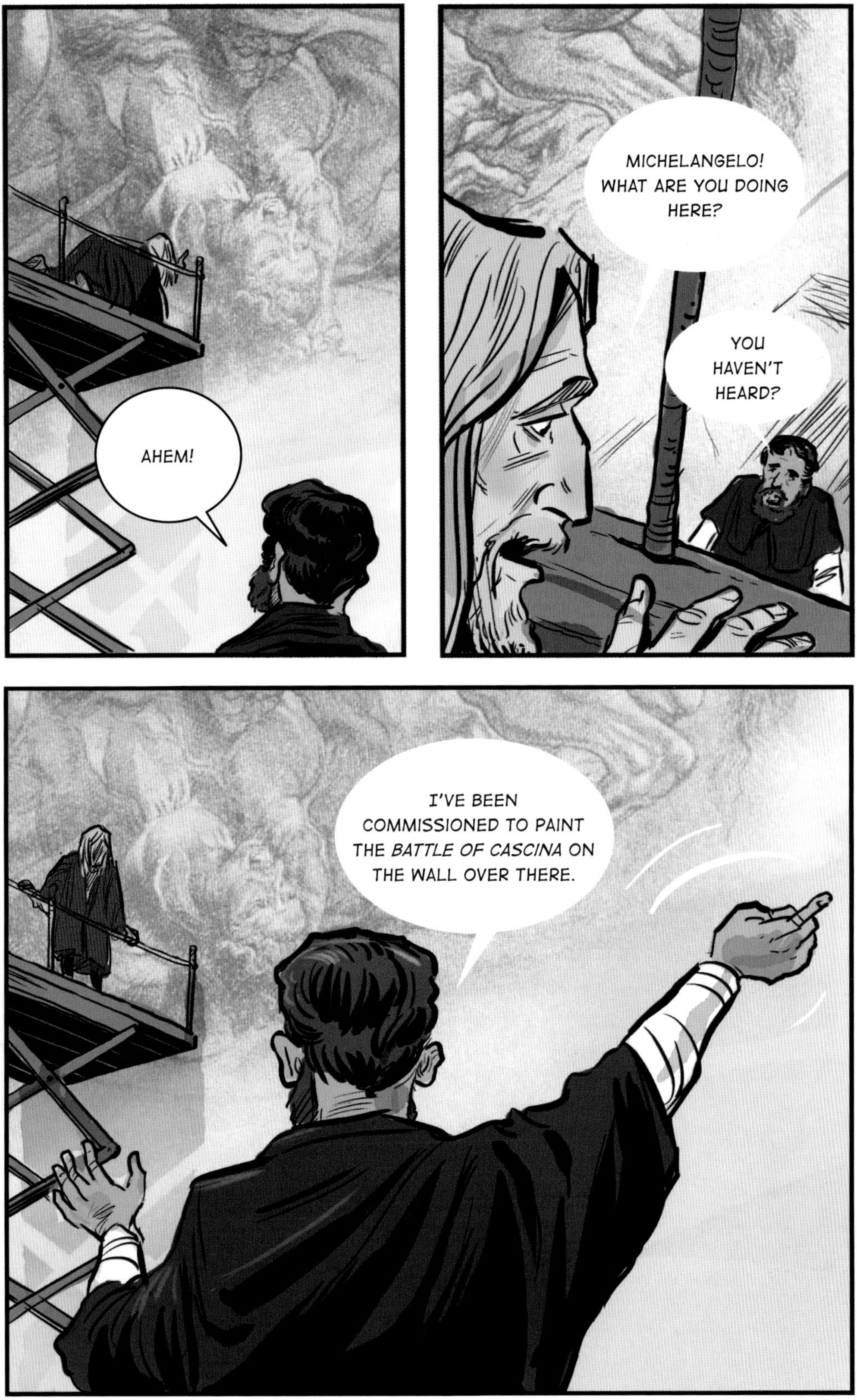
AHEM!
MICHELANGELO! WHAT ARE YOU DOING HERE?
YOU HAVEN'T HEARD?
I'VE BEEN COMMISSIONED TO PAINT THE *BATTLE OF CASCINA* ON THE WALL OVER THERE.

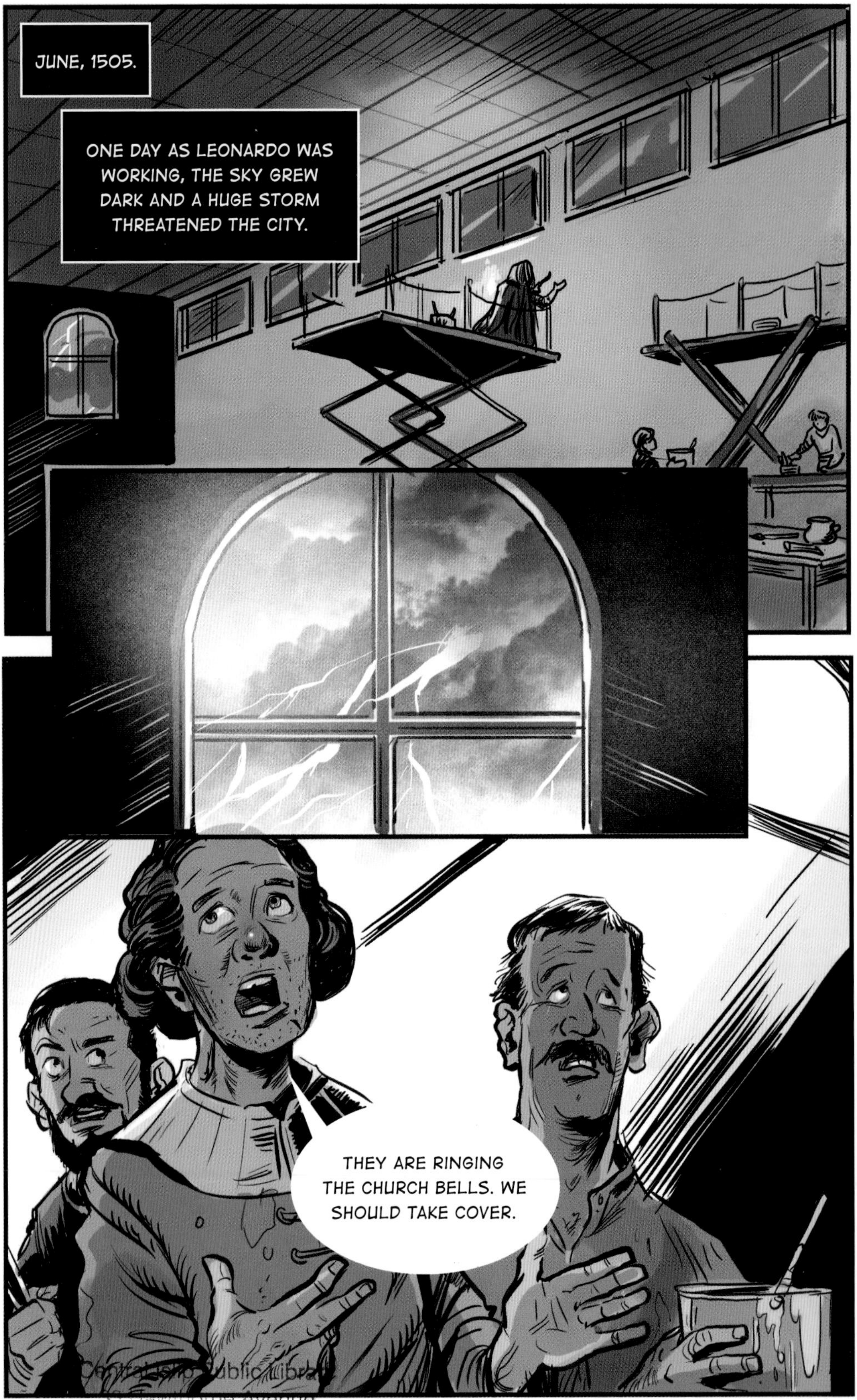
JUNE, 1505.
ONE DAY AS LEONARDO WAS WORKING, THE SKY GREW DARK AND A HUGE STORM THREATENED THE CITY.
THEY ARE RINGING THE CHURCH BELLS. WE SHOULD TAKE COVER.

THE TORRENTIAL RAIN FURTHER DAMAGED THE FLAKING PAINT ON THE MURAL. IT WAS THE FINAL STRAW AND LEONARDO LOST HOPE IN THE PROJECT.

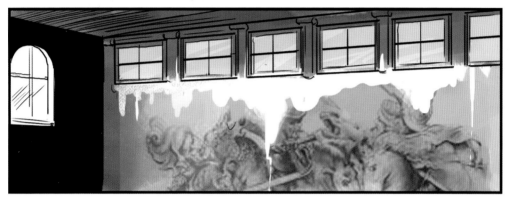

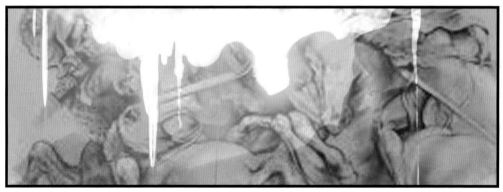

PERHAPS NEITHER OF US WILL SUCCEED IN THIS MISSION.

I'VE BEEN SUMMONED TO ROME BY THE POPE. I'LL BE PAINTING FRESCOES IN THE SISTINE CHAPEL.

MICHELANGELO AND LEONARDO NEVER FINISHED THEIR MURALS FOR THE COUNCIL HALL.

CHAPTER 10

STUDIES IN ANATOMY

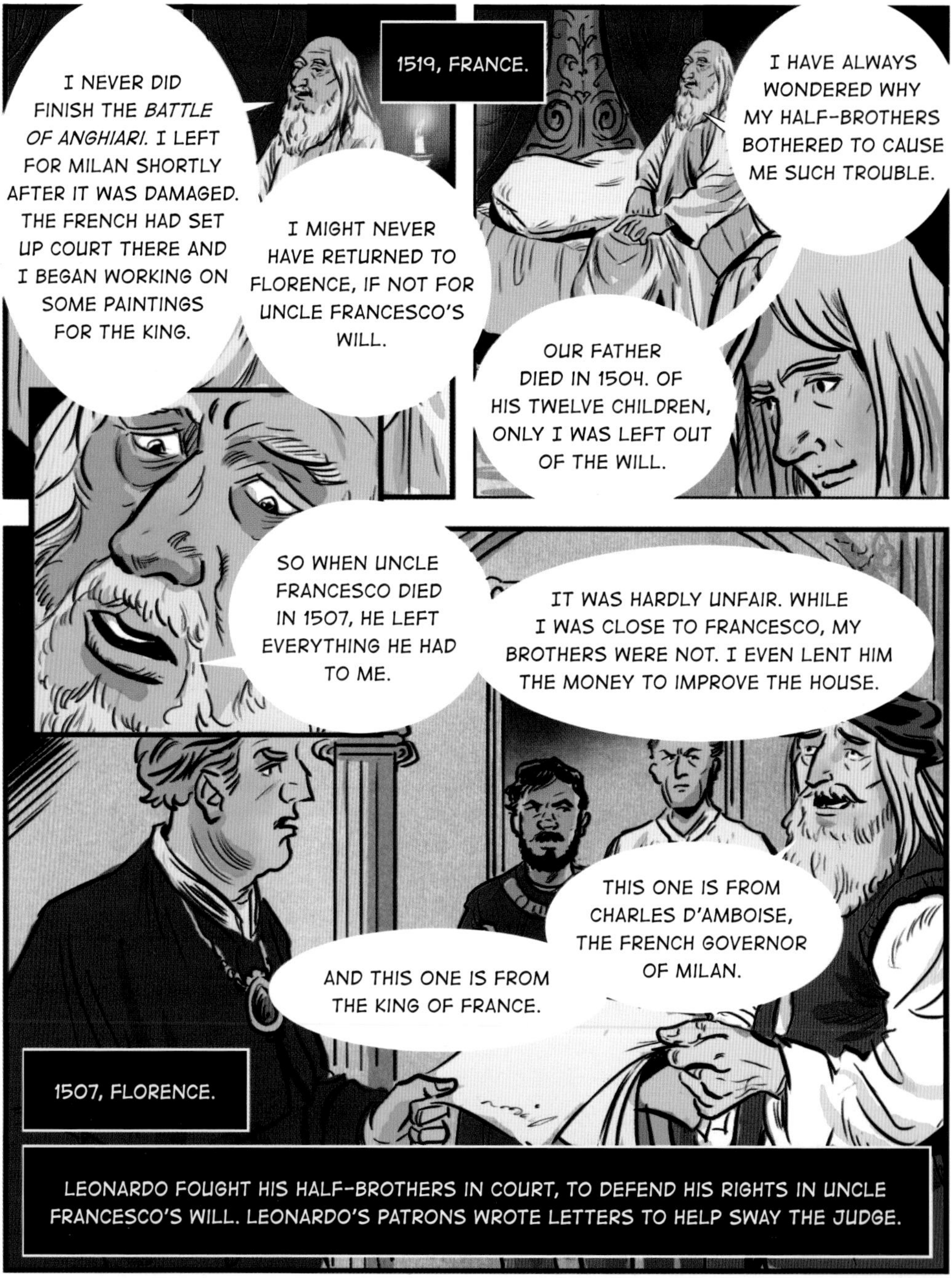
1519, FRANCE.
I NEVER DID FINISH THE *BATTLE OF ANGHIARI*. I LEFT FOR MILAN SHORTLY AFTER IT WAS DAMAGED. THE FRENCH HAD SET UP COURT THERE AND I BEGAN WORKING ON SOME PAINTINGS FOR THE KING.
I MIGHT NEVER HAVE RETURNED TO FLORENCE, IF NOT FOR UNCLE FRANCESCO'S WILL.
I HAVE ALWAYS WONDERED WHY MY HALF-BROTHERS BOTHERED TO CAUSE ME SUCH TROUBLE.
OUR FATHER DIED IN 1504. OF HIS TWELVE CHILDREN, ONLY I WAS LEFT OUT OF THE WILL.
SO WHEN UNCLE FRANCESCO DIED IN 1507, HE LEFT EVERYTHING HE HAD TO ME.
IT WAS HARDLY UNFAIR. WHILE I WAS CLOSE TO FRANCESCO, MY BROTHERS WERE NOT. I EVEN LENT HIM THE MONEY TO IMPROVE THE HOUSE.
THIS ONE IS FROM CHARLES D'AMBOISE, THE FRENCH GOVERNOR OF MILAN.
AND THIS ONE IS FROM THE KING OF FRANCE.
1507, FLORENCE.
LEONARDO FOUGHT HIS HALF-BROTHERS IN COURT, TO DEFEND HIS RIGHTS IN UNCLE FRANCESCO'S WILL. LEONARDO'S PATRONS WROTE LETTERS TO HELP SWAY THE JUDGE.

"PERMISSION TO LEAVE HAS BEEN GRANTED WITH THE GREATEST RELUCTANCE..."

"IT IS IMPORTANT FOR LEONARDO TO BE IN OUR PRESENCE. BRING THE SAID DISPUTE AND LITIGATION TO AN END AND SEE THAT TRUE JUSTICE IS DONE WITH AS LITTLE DELAY AS POSSIBLE."

"...WORKING ON A PAINTING VERY DEAR TO THE KING..."

IT SEEMS YOU HAVE FRIENDS IN IMPORTANT PLACES. I WILL THINK THIS OVER.

LEONARDO EVEN WROTE A LETTER TO THE PRESTIGIOUS CARDINAL IPPOLITO D'ESTE, BROTHER OF ISABELLA D'ESTE, ASKING FOR SUPPORT IN WINNING HIS CASE.

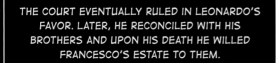

THE COURT EVENTUALLY RULED IN LEONARDO'S FAVOR. LATER, HE RECONCILED WITH HIS BROTHERS AND UPON HIS DEATH HE WILLED FRANCESCO'S ESTATE TO THEM.

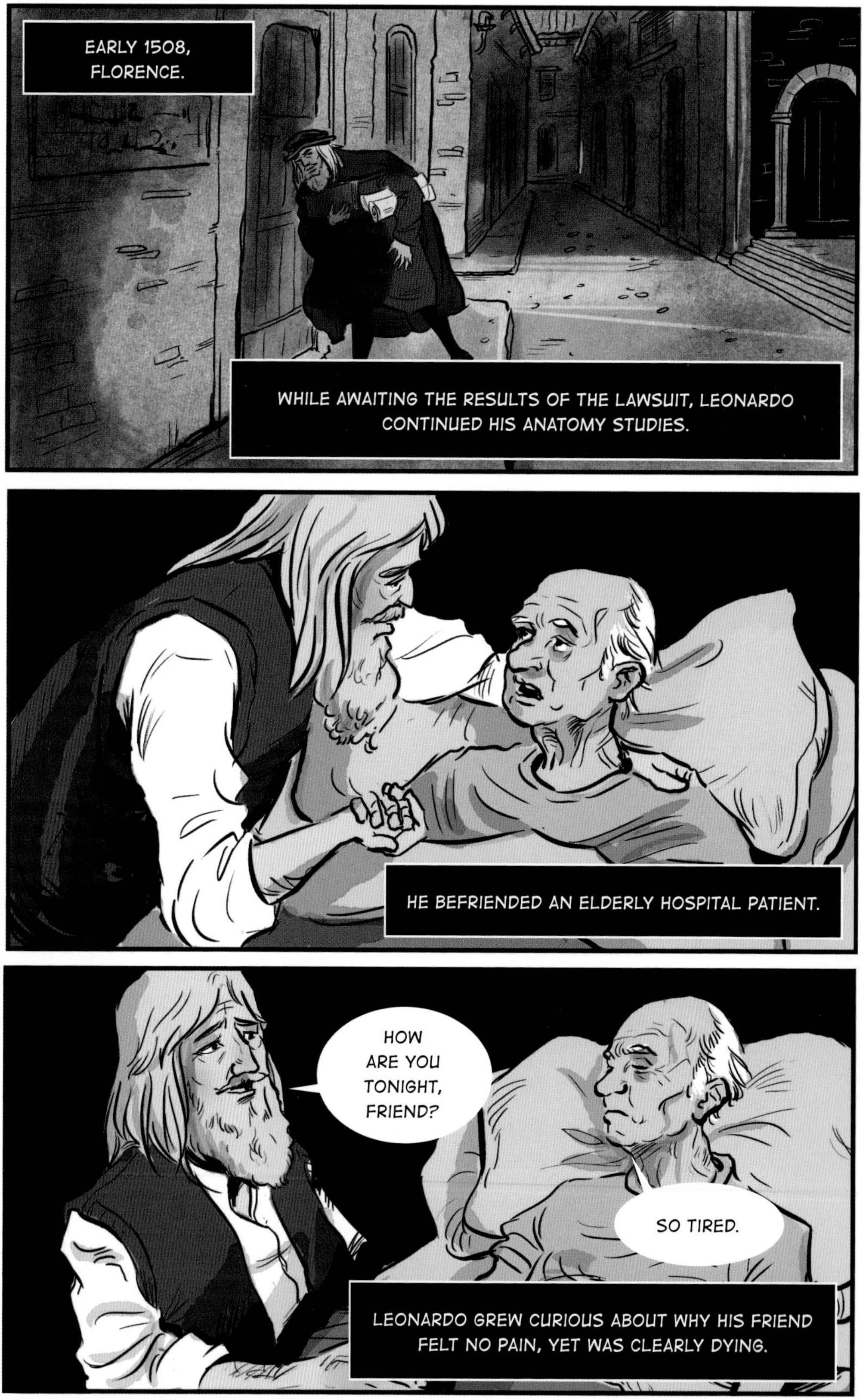
EARLY 1508, FLORENCE.
WHILE AWAITING THE RESULTS OF THE LAWSUIT, LEONARDO CONTINUED HIS ANATOMY STUDIES.
HE BEFRIENDED AN ELDERLY HOSPITAL PATIENT.
HOW ARE YOU TONIGHT, FRIEND?
SO TIRED.
LEONARDO GREW CURIOUS ABOUT WHY HIS FRIEND FELT NO PAIN, YET WAS CLEARLY DYING.

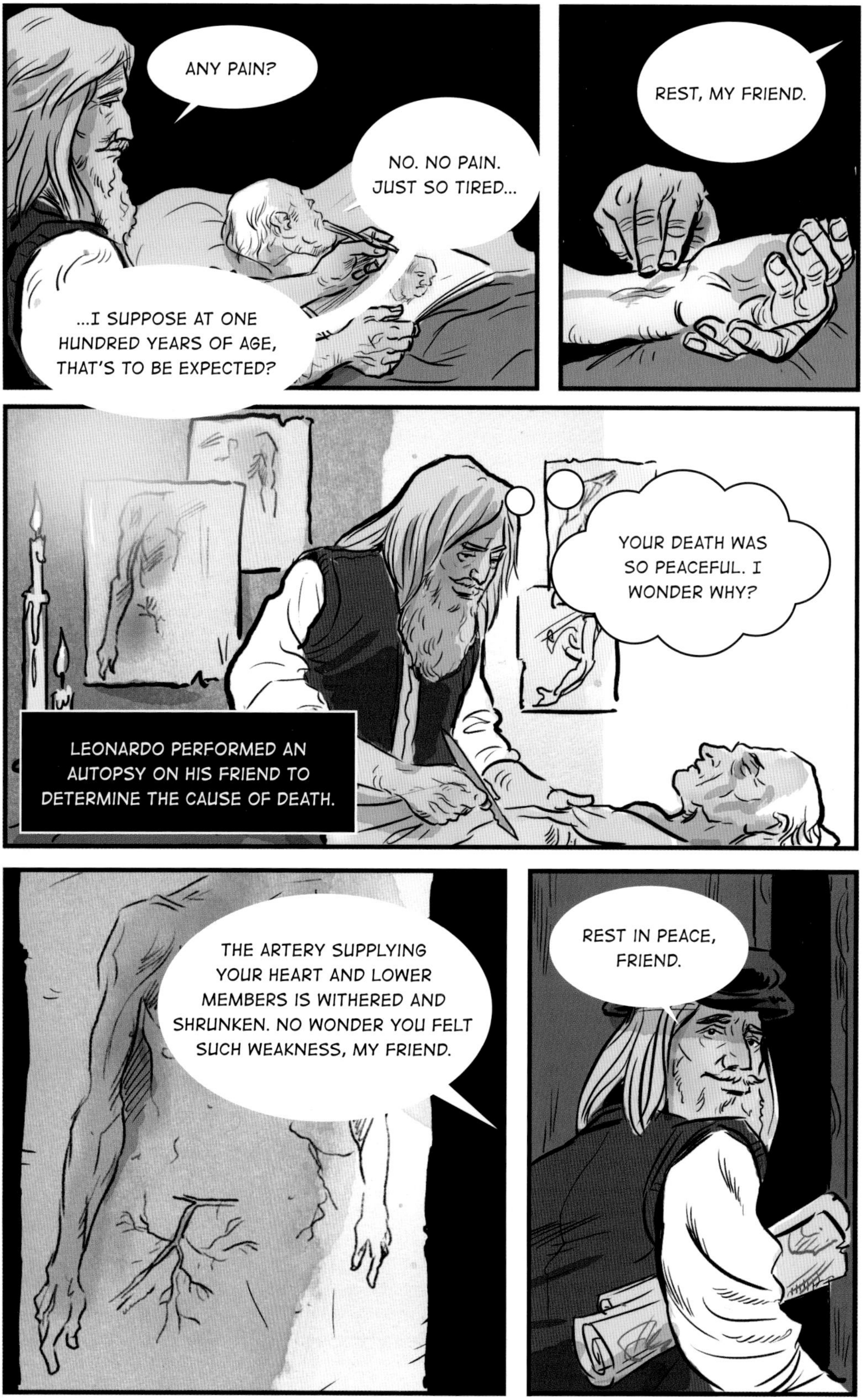
ANY PAIN?
NO. NO PAIN. JUST SO TIRED...
...I SUPPOSE AT ONE HUNDRED YEARS OF AGE, THAT'S TO BE EXPECTED?
REST, MY FRIEND.
YOUR DEATH WAS SO PEACEFUL. I WONDER WHY?
LEONARDO PERFORMED AN AUTOPSY ON HIS FRIEND TO DETERMINE THE CAUSE OF DEATH.
THE ARTERY SUPPLYING YOUR HEART AND LOWER MEMBERS IS WITHERED AND SHRUNKEN. NO WONDER YOU FELT SUCH WEAKNESS, MY FRIEND.
REST IN PEACE, FRIEND.

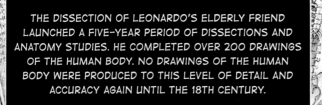

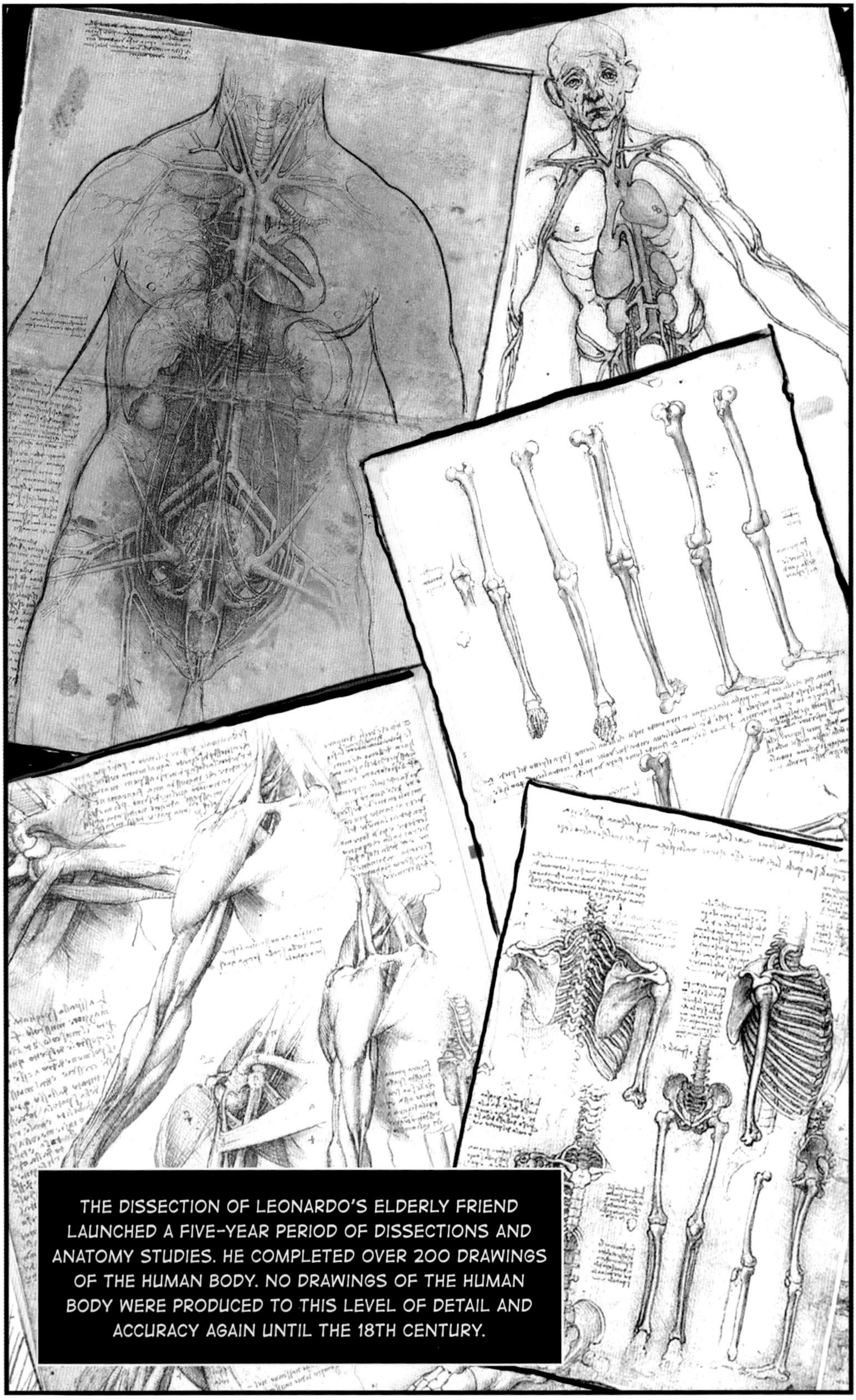

THE DISSECTION OF LEONARDO'S ELDERLY FRIEND LAUNCHED A FIVE-YEAR PERIOD OF DISSECTIONS AND ANATOMY STUDIES. HE COMPLETED OVER 200 DRAWINGS OF THE HUMAN BODY. NO DRAWINGS OF THE HUMAN BODY WERE PRODUCED TO THIS LEVEL OF DETAIL AND ACCURACY AGAIN UNTIL THE 18TH CENTURY.

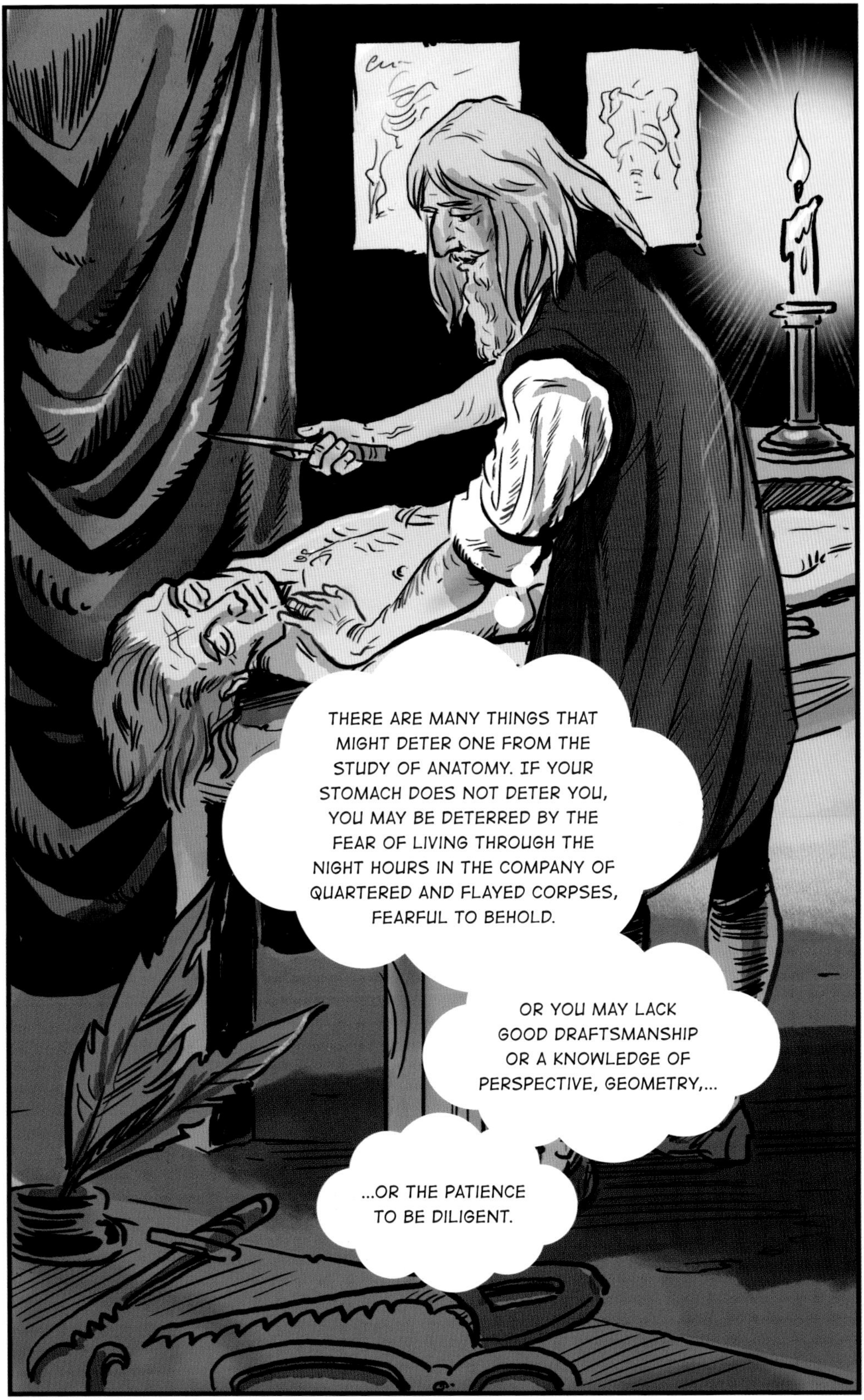
THERE ARE MANY THINGS THAT MIGHT DETER ONE FROM THE STUDY OF ANATOMY. IF YOUR STOMACH DOES NOT DETER YOU, YOU MAY BE DETERRED BY THE FEAR OF LIVING THROUGH THE NIGHT HOURS IN THE COMPANY OF QUARTERED AND FLAYED CORPSES, FEARFUL TO BEHOLD.
OR YOU MAY LACK GOOD DRAFTSMANSHIP OR A KNOWLEDGE OF PERSPECTIVE, GEOMETRY,...
...OR THE PATIENCE TO BE DILIGENT.

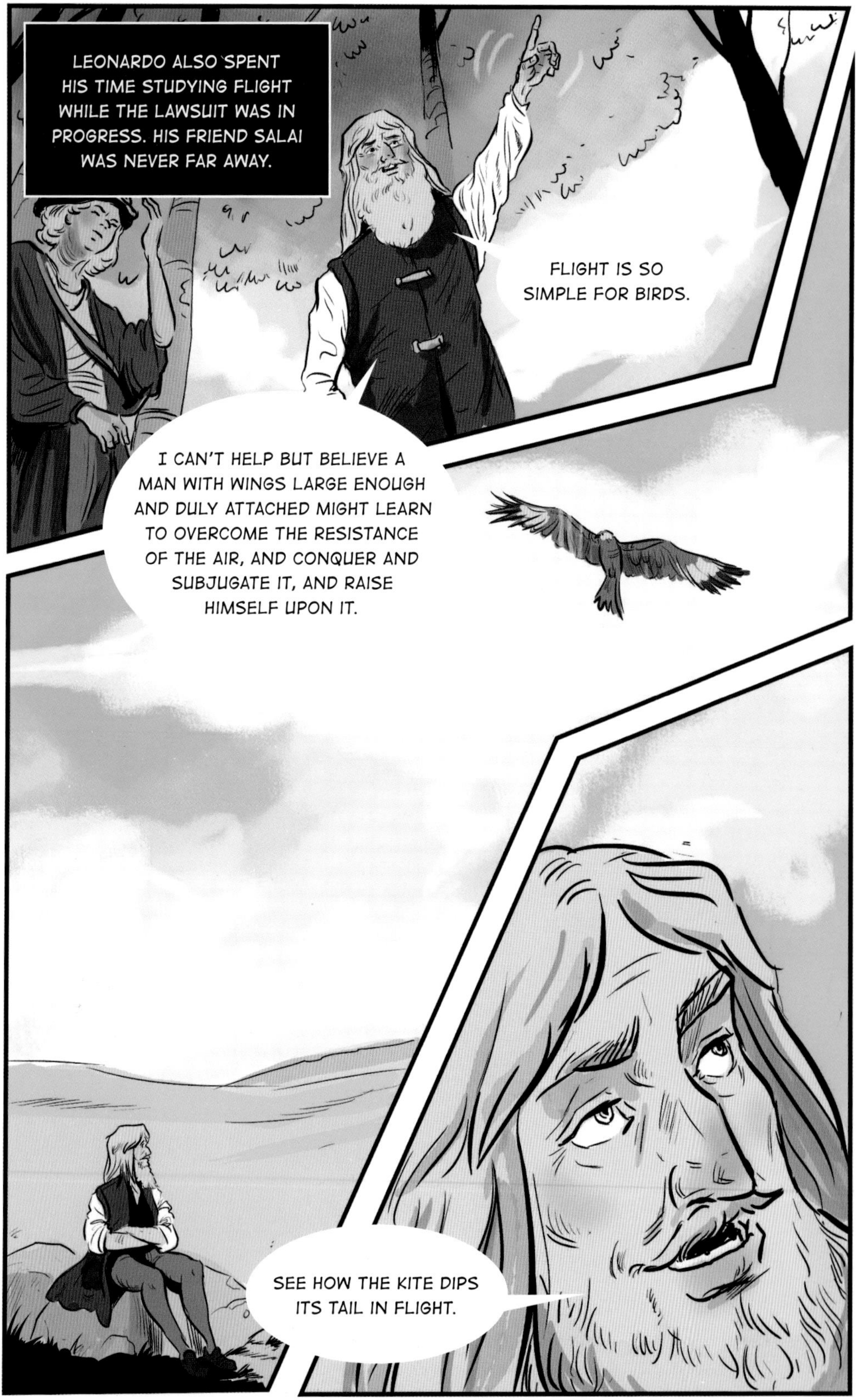
LEONARDO ALSO SPENT HIS TIME STUDYING FLIGHT WHILE THE LAWSUIT WAS IN PROGRESS. HIS FRIEND SALAI WAS NEVER FAR AWAY.
FLIGHT IS SO SIMPLE FOR BIRDS.
I CAN'T HELP BUT BELIEVE A MAN WITH WINGS LARGE ENOUGH AND DULY ATTACHED MIGHT LEARN TO OVERCOME THE RESISTANCE OF THE AIR, AND CONQUER AND SUBJUGATE IT, AND RAISE HIMSELF UPON IT.
SEE HOW THE KITE DIPS ITS TAIL IN FLIGHT.

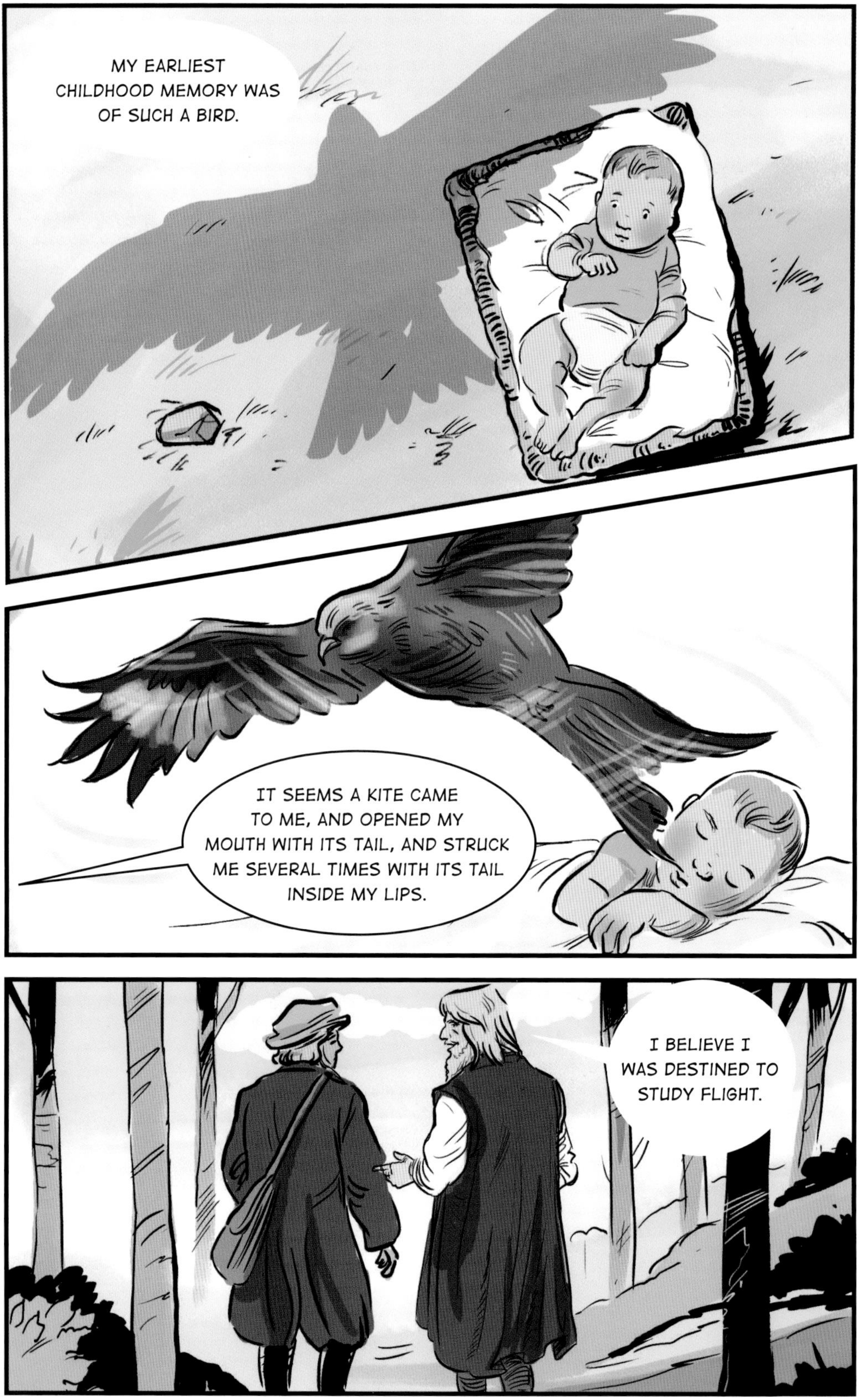
MY EARLIEST CHILDHOOD MEMORY WAS OF SUCH A BIRD.
IT SEEMS A KITE CAME TO ME, AND OPENED MY MOUTH WITH ITS TAIL, AND STRUCK ME SEVERAL TIMES WITH ITS TAIL INSIDE MY LIPS.
I BELIEVE I WAS DESTINED TO STUDY FLIGHT.

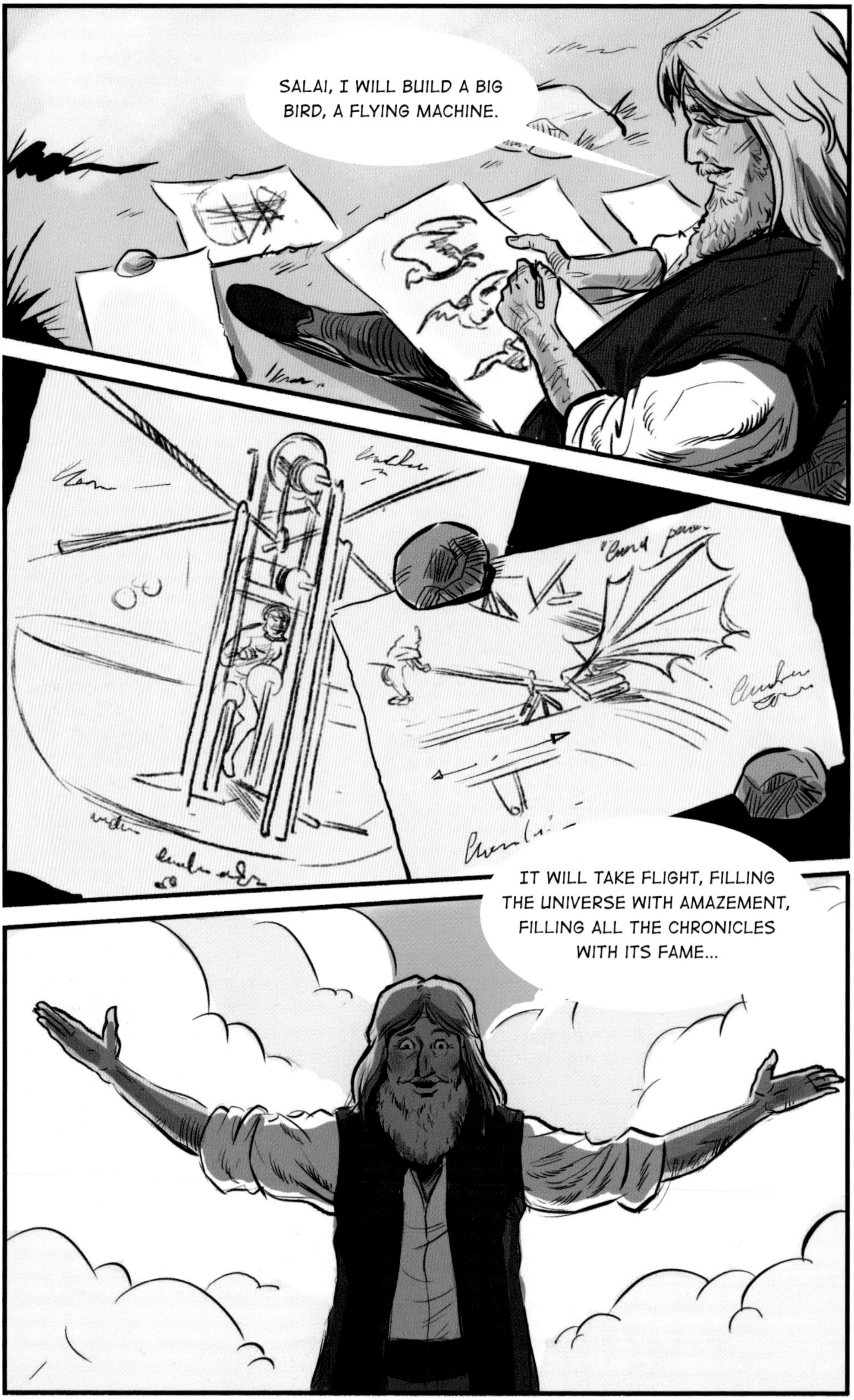
SALAI, I WILL BUILD A BIG BIRD, A FLYING MACHINE.
IT WILL TAKE FLIGHT, FILLING THE UNIVERSE WITH AMAZEMENT, FILLING ALL THE CHRONICLES WITH ITS FAME...

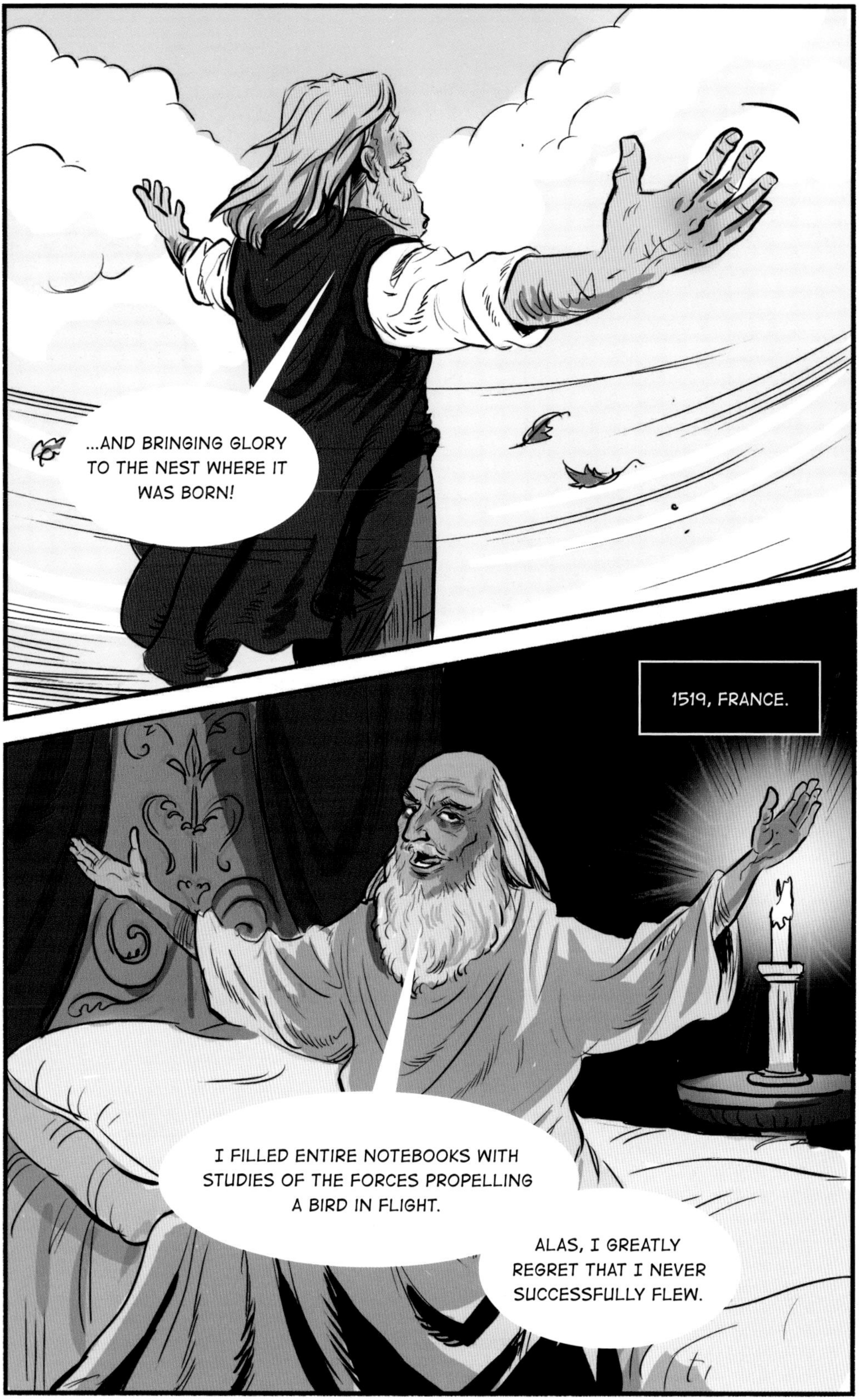
...AND BRINGING GLORY TO THE NEST WHERE IT WAS BORN!
1519, FRANCE.
I FILLED ENTIRE NOTEBOOKS WITH STUDIES OF THE FORCES PROPELLING A BIRD IN FLIGHT.
ALAS, I GREATLY REGRET THAT I NEVER SUCCESSFULLY FLEW.

CHAPTER 11

ROME: A NEW SPONSOR FOR LEONARDO

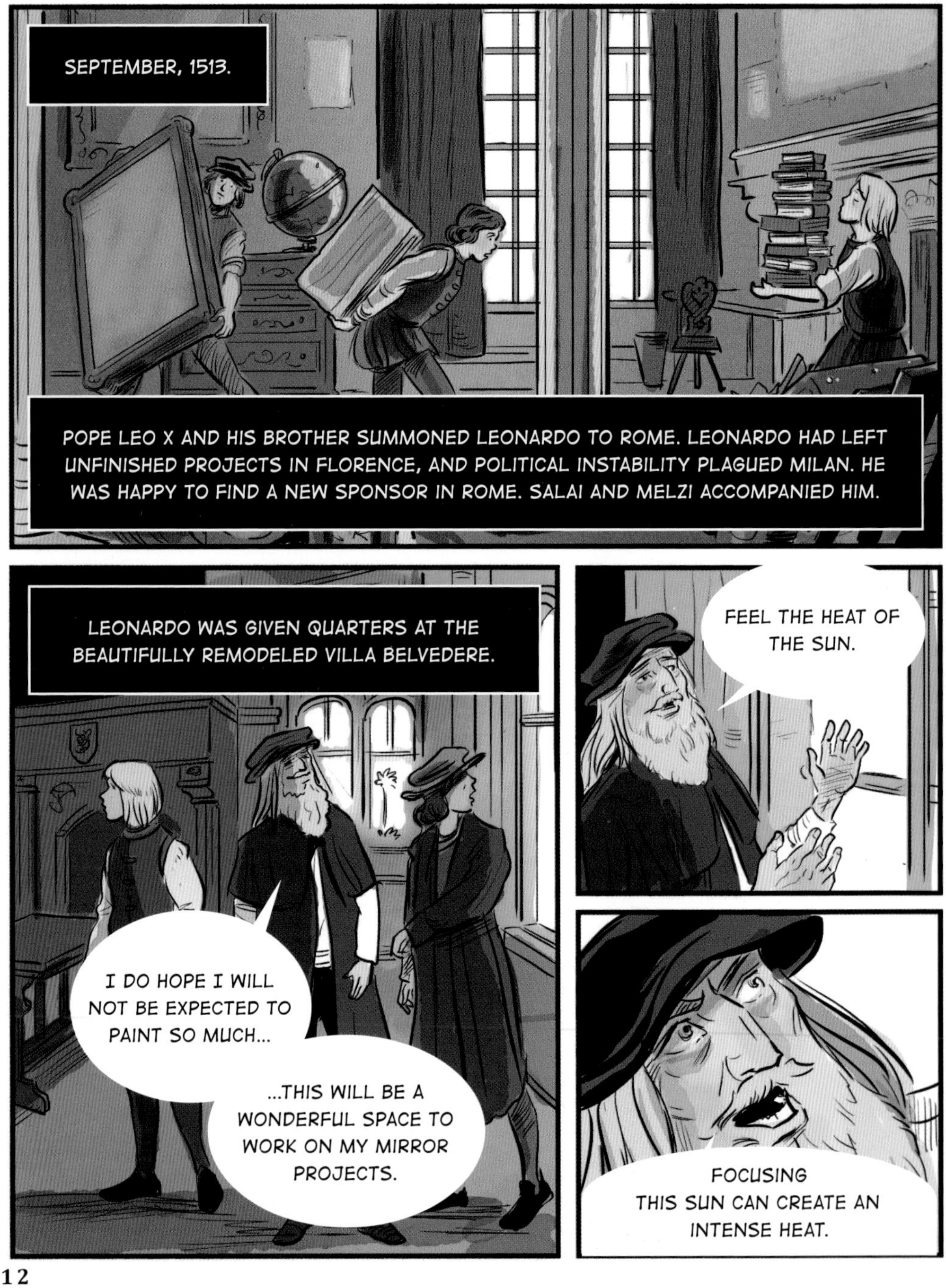
SEPTEMBER, 1513.
POPE LEO X AND HIS BROTHER SUMMONED LEONARDO TO ROME. LEONARDO HAD LEFT UNFINISHED PROJECTS IN FLORENCE, AND POLITICAL INSTABILITY PLAGUED MILAN. HE WAS HAPPY TO FIND A NEW SPONSOR IN ROME. SALAI AND MELZI ACCOMPANIED HIM.
LEONARDO WAS GIVEN QUARTERS AT THE BEAUTIFULLY REMODELED VILLA BELVEDERE.
I DO HOPE I WILL NOT BE EXPECTED TO PAINT SO MUCH...
...THIS WILL BE A WONDERFUL SPACE TO WORK ON MY MIRROR PROJECTS.
FEEL THE HEAT OF THE SUN.
FOCUSING THIS SUN CAN CREATE AN INTENSE HEAT.

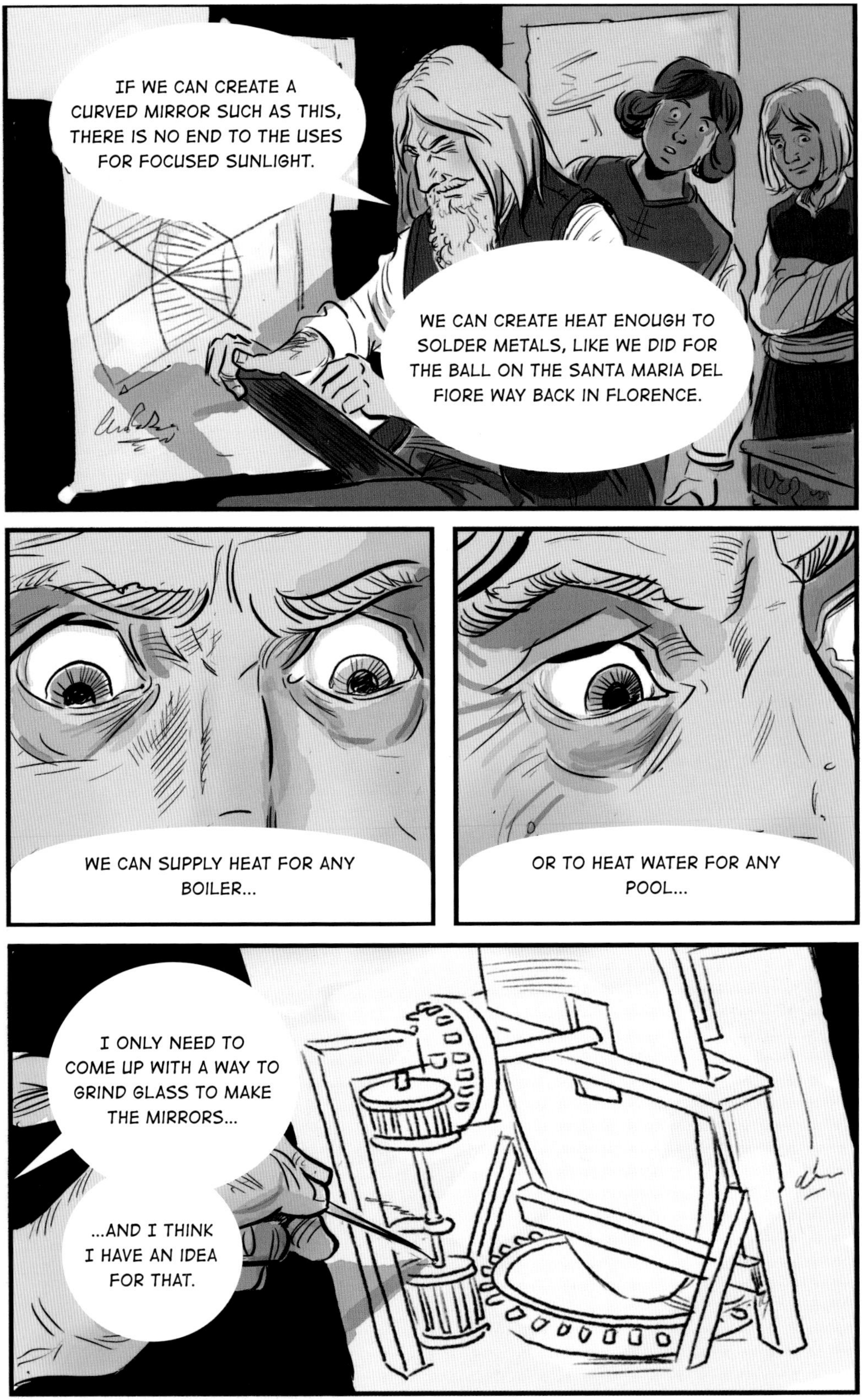
IF WE CAN CREATE A CURVED MIRROR SUCH AS THIS, THERE IS NO END TO THE USES FOR FOCUSED SUNLIGHT.
WE CAN CREATE HEAT ENOUGH TO SOLDER METALS, LIKE WE DID FOR THE BALL ON THE SANTA MARIA DEL FIORE WAY BACK IN FLORENCE.
WE CAN SUPPLY HEAT FOR ANY BOILER...
OR TO HEAT WATER FOR ANY POOL...
I ONLY NEED TO COME UP WITH A WAY TO GRIND GLASS TO MAKE THE MIRRORS...
...AND I THINK I HAVE AN IDEA FOR THAT.

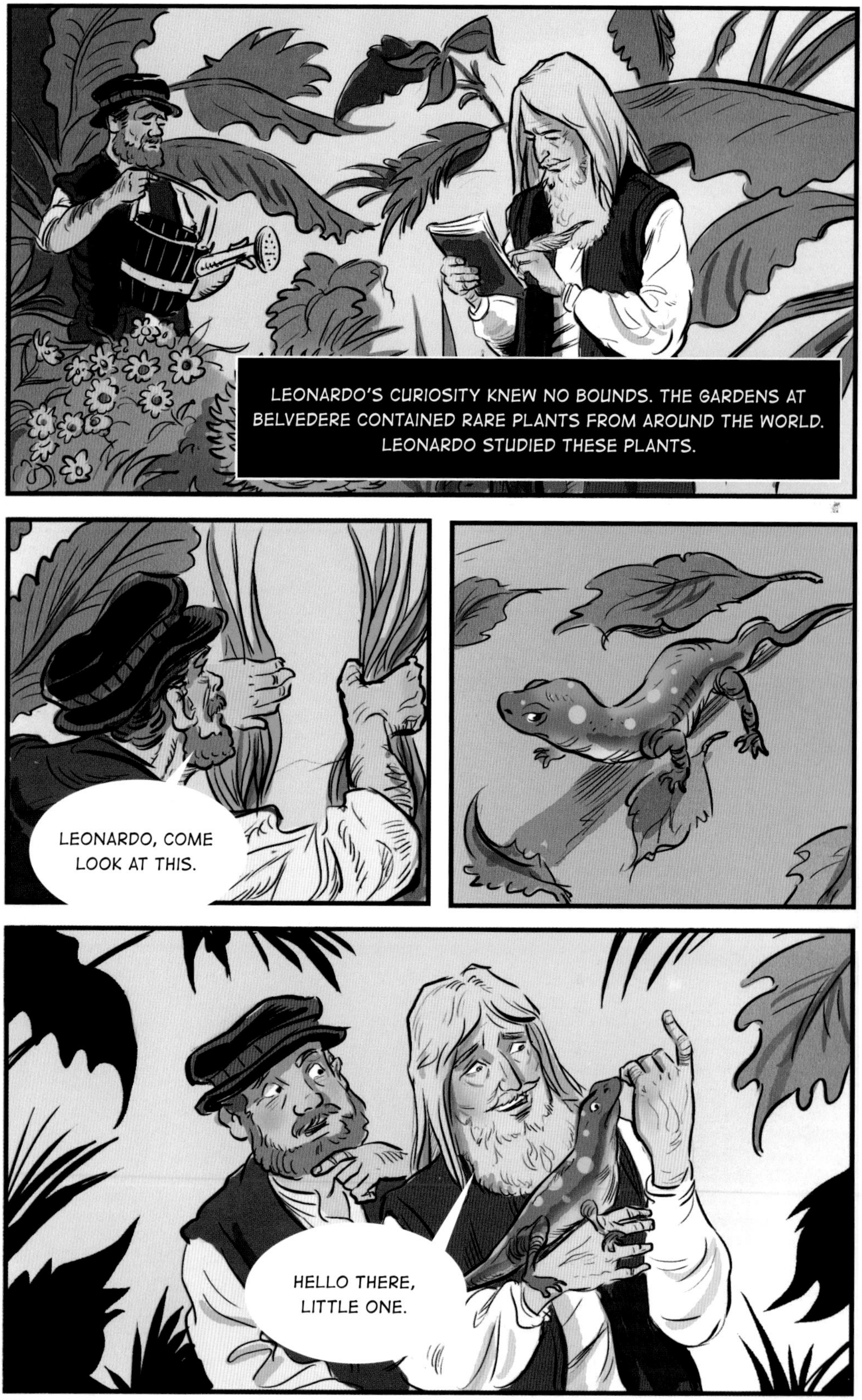
LEONARDO'S CURIOSITY KNEW NO BOUNDS. THE GARDENS AT BELVEDERE CONTAINED RARE PLANTS FROM AROUND THE WORLD. LEONARDO STUDIED THESE PLANTS.
LEONARDO, COME LOOK AT THIS.
HELLO THERE, LITTLE ONE.

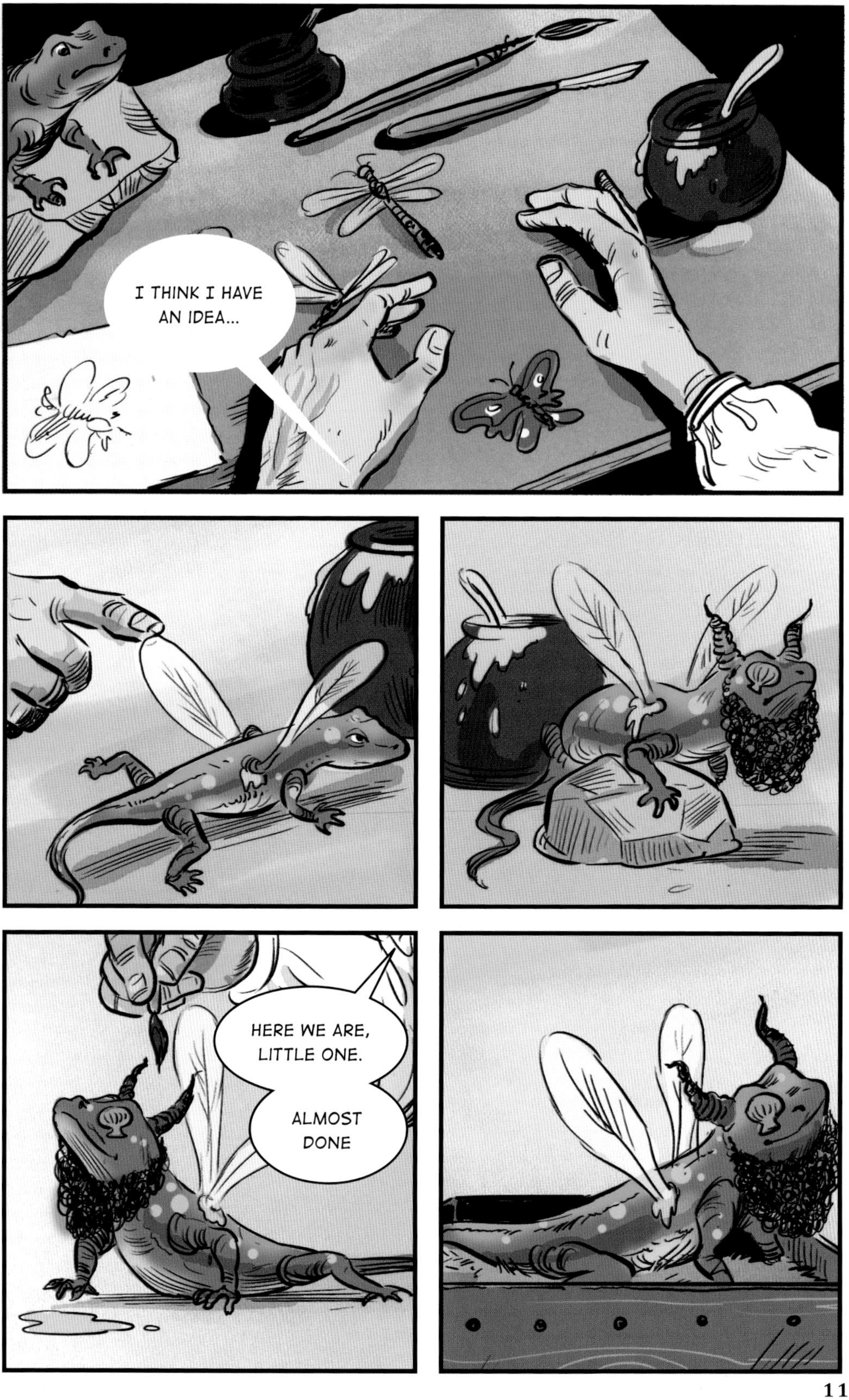
I THINK I HAVE AN IDEA...
HERE WE ARE, LITTLE ONE.
ALMOST DONE

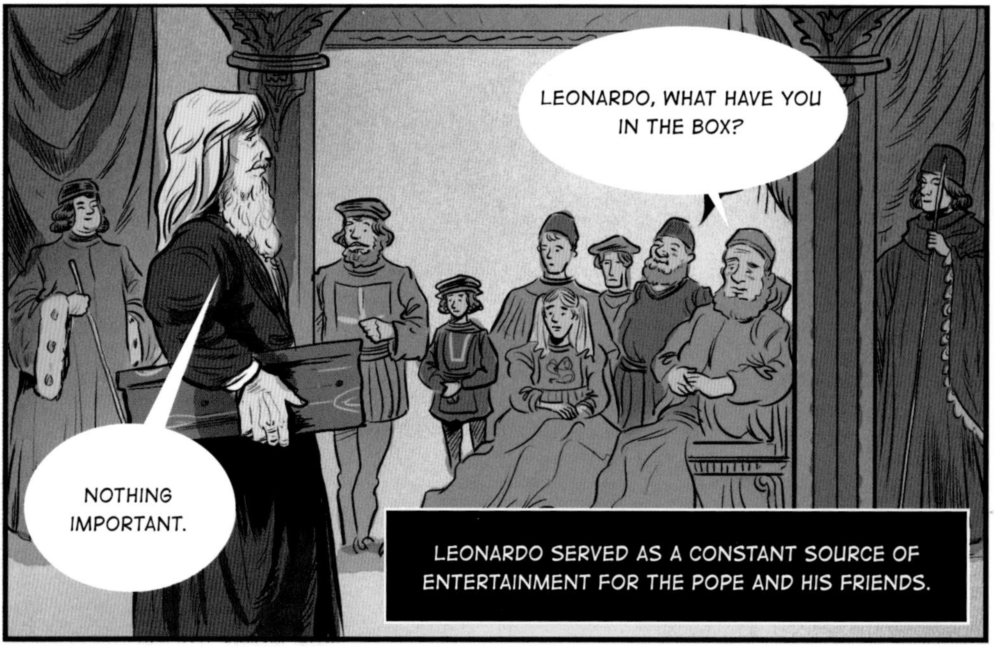
LEONARDO, WHAT HAVE YOU IN THE BOX?
NOTHING IMPORTANT.
LEONARDO SERVED AS A CONSTANT SOURCE OF ENTERTAINMENT FOR THE POPE AND HIS FRIENDS.

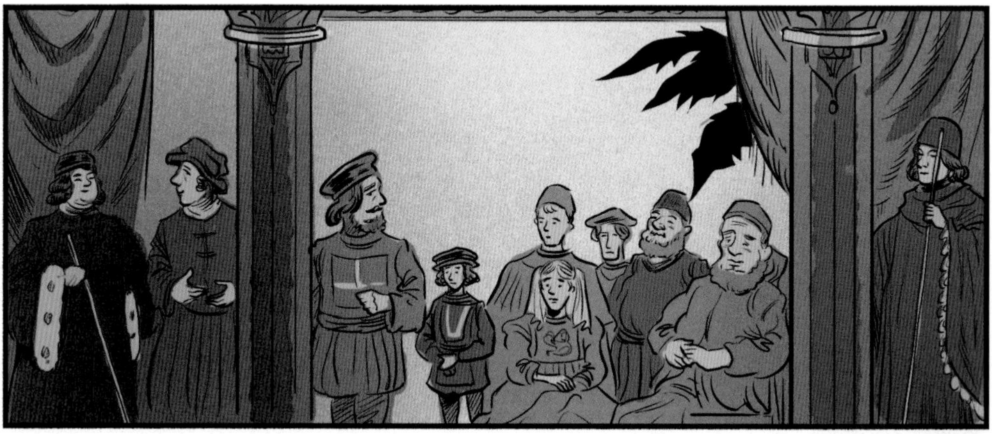

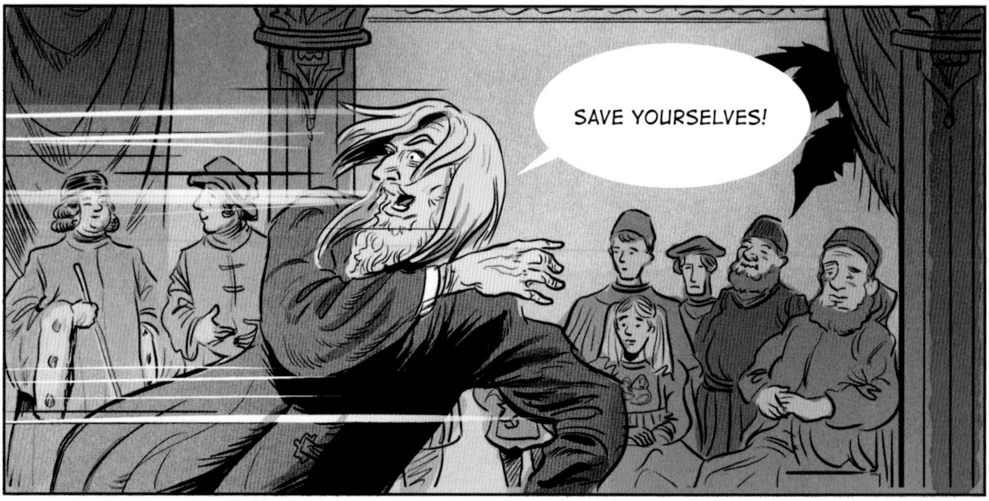
SAVE YOURSELVES!

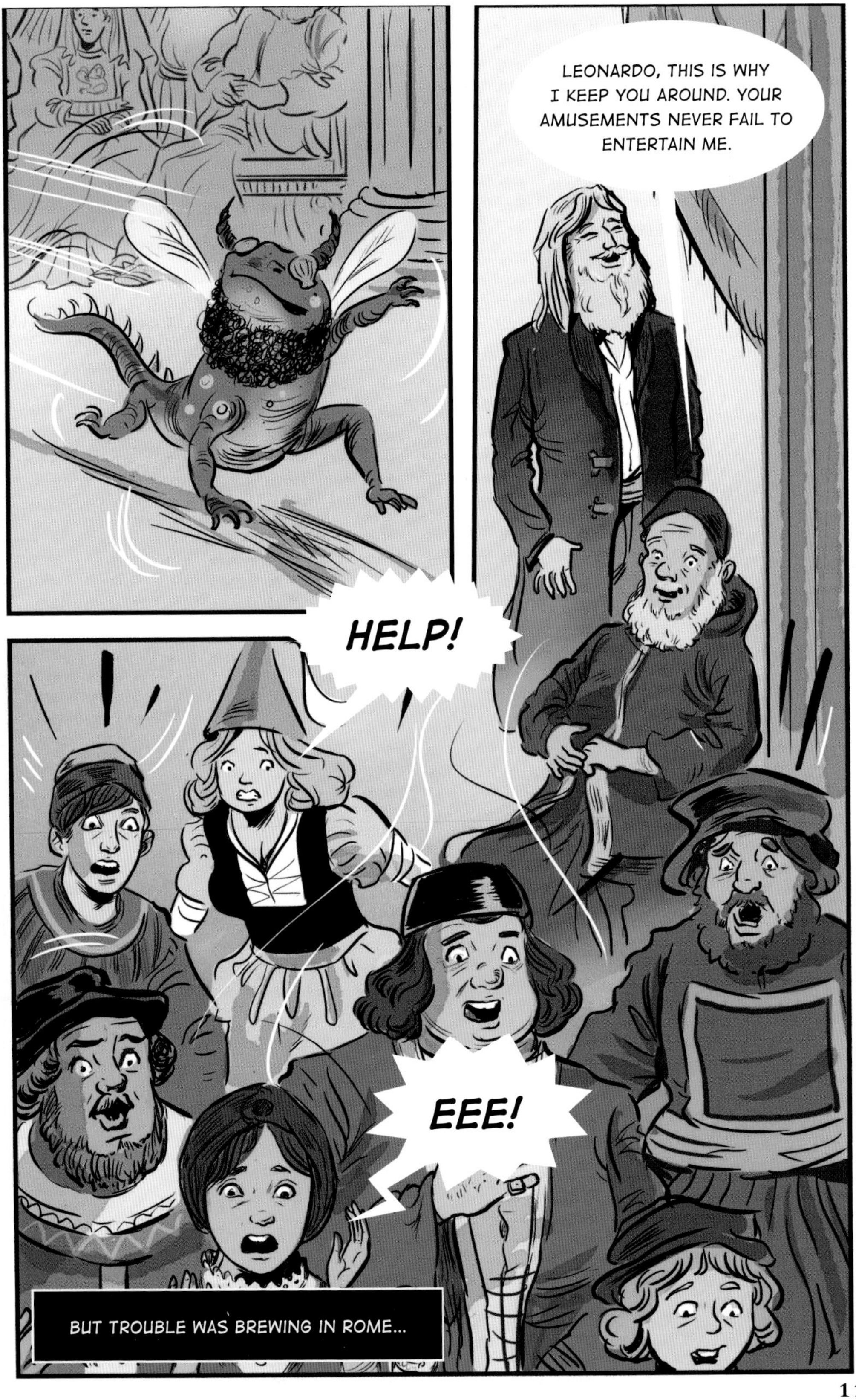
LEONARDO, THIS IS WHY I KEEP YOU AROUND. YOUR AMUSEMENTS NEVER FAIL TO ENTERTAIN ME.
HELP!
EEE!
BUT TROUBLE WAS BREWING IN ROME...

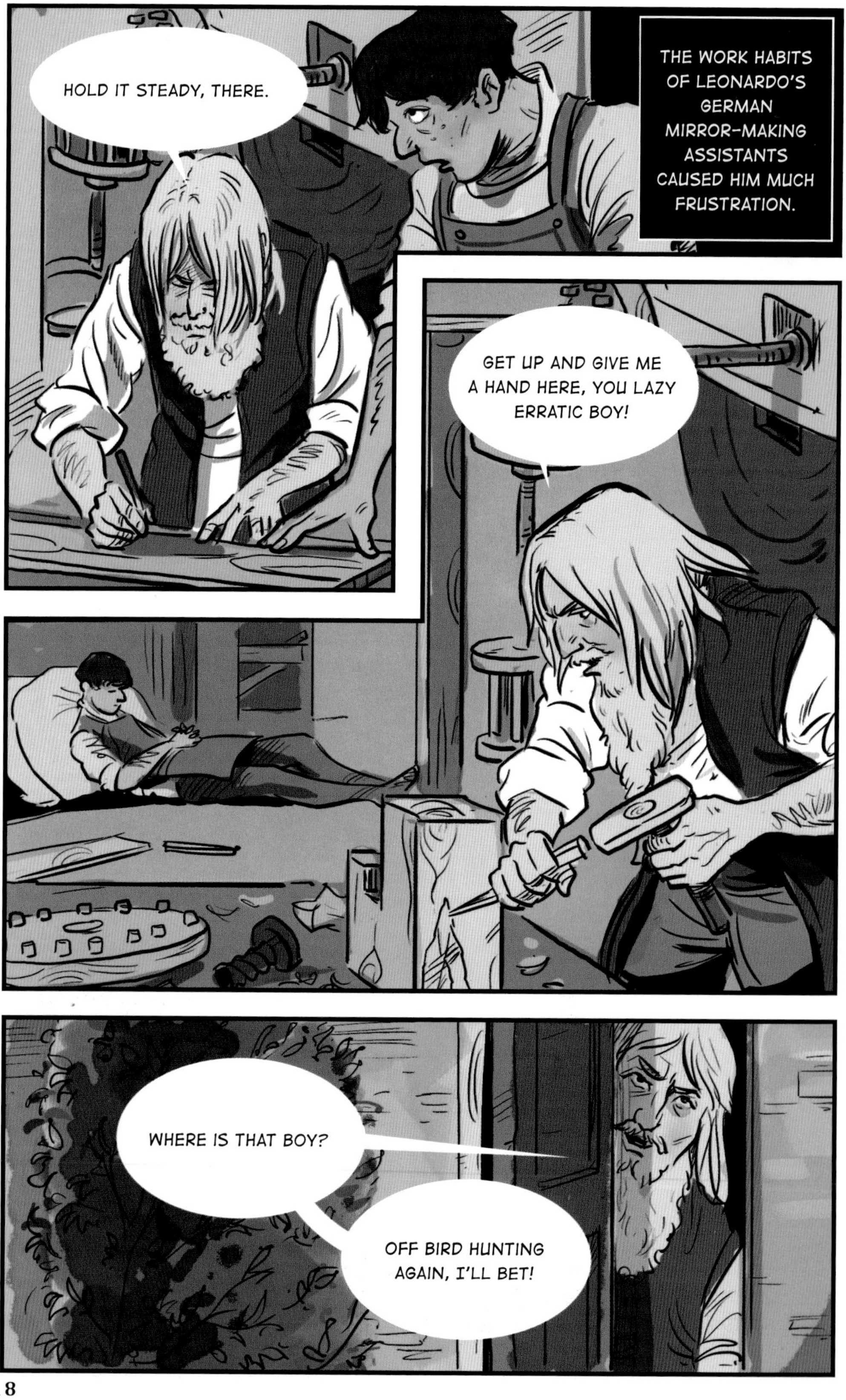
THE WORK HABITS OF LEONARDO'S GERMAN MIRROR-MAKING ASSISTANTS CAUSED HIM MUCH FRUSTRATION.
HOLD IT STEADY, THERE.
GET UP AND GIVE ME A HAND HERE, YOU LAZY ERRATIC BOY!
WHERE IS THAT BOY?
OFF BIRD HUNTING AGAIN, I'LL BET!

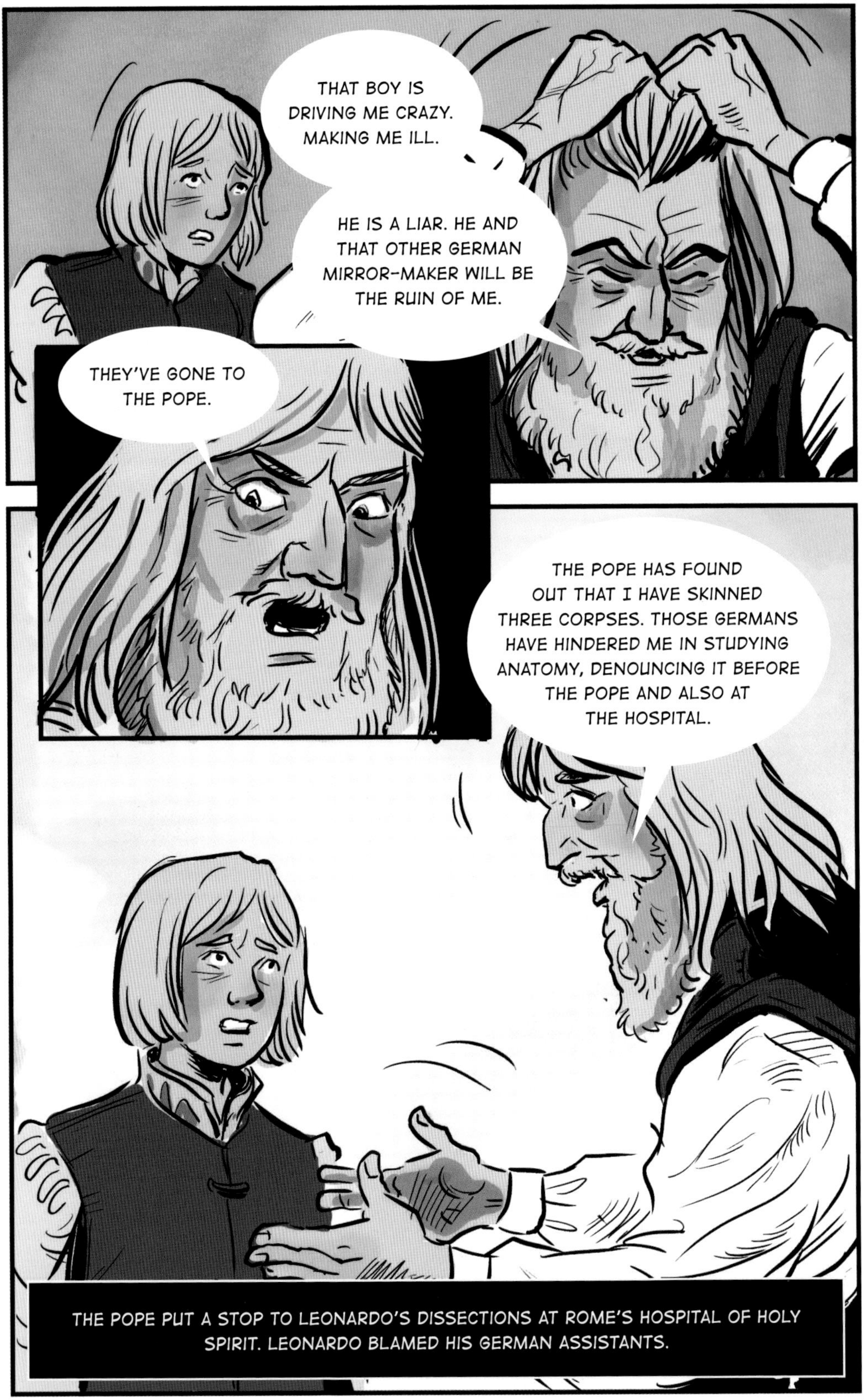
THAT BOY IS DRIVING ME CRAZY. MAKING ME ILL.
HE IS A LIAR. HE AND THAT OTHER GERMAN MIRROR-MAKER WILL BE THE RUIN OF ME.
THEY'VE GONE TO THE POPE.
THE POPE HAS FOUND OUT THAT I HAVE SKINNED THREE CORPSES. THOSE GERMANS HAVE HINDERED ME IN STUDYING ANATOMY, DENOUNCING IT BEFORE THE POPE AND ALSO AT THE HOSPITAL.
THE POPE PUT A STOP TO LEONARDO'S DISSECTIONS AT ROME'S HOSPITAL OF HOLY SPIRIT. LEONARDO BLAMED HIS GERMAN ASSISTANTS.

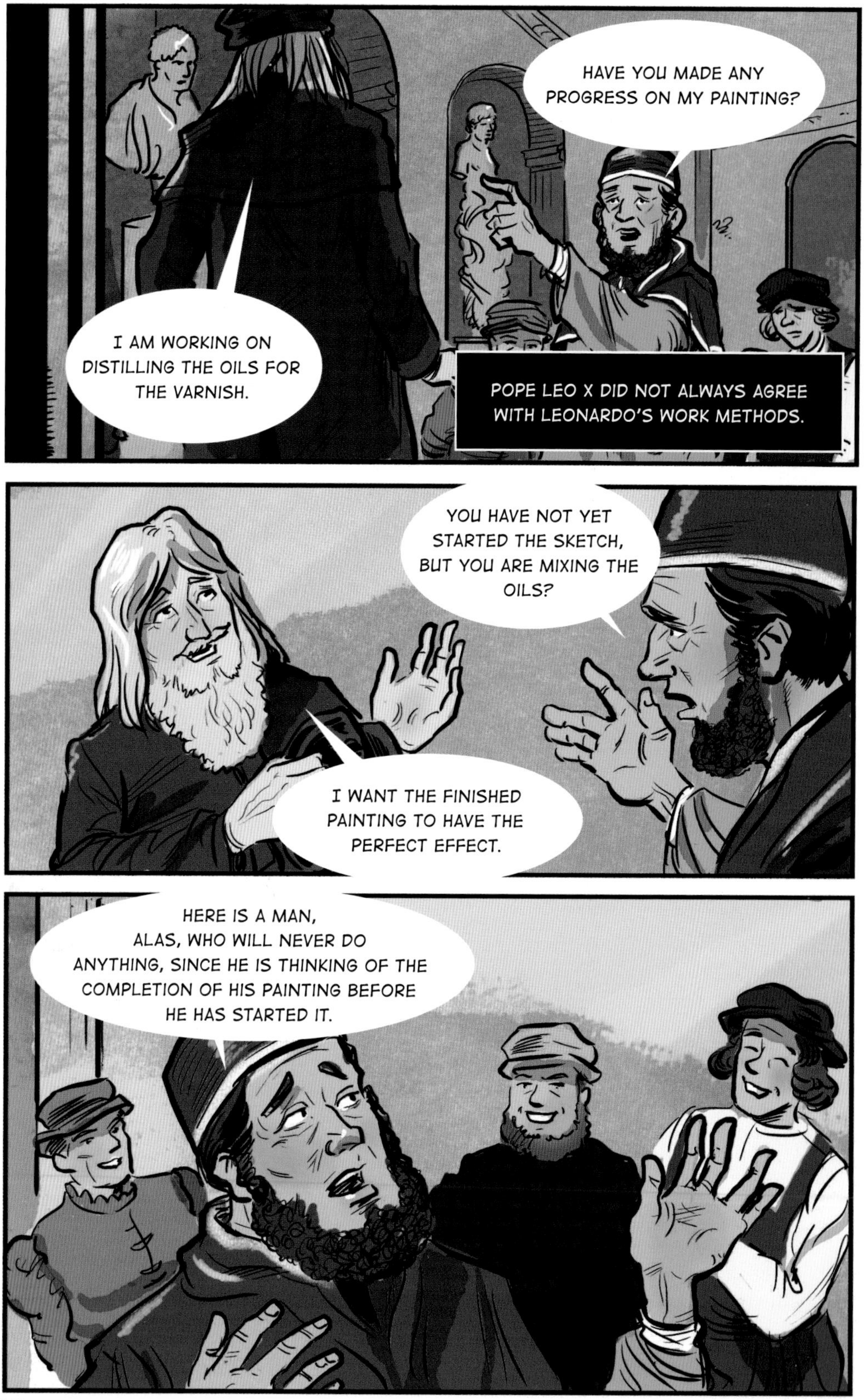
HAVE YOU MADE ANY PROGRESS ON MY PAINTING?
I AM WORKING ON DISTILLING THE OILS FOR THE VARNISH.
POPE LEO X DID NOT ALWAYS AGREE WITH LEONARDO'S WORK METHODS.
YOU HAVE NOT YET STARTED THE SKETCH, BUT YOU ARE MIXING THE OILS?
I WANT THE FINISHED PAINTING TO HAVE THE PERFECT EFFECT.
HERE IS A MAN, ALAS, WHO WILL NEVER DO ANYTHING, SINCE HE IS THINKING OF THE COMPLETION OF HIS PAINTING BEFORE HE HAS STARTED IT.

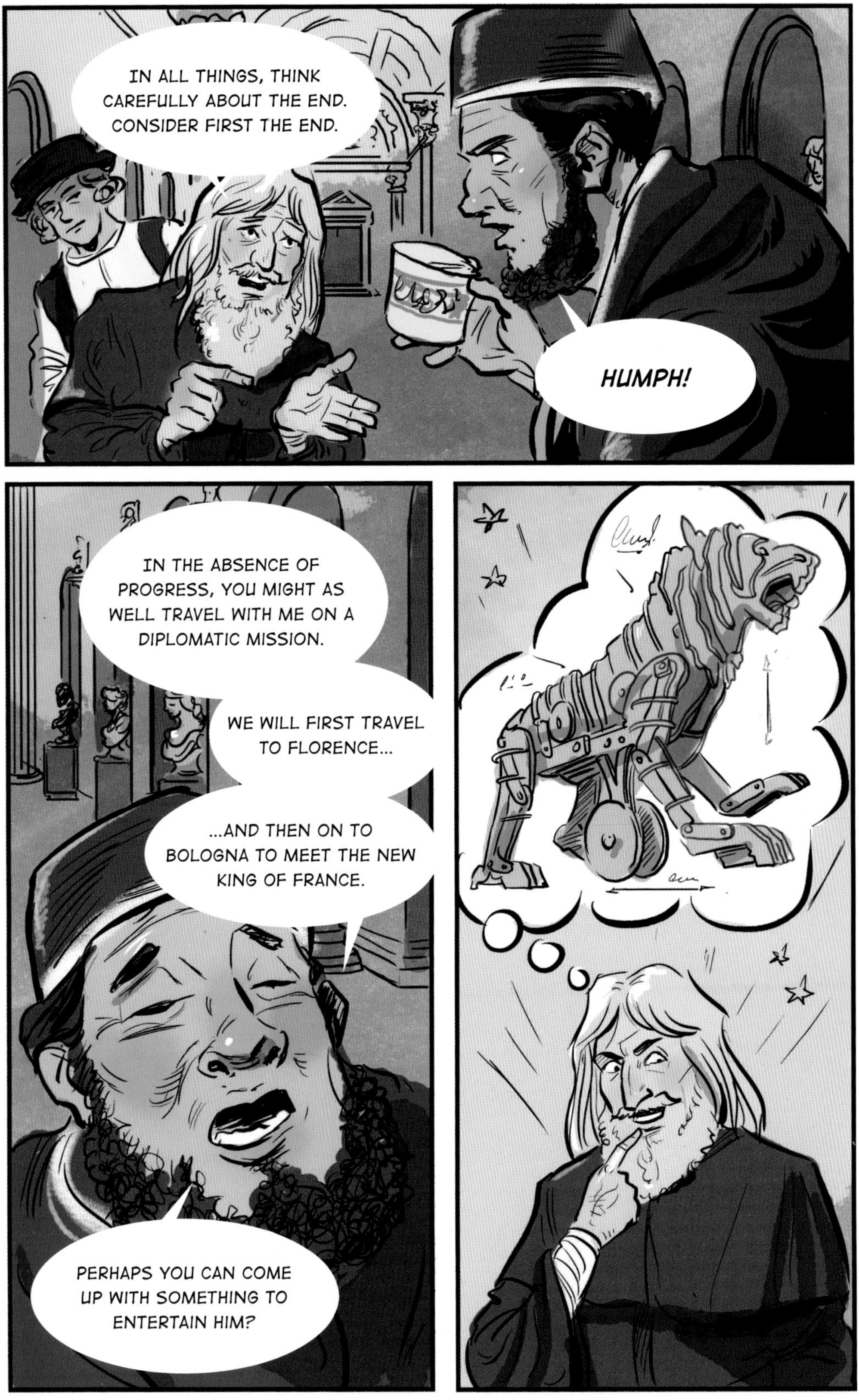
IN ALL THINGS, THINK CAREFULLY ABOUT THE END. CONSIDER FIRST THE END.
HUMPH!
IN THE ABSENCE OF PROGRESS, YOU MIGHT AS WELL TRAVEL WITH ME ON A DIPLOMATIC MISSION.
WE WILL FIRST TRAVEL TO FLORENCE...
...AND THEN ON TO BOLOGNA TO MEET THE NEW KING OF FRANCE.
PERHAPS YOU CAN COME UP WITH SOMETHING TO ENTERTAIN HIM?

CHAPTER 12

FRANCE AND THE *MONA LISA*

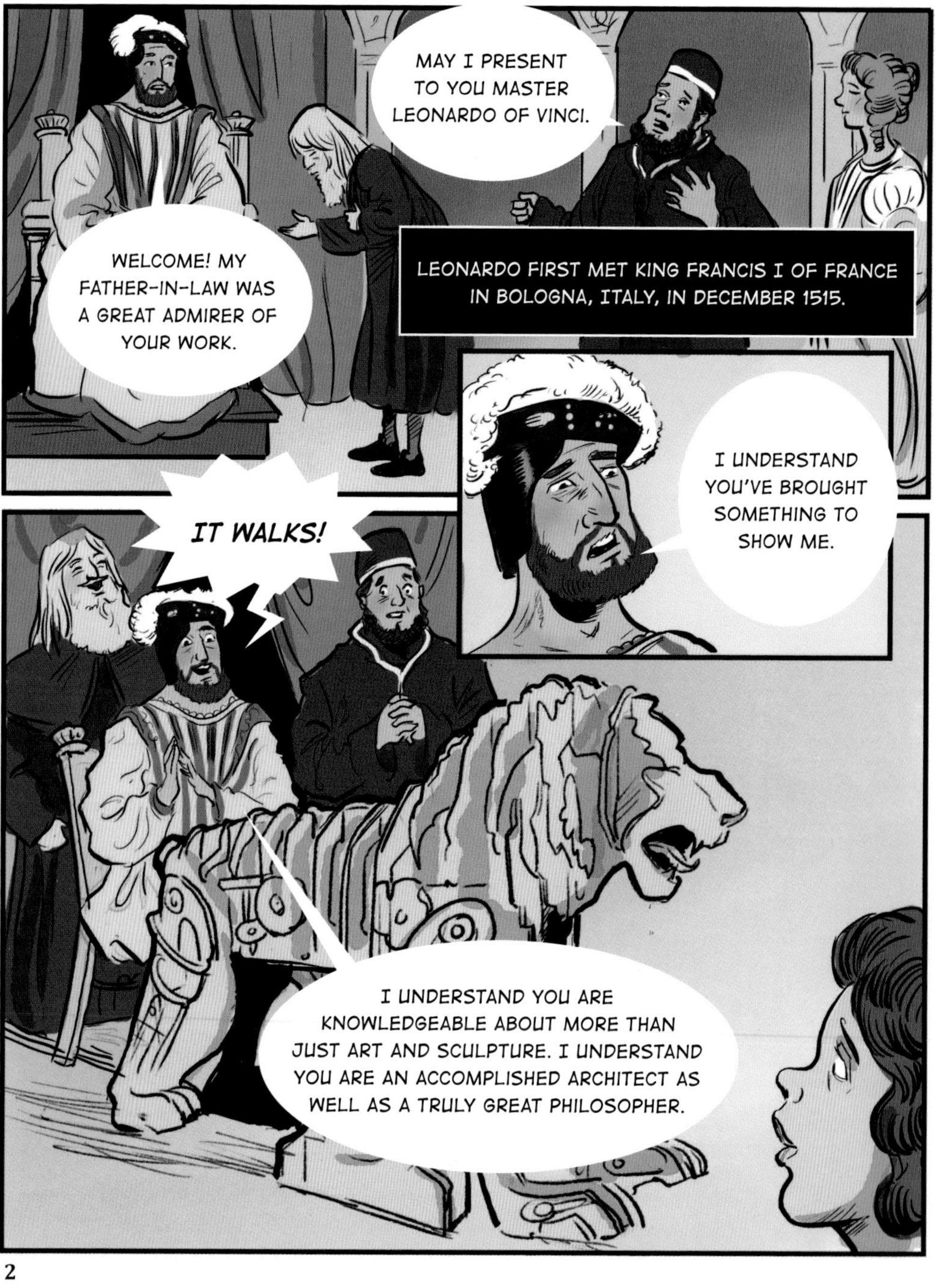
MAY I PRESENT TO YOU MASTER LEONARDO OF VINCI.
WELCOME! MY FATHER-IN-LAW WAS A GREAT ADMIRER OF YOUR WORK.
LEONARDO FIRST MET KING FRANCIS I OF FRANCE IN BOLOGNA, ITALY, IN DECEMBER 1515.
I UNDERSTAND YOU'VE BROUGHT SOMETHING TO SHOW ME.
IT WALKS!
I UNDERSTAND YOU ARE KNOWLEDGEABLE ABOUT MORE THAN JUST ART AND SCULPTURE. I UNDERSTAND YOU ARE AN ACCOMPLISHED ARCHITECT AS WELL AS A TRULY GREAT PHILOSOPHER.

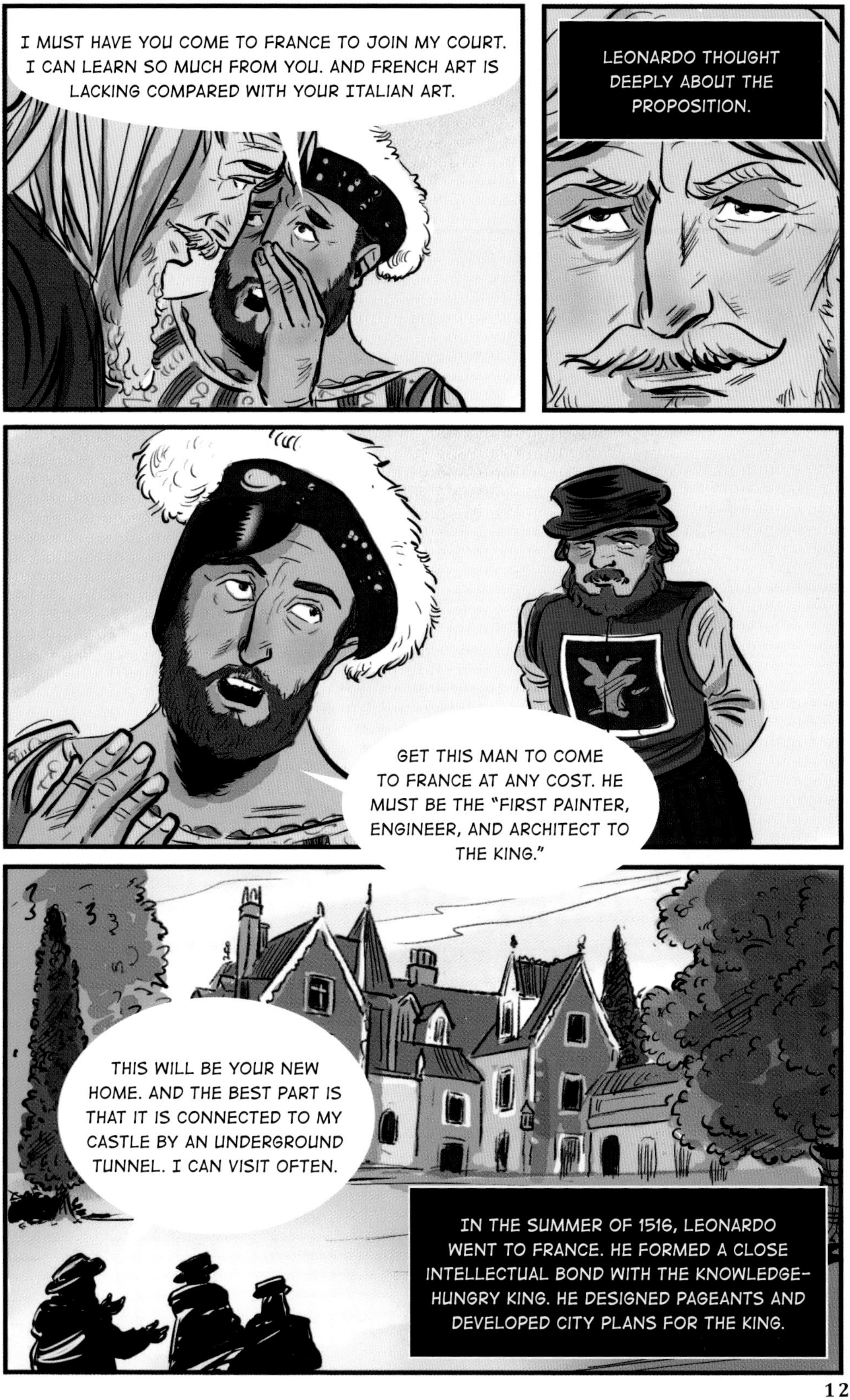
I MUST HAVE YOU COME TO FRANCE TO JOIN MY COURT. I CAN LEARN SO MUCH FROM YOU. AND FRENCH ART IS LACKING COMPARED WITH YOUR ITALIAN ART.
LEONARDO THOUGHT DEEPLY ABOUT THE PROPOSITION.
GET THIS MAN TO COME TO FRANCE AT ANY COST. HE MUST BE THE "FIRST PAINTER, ENGINEER, AND ARCHITECT TO THE KING."
THIS WILL BE YOUR NEW HOME. AND THE BEST PART IS THAT IT IS CONNECTED TO MY CASTLE BY AN UNDERGROUND TUNNEL. I CAN VISIT OFTEN.
IN THE SUMMER OF 1516, LEONARDO WENT TO FRANCE. HE FORMED A CLOSE INTELLECTUAL BOND WITH THE KNOWLEDGE-HUNGRY KING. HE DESIGNED PAGEANTS AND DEVELOPED CITY PLANS FOR THE KING.

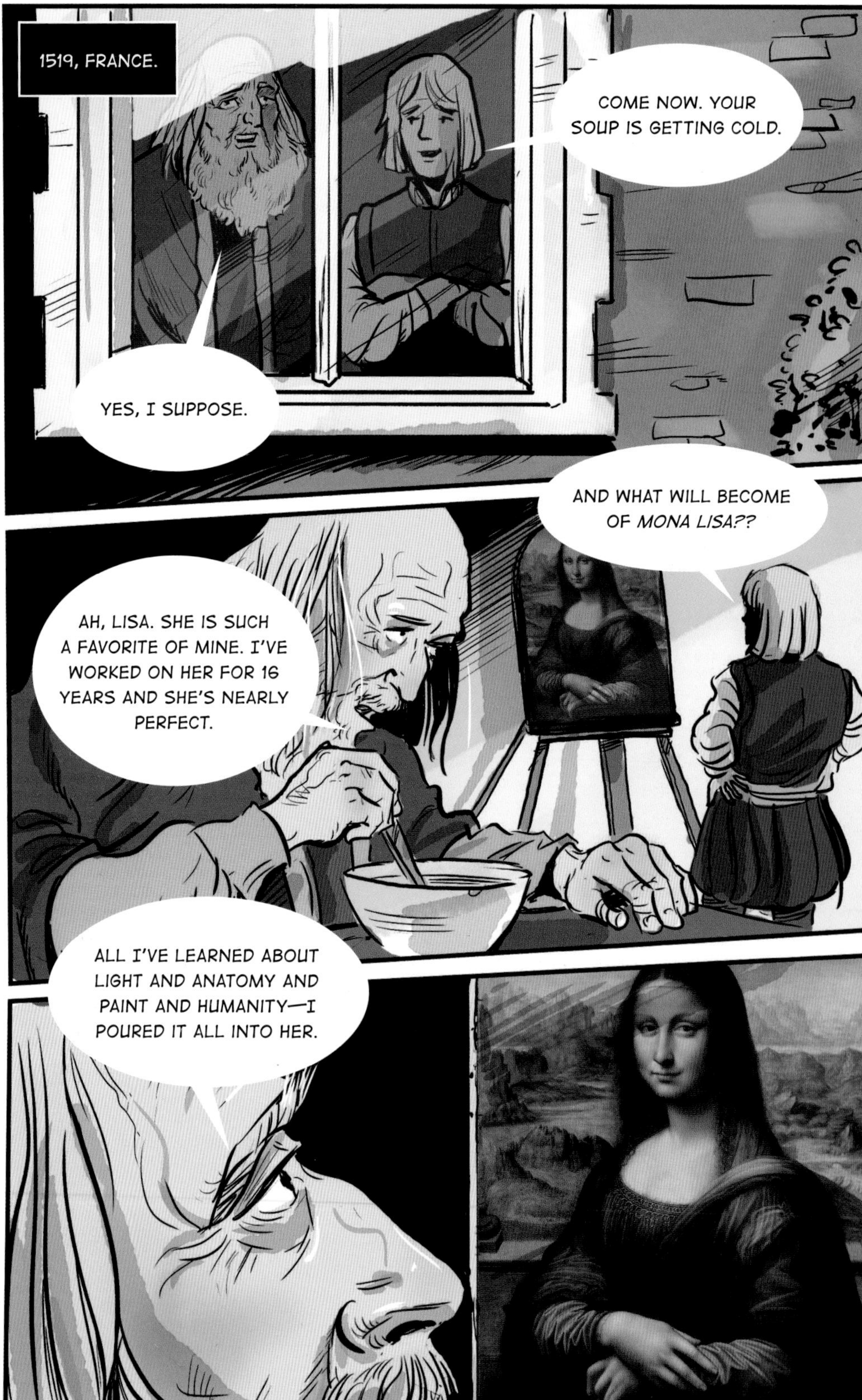
1519, FRANCE.
COME NOW. YOUR SOUP IS GETTING COLD.
YES, I SUPPOSE.
AND WHAT WILL BECOME OF *MONA LISA*??
AH, LISA. SHE IS SUCH A FAVORITE OF MINE. I'VE WORKED ON HER FOR 16 YEARS AND SHE'S NEARLY PERFECT.
ALL I'VE LEARNED ABOUT LIGHT AND ANATOMY AND PAINT AND HUMANITY—I POURED IT ALL INTO HER.

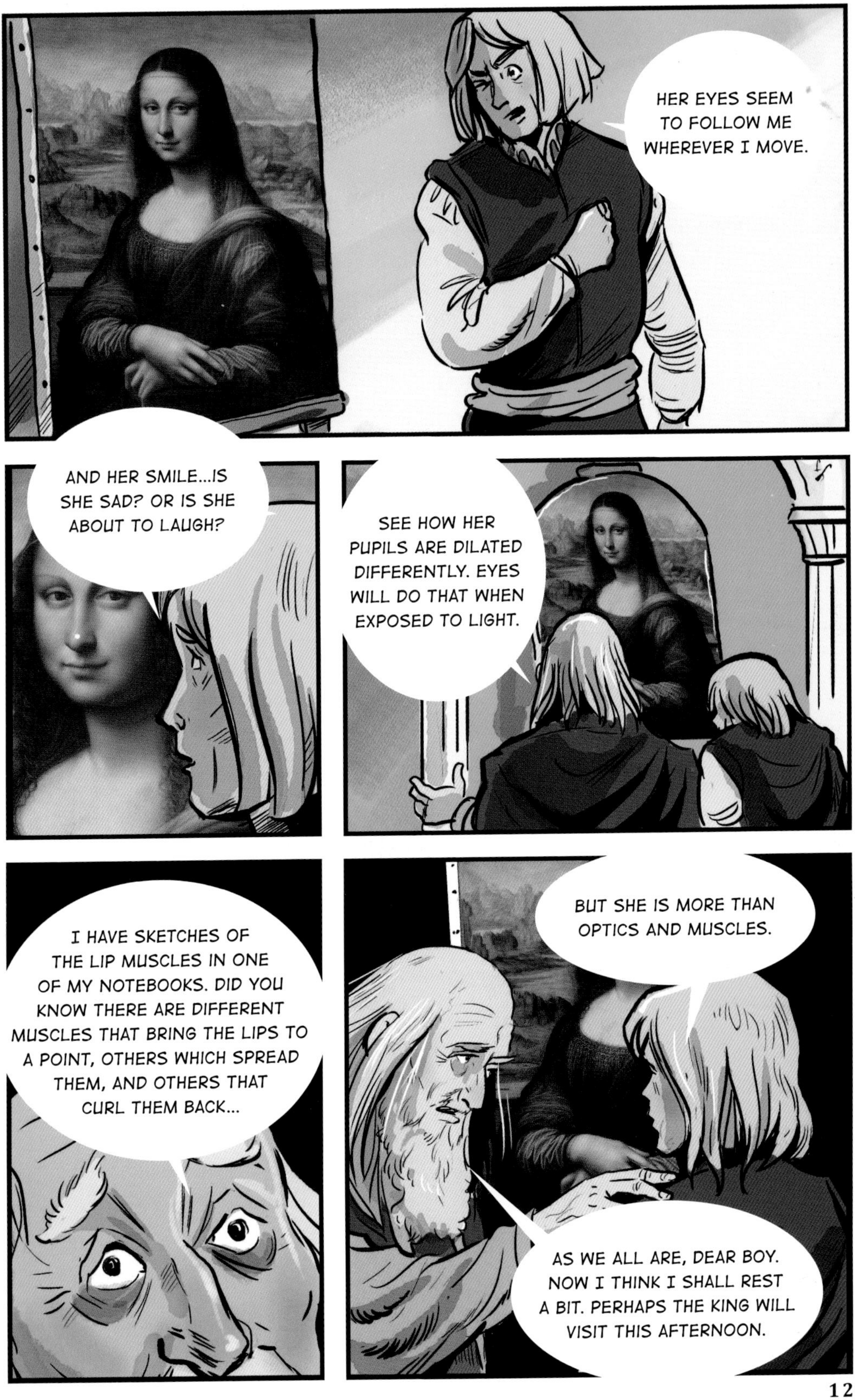
HER EYES SEEM TO FOLLOW ME WHEREVER I MOVE.
AND HER SMILE...IS SHE SAD? OR IS SHE ABOUT TO LAUGH?
SEE HOW HER PUPILS ARE DILATED DIFFERENTLY. EYES WILL DO THAT WHEN EXPOSED TO LIGHT.
I HAVE SKETCHES OF THE LIP MUSCLES IN ONE OF MY NOTEBOOKS. DID YOU KNOW THERE ARE DIFFERENT MUSCLES THAT BRING THE LIPS TO A POINT, OTHERS WHICH SPREAD THEM, AND OTHERS THAT CURL THEM BACK...
BUT SHE IS MORE THAN OPTICS AND MUSCLES.
AS WE ALL ARE, DEAR BOY. NOW I THINK I SHALL REST A BIT. PERHAPS THE KING WILL VISIT THIS AFTERNOON.

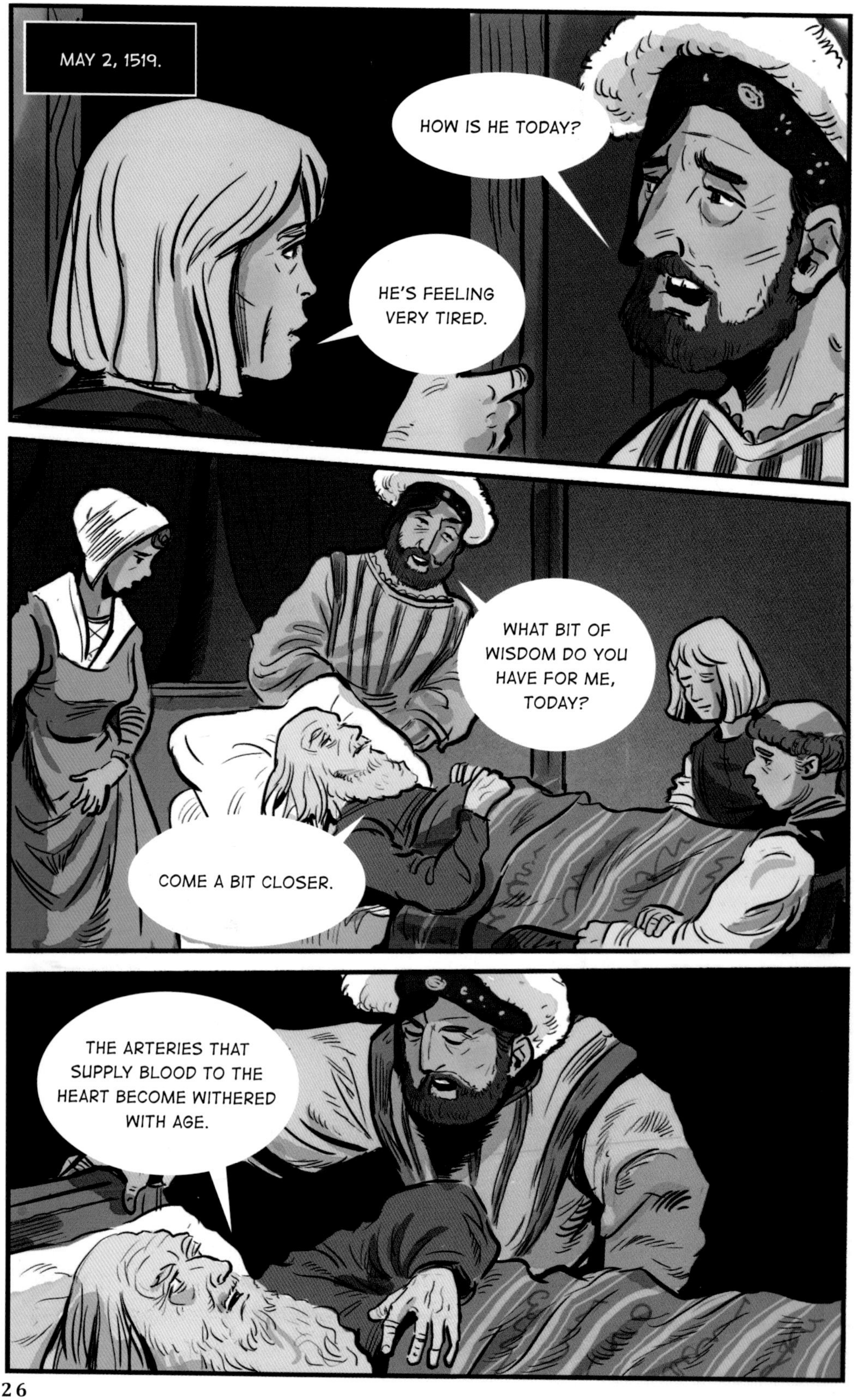
MAY 2, 1519.
HOW IS HE TODAY?
HE'S FEELING VERY TIRED.
WHAT BIT OF WISDOM DO YOU HAVE FOR ME, TODAY?
COME A BIT CLOSER.
THE ARTERIES THAT SUPPLY BLOOD TO THE HEART BECOME WITHERED WITH AGE.

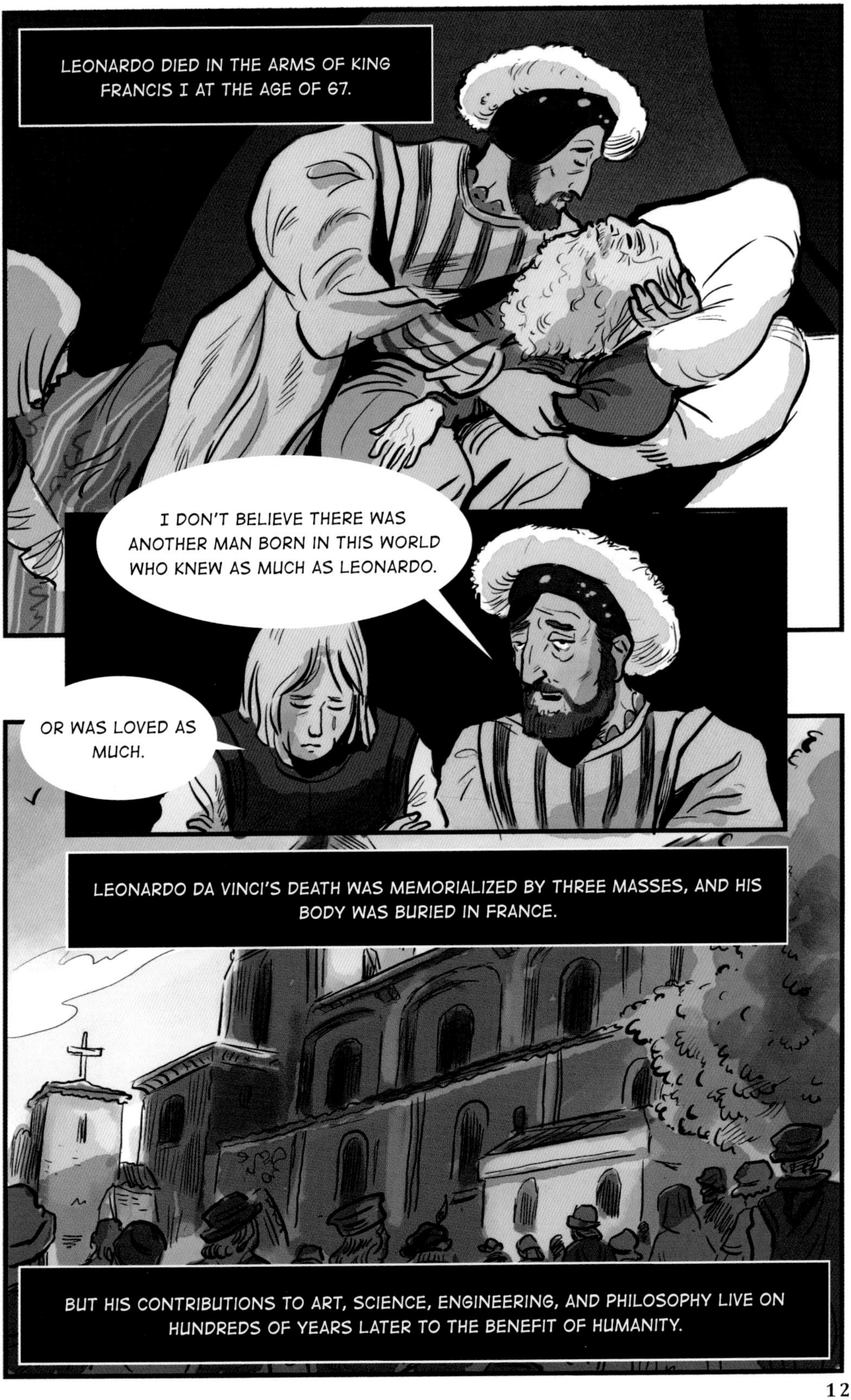
LEONARDO DIED IN THE ARMS OF KING FRANCIS I AT THE AGE OF 67.
I DON'T BELIEVE THERE WAS ANOTHER MAN BORN IN THIS WORLD WHO KNEW AS MUCH AS LEONARDO.
OR WAS LOVED AS MUCH.
LEONARDO DA VINCI'S DEATH WAS MEMORIALIZED BY THREE MASSES, AND HIS BODY WAS BURIED IN FRANCE.
BUT HIS CONTRIBUTIONS TO ART, SCIENCE, ENGINEERING, AND PHILOSOPHY LIVE ON HUNDREDS OF YEARS LATER TO THE BENEFIT OF HUMANITY.

ACKNOWLEDGMENTS

Tammy L. Enz: My thanks go out to the many authors of biographies of Leonardo da Vinci's life that assisted in my formation of this graphic novel. I am especially inspired by Walter Isaacson's *The Secret Lives of Leonardo da Vinci*. Also thanks to my family for their support and encouragement. Living in a home surrounded by artists, engineers, and tinkerers truly inspires me to write about a subject such as Leonardo da Vinci.

Dave Shephard: A great many thanks must be made to friends and family for wearing false beards and posing in Renaissance costume, particularly in public places. I know that was awkward. Also, special thanks to those who volunteered to enact the flying sequence. Huge thanks must be given to the editorial team at The Bright Press who managed to condense an epic life of huge achievements into 128 pages. It could have been so much longer. Which leads me to thank Leonardo da Vinci, who has elevated himself to my top dream dinner guest as a result of this novel. A truly extraordinary man and one I suspect would have been very fine company.